The Economics of Organizational Design

The Economics of Organizational Design

Theoretical Insights and Empirical Evidence

Massimo G. Colombo
Politecnico di Milano

and

Marco Delmastro
Autorità per le Garanzie nelle Comunicazioni

First published in 2008 by
PALGRAVE MACMILLAN
Houndmills, Basingstoke, Hampshire RG21 6XS and
175 Fifth Avenue, New York, N.Y. 10010
Companies and representatives throughout the world.

PALGRAVE MACMILLAN is the global academic imprint of the Palgrave Macmillan division of St. Martin's Press, LLC and of Palgrave Macmillan Ltd. Macmillan® is a registered trademark in the United States, United Kingdom and other countries. Palgrave is a registered trademark in the European Union and other countries.

ISBN-13: 978–1–4039–8741–9 hardback
ISBN-10: 1–4039–8741–6 hardback

This book is printed on paper suitable for recycling and made from fully managed and sustained forest sources. Logging, pulping and manufacturing processes are expected to conform to the environmental regulations of the country of origin.

A catalogue record for this book is available from the British Library.

A catalog record for this book is available from the Library of Congress.

10   9   8   7   6   5   4   3   2   1
17 16 15 14 13 12 11 10 09 08

Printed and bound in Great Britain by
CPI Antony Rowe, Chippenham and Eastbourne

To Elise, Emilia, Ludovica and Raffaella

Contents

List of Figures and Boxes

Figures

Boxes

List of Tables

List of Abbreviations

AMTs	advanced manufacturing technologies
BIC	*Bilans industriels et commerciaux*
CAD	computer aided design
CAM	computer aided manufacture
CEO	chief executive officer
CF	control function
CNC	computerized numerical control
COI	*Changements Organisationnels et Informatisation*
DOF	degrees of freedom
EDI	electronic data interchange
EQW–NES	Educational Quality of the Workforce National Employers' Survey
ER	*Enquête Reponse*
ESE	*Enquête sur l'emploi*
ESOP	employee stock ownership plants
FMS	flexible manufacturing systems and cells
GLS	generalized least square
GMM	General Method of Moments
GRATE	gross rate of return on capital
HR	human resources
HRM	human resource management
HRMPs	human resource management practices
ICTs	information and communication technologies
IMS	inflexible manufacturing line systems
IT	information technology
IV	instrumental variable
IWPs	innovative work practices
JIT	just-in-time
JV	joint venture
LAN	Local Area Network
LISREL	linear structural relationship
M&A	merger and acquisition
MNE	multinational enterprise
NC	numerical control
OLS	ordinary least square
PA	programmable automation

PCA	principal component analysis
QC	quality circles
R&D	research and development
ROI	returns on investment
SMT	self-managed teams
SOE	state-owned enterprise
SOVs	structural organizational variables
TQM	total quality management
WERS	Workplace Employee Relations Survey
WG	within-group
WIRS	(British) Workplace Industrial Relations Survey

Acknowledgments

This book is an outgrowth of the research that we have been doing over the past several years on the organization of firms. Our research work has benefited enormously from interactions with colleagues and friends. To try to list all the people from whom we received insights, ideas, and encouragement would greatly lengthen the book. However, there are some individuals who have been especially helpful through the comments, criticism and suggestions they provided after reading our research papers and draft chapters of this book. First, Keith Cowling and Mike Waterson had a great impact on the work of Marco Delmastro, especially when he was at the University of Warwick doing his PhD. Not only have they provided theoretical aid and fruitful discussions, but Marco is also personally indebted to Keith for the support he gave when he felt lost in his work. Second, the following persons deserve special mention: Alberto Bacchiega, Paolo Bertoletti, Clelia Di Serio, Luca Grilli, Dennis Leech, Colin Mayer, Rocco Mosconi, Larissa Rabbiosi, and Fabio Sartori. Third, we want to thank Samantha Cagnoni, Andrea Scazzosi, Giuliana Sovran and especially Diego D'Adda for their outstanding research assistance through the development of our research. Our editor at Palgrave Macmillan, Alec Dubber, has shown immense patience with our tardiness and is owed special thanks.

Since this book completes several years of research in this field, some limited parts of it are revised versions of papers published elsewhere. In particular:

- Sections 1.2.1 and 1.3.2 of Chapter 1 are based on a related paper that has been published by the authors in the *Journal of Economic Behavior & Organization*, vol. 40 (3), pp. 255–274, 1999, with the title "Some stylized facts on organization and its evolution." These parts of the paper are reprinted with the permission of Elsevier.
- Section 2.2.4 of Chapter 2 is based on a related paper that has been published by the authors in the *Journal of Industrial Economics*, vol. LII (1), pp. 53–80, 2004, with the title "Delegation of authority in business organizations: an empirical test." These parts of the paper are reprinted with the permission of Blackwell Publishing.
- Section 3.3.4 of Chapter 3 is based on a related paper that has been published by Marco Delmastro in the *International Journal of Industrial*

Organization, vol. 20 (1), pp. 119–137, 2002, with the title "The determinants of the management hierarchy: evidence from Italian plants." These parts of the paper are reprinted with the permission of Elsevier.

- Section 4.4.3 of Chapter 4 is based on a related paper that has been published by the authors in the *Journal of Economics and Management Strategy*, vol. 11 (4), pp. 595–635, 2002, with the title "The determinants of organizational change and structural inertia: technological and organizational factors." These parts of the paper are reprinted with the permission of Blackwell Publishing.

Lastly, this book would not have been possible without the patient support and the encouragement provided by our families, to whom we are especially indebted.

Preface

In the past 30-years the theoretical economic literature has shown a growing interest in organizational design. However, this literature has had very limited interaction with applied work on the internal organization of firms. Part of the problems lies in the difficulty of extracting from these theoretical studies testable hypotheses that could be validated or negated through rigorous empirical tests. Nonetheless, "Part of the problem underlying the lack of interaction [of theoretical studies] with applied work is that most of the evidence concerning internal organization of firms comprises case studies and business reports, instead of large scale empirical datasets" (Mookherjee 2006, p. 385). As will be documented in this volume, this statement is only partially true, as the empirical evidence on organizational design though rather heterogenous, is more extensive than what is generally thought by economic theoreticians. In fact, during the past three decades there has been no shortage of books and articles aimed at analyzing various aspects of organizations in disciplines as diverse as management, organization science, industrial economics, business history, personnel economics, and sociology. Often, however, scholars were interested in different aspects of organizational design, and they resorted to different methodological tools. As a result, this literature is rather fragmented, and the empirical findings on the organization presented by researchers working in one discipline have rarely been considered by researchers working in another.

Thus, the first objective of this volume is to systematize and synthesize the existing quantitative evidence on organizational design coming from different disciplines so as to favor mutual fertilization between theoretical and empirical work.

With this goal in mind, drawing from studies that have adopted different approaches, we have developed a new empirical framework aimed at defining a limited set of quantitative indicators of organizational design that are suitable for use in econometric work.

We use the results of both existing quantitative empirical studies and our own framework to test theoretical predictions about the determinants of organizational design, its evolution, and its effects on firm performance that have been derived from the theoretical economic literature. In so doing, we also indicate future directions of research.

It is our conviction that quantitative empirical studies are the key "raw material" for developing more rigorous theories of organizational design. In fact, systematic theory must be grounded in and derived from systematic empirical facts, a principle that unfortunately has rarely been followed so far in this field.

How to use the book

This work represents, as already said, a bridge between theory and empirics. Hence, it is intended for a broad audience of readers. The first audience consists of scholars with an interest in the theory and empirics of organizational design. This group includes researchers at universities and other scientific institutions and graduate students interested in issues relating to the organization of firms from different perspectives: industrial economics, the theory of the firm, business history, management, and organization studies. The second audience consists of management practitioners. This group includes corporate managers, business consultants, and whoever evaluates and/or takes decisions on how to organize people and resources within a firm. Finally, this book is also addressed to psychologists, sociologists, political scientists, and historians with an interest in quantitative social research.

Some parts of the book are rather technical, but this should not deter the interested reader. In fact, we have used an asterisk (*) to indicate these more technical (usually econometric) sections that the reader may skip without losing the general progression and the main concepts of the chapter. Indeed at the end of each of these more technical parts we have inserted a section that sums up the main results.

Every chapter develops a self-contained discussion of an aspect of organizational design. However, the reader should read first Chapter 1 where the general concept of organizational design and the empirical methodology to analyze it are developed. Then, from Chapter 2 to Chapter 5 we tackle single issues which are at the core of the current debate on organizational design – i.e. the allocation of decision-making authority (Chapter 2), the corporate hierarchy (Chapter 3), the dynamics of organizational design (Chapter 4), and the relation between organizational design and firm performance (Chapter 5). These chapters contain both conceptual and empirical sections. We anticipate that many readers will be interested in relating the conceptual models illustrated in each chapter to the theoretical literature on the economics of organizational design. With those readers in mind, in the Introduction to the volume we have briefly illustrated the key intuitions on which the different theoretical approaches to the study of the economics of organizational design hinge. In addition, the Introduction highlights the (allegedly original) contribution of this book to the extant literature and provides a preliminary account of both the aspects of organizational design taken into consideration and the quantitative methodology that we have developed in order to study them. In the Conclusion we synthesize the key stylized facts on organizational design that emerge from this volume and indicate other potential issues for further research.

Introduction: A New View of Organizational Design

> The last two decades have seen a set of innovations in the organization of the firm that is similarly fundamental and that may ultimately be as momentous [as the rise of the multidivisional form in the first two decades of the twentieth century] ... [Firms] have eliminated layers of management and associated staff positions, redefined the units into which they divide themselves internally, dispersed functional experts to the business units, and increased the authority and accountability of line managers. By these measures, coupled with improved information and measurement systems and redesigned performance management systems, they have sought to increase the speed of decision-making and to tap the knowledge and energy of their employees in ways that have not been tried before.
>
> (Roberts 2004, p. 2)

Statements like this are rather common in works on the organization that mix real facts based on anecdotal business evidence and case studies with conceptual and theoretical insights. It is our opinion that this popular approach though fruitful, suffers from a serious methodological weakness in that it fails to provide a generalizable framework for the study of organizational design. In fact, its conclusions are limited by some general caveats.

From a historical point of view, it is questionable that we are today experiencing a special phase leading to a discrete change that involves the emergence of a new organizational paradigm. In fact, one should acknowledge that in the twentieth century there has been an incessant transformation of organizational structures and practices, due to changes in both external (e.g. technology, market demand, labor relations) and internal (e.g. ownership structure, goals, unionization ratio) conditions. In order to qualify the above-mentioned organizational changes as "revolutionary" rather than "evolutionary," a far more comprehensive and generalizable empirical evidence is needed than the qualitative and rather fragmented picture on which most studies rely.

In addition, since the organization is a very difficult concept to define, analyze, and operationalize, scholars should carefully avoid overwhelming simplifications. On the one hand, organization studies should dissect the complexity of structures and procedures and try to provide comprehensive, robust, micro-level evidence on, at least, some key dimensions of the organization, instead of center-ing attention around theoretically derived archetypes. For instance, in the real world there is no matrix organization, there is instead a continuum of forms that differ one from another as to the specific "value" taken by several organizational dimensions. On the other hand, one should learn from well-known classifications instead of being trapped by them in scientific "culs de sac." U-form, M-form, and lean organization (or J-form) are now standard concepts in the theory of business organizations. In our opinion, the huge work in business history and organization studies that has provided evidence on these forms should be used as a starting (and not an ending) point of empirical and theoretical research. The use of the concept of organizational form indeed is unsuitable to quantitative studies on the organization. In other words, the definition of organizational forms implies a holistic approach to the organization that is not com-patible with the statistical analysis of its individual dimensions – e.g. allocation of power, management hierarchy, incentive structure, routines, procedures, and practices. We need complexity in order to study complexity.

In particular, we claim that what we need is a framework in which organization can be quantitatively analyzed in a multi-dimensional space, an idea which is not new in the organization literature. For any organization, the value of a set of indicators measuring different dimen-sions of organizational design will jointly define an empirically derived profile. The individual dimensions and their variations both across differ-ent organizations and over time, can then be studied quantitatively through appropriate statistical and econometric techniques. The emer-gence of this (static and dynamic) quantitative evidence on organiza-tional design is a necessary condition for the rigorous empirical assessment of the explanatory power of arguments proposed by the theo-retical literature.

In this volume we have adhered to this research design. First, we have tried to systematize, combine, and condense the existing quantitative empirical evidence on (selected dimensions of) organizational design coming from disciplines as diverse as industrial economics, personnel economics, business history, organization and management studies, industrial relations, and sociology. In fact, the lack of a synthesis of quantitative work in different disciplines is a major drawback of the extant empirical literature on organizational design which we have attempted to remedy in this volume. Second, drawing on these studies, we have proposed a new empirical framework aimed at defining (a limited set of) standardized quantitative indicators of organizational design that are suitable for use in econometric work. Third, we have used the stylized facts that result from both existing quantitative empirical studies and our own framework to test theoretical predictions that are derived from the theoretical economic literature about the determinants of organizational design, its evolution, and its effects on firm performance. In so doing, we have also indicated promising directions for future research in this field.

Nonetheless, in order to render this research design manageable, we have been forced to impose some constraints on ourselves.

First, attention has been limited to organizations which induce or coerce participation, and not to organizations of a voluntary nature, such as religious or ideological associations. Hopefully some of the propositions advanced here can fruitfully be applied to these organizations as well.

Second, we have exercised considerable discretion, selecting only a limited number of dimensions of organizational design which have both been analyzed by previous empirical studies and appear key for the purpose of creating a more solid bridge between economic theory and empirical findings. This means that we have omitted some other aspects, no matter how widely they are used or how powerful they have proved to be for other purposes. We claim that failure to adopt this selective strategy has been a major drawback of the quantitative empirical literature in this field. In fact, as will be indicated below in greater detail, some seminal research programs on organizational design in the 1960s have attempted to delineate empirically all the possible interesting variables in organizations. In so doing, they have not given sufficient consideration to the potential operational problems of acquiring reliable data on them and relating them to each other and to the characteristics of the environment.

Before addressing the core aspects of our framework and relating them to theoretical models, some preliminary remarks are in order.

I.1   Preliminary issues in the study of the organization

I.1.1   The concept of organization

Organization is a complex multi-dimensional concept that has been subject to numerous definitions. In this volume, we do not embrace any particular view of the organization. We adopt a very general approach in which an organization can be defined as a collectivity with a relatively identifiable boundary, a normative order, authority ranks, communications systems, and membership coordinating systems; this collectivity exists on a relatively continuous basis in an environment and engages in activities that are usually related to a goal or a set of goals (Hall 1972, p. 9).

In this sense, we use not only an agnostic definition of organization but also a very general conceptual framework through which different theoretical approaches (in both industrial economics and organization science) can be validated empirically. Strangely enough, industrial economics and organization science have developed parallel but unrelated theories of organization (see below for a review of theoretical models).

First of all, organizations are systems for *collective action*. They develop a structure and pattern of functioning which equip them, more or less well, for coping with externally given constraints and uncertainties in order to achieve their objectives. In this view, control is essentially apolitical and defined as independent of interest factors (see the so-called contingency theory in organization science, Burns and Stalker 1961; Woodward 1965; Lawrence and Lorsch 1967; Galbraith 1973, and below for works in the information processing stream of the theoretical economic literature).

In other views, the analysis instead focuses on questions related to the existence in organizations of agents with different interests and the way in which the *distribution of power and influence* affects the pursuit of a common goal. In this case, the mechanisms by which these groups are held together and through which they pursue their own interests to the detriment of the organization's goal become critically important to the understanding of organizational processes and outcomes (see, among many others, Emerson 1962 and Pettigrew 1973 in organization science, and below for works in the decentralization of incentives stream of the theoretical economic literature).

Some other scholars have developed theories that are based on the assumption that the structure of organizations is the outcome of a process of negotiation between *different organizational participants* (see Elger 1975 in organization science, and below for works in the transaction cost economics stream of the theoretical economic literature).

As was mentioned above, we acknowledge the existence of these different conceptual approaches but we do not take any of their considerations for granted, since our goal is to test empirically their predictions.

At this preliminary stage, we want only to clarify that, purely for empirical reasons, our notion of organization excludes:

- informal arrangements (or so-called "informal organizations")
- organizations of a voluntary nature.

I.1.2   Unit of analysis

Overall complex structures consist of many differentiated but interdependent subsystems. For instance, there may be a number of functional divisions within the same corporation, and also a number of branches, plants, or factories at various distances from the headquarters.

These subunits can be analyzed separately so as to simplify the empirical analysis of organization. However, one has to acknowledge the fact that these subsystems are linked together as an overall organizational system through information and resource flows. Indeed, as systems become large they differentiate into parts, and the functioning of these separate parts has to be integrated if the entire system is to be viable.

In this vein, the present volume will illustrate results on both the whole organization of complex structures and that of single subunits. In the latter case, subunits are, however, considered as parts of a greater system of relations.

In particular, our empirical exercise will concentrate on manufacturing plants (see the Appendix at the end of the volume). On the one hand, the focus on subunits will allow us to investigate the organization in greater detail. On the other hand, we will conduct the analysis taking into consideration the relation between subunits and the whole organization through the use of firm-level variables (e.g. ownership status, characteristics of the group).

I.2   An overview of a new approach to the study of organization

I.2.1   The roots of the new approach

Of course, we hope that this volume will be regarded as an original contribution, but the claim of originality is a difficult one to establish. In the building of a science, each of us starts from the contributions of others. In this volume, we have tried to build as much as possible on the contributions of diverse disciplines.

I.2.1.1   Organization science

First, those familiar with organization theory, particularly studies conducted in the mid-1960s, will recognize that our debts fan out from a bunch of seminal studies. Indeed, in those years several important contributions started to shed light on the functioning of the organization. We share the same general approach to the study of organization: a comprehensive investigation of structures based on empirical facts provided by a quantitative account of some dimensions of organizational design.

We build on the pioneer work on organization developed in the 1960s by Derek Pugh and his colleagues at the University of Aston (see Pugh *et al.* 1963, 1968, 1969a, 1969b), and we design a stylized but thorough description of the organization using a vector of quantitative variables similar to that proposed by the Aston group, but of smaller size.

Likewise, Joan Woodward (1965) analyzed deeply the organization of firms, providing comprehensive evidence on some important dimensions. For instance, she established a (linear) relationship between a firm's technical complexity and aspects of its organization chart and personnel ratios, such as the length of the line of command and the span of control of the Chief Executive Officer (CEO) and of other managers. She also explained why firms involved in unit production were more successful if they had short lines of command and wider spans of supervisory control.

A similar analysis was conducted by Burns and Stalker (1961), who found that organizations in more stable industry contexts tended to rely more on formal rules and procedures; decisions were reached at higher levels of the organization and the span of supervisory control was narrower. On the contrary, effective organizations in more dynamic industries were characterized by wider spans of control, less formal procedures, and decentralization of decision-making to middle levels of the organization. In this vein see also Blau and Schoenherr (1971) and Starbuck (1971), among others.

I.2.1.2   Business history

Second, our contribution builds on the huge amount of empirical evidence on organization provided by the business history literature. In particular, we have tried to operationalize and to measure through quantitative indicators aspects that qualitative studies developed by business history scholars generally consider as key dimensions of organizational forms.

In particular, Boxes I.1–I.4 show that this work has extensively documented that organizational forms may be expressed by a bunch of key dimensions. Among them we have selected three:

- the corporate hierarchy and its structure (i.e. the span of control and the depth of the hierarchy)
- the allocation of power (i.e. formal and real decision authority)
- organizational routines, procedures, and practices.

Box I.1   The passage from the pre-modern to the modern form of organization

Business history studies have extensively documented that the passage from the pre-modern to the modern form of organization was characterized by both the rise of a managerial hierarchy and the specialization of workers in fixed, planned and repetitive tasks (see Marglin 1974). In the pre-factory organization workers were directly linked to the owner/entrepreneur and they frequently changed their tasks and positions along the layout of production. The modern corporation is based upon two opposing features: "it contains many distinct operating units and it is managed by a hierarchy of salaried executives" (Chandler 1977).

The evolution of the factory system followed the opposite pattern of that of agriculture (the so-called "Dahlman Paradox," see Leijonhufvud 1986). The modern factory arose from a process of coordination and consolidation of dispersed units of production within the same centralized production system. This was mainly due to the technological advances of the second industrial revolution and to an expanding market. Modern firms developed a structure that gathers and processes information and takes decisions faster and better than the pre-modern factory did (O'Donnell 1952).

Economies of scale and scope of managerial work depend crucially on technology. As a consequence, the advances of the second industrial revolution allowed an increase in the optimal depth of the organization of firms, by sharply decreasing costs of communication and transportation (see Chandler 1977).

In addition the passage from a craft to a hierarchical system of organization induced both a drastic change in the allocation of decision-making and the adoption of new organizational practices (see Montgomery 1987). Using Taylor's (1967) own words "it is only through enforced standardization of methods, enforced adoption of the best implements and working conditions, and enforced cooperation that this faster work can be assured. And the duty of enforcing the adoption of standards and enforcing this cooperation rests with the management alone."

In sum, the modern form of organization is characterized by the rise of a managerial hierarchy, the re-allocation of decision-making power within this hierarchy, and the use of new organizational practices.

Box I.2   The U-form

This structure is characterized by both the presence of a deep managerial hierarchy and the key role of vertical coordination and control; decision-making is highly centralized at the pinnacle of the hierarchy, where corporate offices (e.g. the board of directors, the executive committee) operate. Managers that hold each functional department (e.g. sales, production, finance, R&D) are also members of the top management, so that real and formal authority is mainly centralized at upper levels.

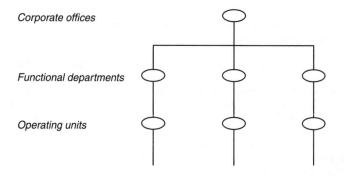

The central management defines long-run and short-run strategies, drawing upon the information coming from lower levels. The vertical and upward structure of the information flow is a key element of this organization. At the bottom of the hierarchy, lower-level managers supervise the implementation of strategies operated by line workers.

The organization depends heavily on the availability of computable data upon which the firm's strategies are based. In this respect, the development of new accounting methodologies for planning and monitoring operations (Johnson 1975) and the use of new organizational practices (Montgomery 1987) are essential elements of the functional organization.

In sum, the U-form is a complex structure composed of a deep hierarchy of managerial executives who are ranked vertically. Strategic decision-making is highly centralized and is based on a bottom-up information network.

Box I.3   The M-form

The multi-divisional form is an evolution of the functional structure (U-form) in which organizational complexity increases and authority is partially allocated downwards. Middle management is now composed of heads of divisional offices as well as functional departments. So the organization is first subdivided by divisions (product and market divisions) and then is functionally structured. Given the introduction of new hierarchical levels, the depth of the management hierarchy expands.

Corporate offices

Divisional offices

Functional
departments

Operating units

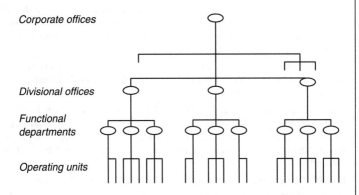

Besides changes in the number and structure of hierarchic relations, the multi-divisional form implies a step towards decentralization of decision-making. The corporate office still remains in charge of long-run strategies. However, divisions are partially autonomous, especially for short-run decisions, and they are managed functionally by a general manager. This partial transfer of authority aims at exploiting local knowledge and increasing the initiative and participation of middle managers (see Chandler 1962).

It has been also pointed out (Johnson 1978) that this new type of organization has needed new accounting procedures as well as a new information and communication network. Of course, information flows and authority links remain vertically structured.

To sum up, the M-form is a complex organization in which functional structures (divisions) are subsystems of a more complex and integrated system of authority relations and information flows. Decision-making is partially delegated down the management hierarchy in order to exploit capabilities of division managers, stimulate their participation to firm's objectives, and speed up implementation of strategic decision-making.

Box I.4   The lean organization (J-form)

The so-called "lean" type of organization (or J-form, see Aoki 1986) represents a step towards a decrease of bureaucratization (Womack *et al.* 1990); in this structure tasks are loosely defined in order to achieve flexibility and exploit local learning and dispersed capabilities. In addition "increased use of technologies, such as email, voice mail and shared databases, has, over time, reduced the need for traditional middle management, whose role was to supervise others and to collect, analyze, evaluate, and transmit information up, down, and across the organizational hierarchy" (Bahrami 1992). The new applications of the information and communication technology (ICT) paradigm have flattened managerial hierarchies just as the second industrial revolution increased their depth; thus the depth of the corporate hierarchy decreases.

It has also been noted (Krafcik 1988) that this type of organization is characterized by a higher span of control, possibly due to the fact that ICTs allow managers to monitor more employees.

Decision-making is further decentralized (Jaikumar 1986; Drucker 1988); flexibility and agents' initiative are achieved through partial delegation of authority, i.e. by the so-called "white collarization of blue collars" (Koike 1990). Hence this structure needs a skilled workforce also at the bottom of the hierarchy.

Finally, the new organization is closely intertwined with the adoption of new organizational practices: innovative work practices (IWPs) and human resource management practices (HRMPs).

To sum up, the lean type of organization is characterized by a drastic reduction of the number of corporate tiers, an increase in the span of control of managers, a further delegation of decision-making power and the use of new work and incentive practices.

I.2.1.3   Management studies

Third, we acknowledge management studies that have documented the rise of a new form of organization: the so-called "lean" type of organization (see Box I.4). In so doing, they have by and large stressed the role played by the same key dimensions of organizational design that have been mentioned above: (re-)allocation of decision authority, (shrinking of the) corporate hierarchy, and (use of innovative) organizational procedures and practices. We are thus indebted to these studies that have been used here as focusing devices. Moreover, the book provides a condensed, comprehensive illustration of stylized facts on these aspects of organizational design, thus providing an original contribution to this debate.

I.2.1.4 Economic theory

In the past three decades there has been growing interest in organizational design from economic theoreticians. We share Roberts' (2004) view that "economics has much to say about the problem of organizational design" (p. 12). He defines his own work as mixing "case studies and shorter examples with fundamental conceptual and theoretical material" (p. ix). As was mentioned earlier, this approach indeed is rather popular in the extant literature on organizational design. In this volume we have the ambition to go a step further.

In fact, in spite of the claim that economic theory provides useful predictions on the determinants of firms' organizational design and its evolution over time, there is a surprising shortage of robust quantitative tests of the explanatory power of different theories. In turn, this represents an insurmountable obstacle to the further development of theoretical models, and more generally of our knowledge about the "how" and "why" of firms' organizational design. The main objective of this volume is to contribute to closing this gap. For this purpose, we provide a critical review and a synthesis of the multi-disciplinary quantitative empirical evidence on selected aspects of firms' organizational design and we propose and use a new empirical methodology that is suitable to econometric tests (see below).

In Chapters 1–4, for each organizational dimension under scrutiny, a conceptual model that leads to precise theoretical predictions is first illustrated. In order to allow the interested reader to better relate these models to the theoretical debate in the economics of organizational design, in a later section of this Introduction we briefly highlight relevant aspects of the different streams of the theoretical literature.

I.2.2 A new approach to the study of organizational design

Above and beyond the contribution of existing empirical quantitative studies, in this volume we present new facts based on a new empirical approach to the study of organizational design. While a detailed description of this approach is postponed to Chapter 1, it is important to delineate here the main principles by which it is inspired.

We have designed a framework in which organization is quantitatively analyzed in a multi-dimensional space. For any structure or subsystem, the value of a vector including a *selected* set of organizational dimensions will jointly define empirically a profile of organizational design. We are thus able to investigate quantitatively individual dimensions of organizational design, correlating them to each other and to other aspects of the firm (e.g. ownership status, technology) and of its environment (location, demand, labor market, social context). Dynamically, changes over time in these dimensions provide evidence on the evolutionary path of organizational design.

The key advantage of this approach is that it is suitable for use in statistical and econometric analyses based on large-scale data sets. In addition, while providing a set of standardized quantitative indicators, it can be replicated in different empirical settings. In so doing, it extends our capacity to measure (and thereby investigate) some key characteristics of firms' organizational design. In our view, this is a substantial departure from case studies that attempt little in the way of measurement of variables and quantification of relationships; hence they do not offer the opportunity to systematically confirm findings from one study with those of another one or to assess the reliability of the relationships detected between variables.

It is important to emphasize that in order to render this approach manageable, we have had to concentrate on some key dimensions of organizational design, basically due to operational constraints, and we have developed appropriate indicators only for these dimensions. It is fair to acknowledge that there are other aspects of organizational design that have been omitted here. In principle, our empirical framework could be easily extended to other dimensions. However, the aspects that we do consider are central to the debate in economics, management, and business history. In fact, we take as our major concern the issues of hierarchical relations and of power and its distribution in organized structures. After all, this is what social organization is all about.

Indeed, the fundamental conception of formal complex organizations entails two dimensions: the subdivision of the total responsibilities among employees so as to simplify individual tasks and permit the application of expert knowledge in the performance of specialized duties, on the one hand, and a hierarchy of official authority to effect the coordination needed as the result of this subdivision, on the other (see Roberts 2004, pp. 17–18).

In so doing, we have first of all developed standardized scales and measures of the structural dimensions of organizational design. For instance, the detailed examination of control systems resulted in the development of a typology based on two parameters: the degree to which control is exercised personally or indirectly; and the degree to which control systems are integrated or dispersed (Woodward 1965). Accordingly, we have derived measures of the amount and forms of control exercised by managers at the different levels of the corporate hierarchy.

Furthermore, we have added to the variables measuring the architectural features of organizational design indicators relating to organizational procedures and practices. These latter present complementary relations with the structure *a là Weber,* because they define the ways in which workers should perform their tasks (*systems of formal and informal routines*) and they try to align employees' interests to the goals of the firm (*incentive structure*).

But organizations do not operate in a vacuum. They affect their internal and external environment and are affected by them. We will go into the relation between design, structure and performance of organizations, and technology, asserting that the previous ones vary systematically in different technological contexts. In addition, organizations are in constant interaction with other organizations, clients and customers, and general societal conditions (the external environment). In a variety of ways we will also assert that the design, structure, and performance of organizations reflect variations in external environmental conditions, so that industry, location, and cultural contexts play a key role in shaping organizational design.

We stop this brief presentation of our new approach at this stage. In Chapter 1 we will further specify our empirical methodology and provide preliminary descriptive evidence on firms' organizational design and its evolution in the past two decades. Then, in Chapters 2 and 3, we will study the relation between architectural features of organizational design and the internal and external environment (the allocation of decision-making authority in Chapter 2, and the corporate hierarchy in Chapter 3). In Chapter 4 we will investigate the determinants of the dynamics of organizational design. Chapter 5 will shed new lights on the impact of organizational design on firm performance. Finally, the main contributions of this volume are synthesized in the conclusion.

I.3   The substance of the economics of organizational design

In this section we will synthesize the key approaches of the economic theoretical literature on organizational design. Note that the aim is not to provide another survey of this literature. Rather we will simply illustrate the key intuitions behind the most popular approaches, and the fundamental indications they provide to empirical studies. Accordingly, we will be selective rather than comprehensive, and in so doing we will not do justice to the richness of the theoretical debate – for this purpose, the interested reader will find appropriate references. Inclusion of a particular contribution will be driven by our subjective appreciation of its relevance in terms of predictions regarding the determinants of firms' organizational design, its evolution over time, and the economic impact of its adoption.

We will start from the pioneer insights on authority and hierarchical design provided by transaction cost economics. Then we will consider the information processing and decentralization of incentives streams of literature, which offer different, but largely complementary, explanations of the determinants of firms' organizational design. Lastly, we will briefly analyze different bodies of literature that, starting from different premises and following different approaches, have addressed the question of why organizational design is sticky and tends not to be changed by firms over time.

I.3.1 Transaction cost economics

Since the seminal work of Simon (1962) economists have described the firm as a system that is composed of interrelated subsystems, each of the latter being, in turn, *hierarchic* in structure until we reach some lowest level of elementary subsystem. According to Williamson (1975) hierarchical organizational designs arise because of the efficiency advantages of authority relations based on decisions by fiat. These advantages stem from the ability of hierarchical designs (i) to economize on communication and information processing costs,[1] and (ii) to mitigate problems engendered by individuals' opportunism. In particular, in Chapter 3 of his book Williamson compares the efficiency properties of simple hierarchy and peer group organizations. The latter organizations involve collective production, information processing, and decision-making activities, and provide income-sharing arrangements between participants, but do not entail subordination. Conversely, in a simple hierarchy one individual (the "boss") is assigned the task of giving instructions to other individuals (the "employees") and monitoring their behavior: "The employee stands ready to accept authority regarding work assignments provided only that the behavior called for falls within the "zone of acceptance" of the [employment] contract" (Williamson, 1985, pp. 218–219). In joining a hierarchy he also accepts the authority of the boss to monitor his behavior *ex post*.

Therefore, a simple hierarchy enjoys both information processing and monitoring advantages. First of all, information flows and decision-making activity are centralized in the hands of the supervisor. In accordance with Arrow (1974, p. 68) this arrangement yields the benefits of coordinated decision-making and saves on the costs of transmitting and processing information. In addition, if the requisite information processing and decision-making capabilities are not uniformly distributed among individuals, it also captures specialization economies as the supervisory function will be assigned to the most talented individual. Second, the tasks assigned to the supervisor also involve *ex post* auditing and experience-rating. As is discussed by Alchian and Demsetz (1972) this limits the free rider problem inherent in the peer group arrangement.

Williamson adds that more complex multi-stage hierarchies are composed of a sequence of simple hierarchies and enjoy similar advantages to those highlighted above: "there are striking parallels between the reason for workers to be joined in simple hierarchies and the decision to merge simple hierarchies into a multistage hierarchy rather than mediate transactions between them by market means" (Williamson 1975, p. 56).

I.3.2 The information processing stream

The information processing stream analyzes the issue of coordination of imperfectly informed agents.[2] The rationality of agents is bounded *à la* Simon, in the sense that the scarce resource is not information,but information processing capacity (Simon 1945). Accordingly, in this stream of literature emphasis is placed on the costs involved in information processing and communications. Conversely, the problems of conflicting objectives among individuals, and the need for suitable incentives to deal effectively with these problems, are ignored (see below).

In particular, the information processing stream highlights that there are different sources of organizational failures in hierarchical organizations that centralize the decision-making function. First, centralized hierarchies suffer from information transmission leaks (Keren and Levhari 1979, 1983, 1989) and delays (Radner 1993; Van Zandt 1999b) in transmitting information from the pinnacle to the bottom of the hierarchy. The larger the depth of the hierarchy, the larger the leaks and delays. Hence, even if one abstracts from incentive problems, general strategies defined by the superior (i.e. the top management of a firm) might differ from those implemented by subordinates simply because of distortions in intra-firm communication. In addition, these strategies may fail to produce the expected benefits because of implementation delays which render decisions obsolete. In particular, decentralization of decisions reduces delays because it allows tasks to be performed concurrently.

Second, due to information overload, centralized organizations make decisions at a slower pace than decentralized ones. Accordingly, Sah and Stiglitz (1986, 1988) show that when decision authority is concentrated at the top of the hierarchy, a relatively lower number of projects can be selected in comparison with a situation in which it is decentralized. Decentralization then emerges as an efficient arrangement in situations where projects are on average of good quality.

Third, if the tasks that need to be performed by an organization are heterogeneous, by delegating decision-making to the agent who has the best information relating to a given decision firms can fully exploit economies arising from local capabilities and specialization of tasks (Geanakoplos and Milgrom 1991). Moreover, with task specialization by repeatedly processing the same type of information an agent can lower her unit time of processing this type of information. Nonetheless, the different types of information processed by different agents then need to be aggregated in order to create effective decision-making. In other words, the benefits of specialization are limited by the need to coordinate specialized tasks. Greater specialization leads to an increase of communication costs within the organization because of coordination needs (Bolton and Dewatripont 1994). In accordance with these arguments, organizational design is shaped by the trade-off between specialization and communication; this explains the ubiquity of hierarchical organizations.[3] More recently, Dessein and Santos (2006) assume that the information that organizations need to adapt to a changing environment is local in nature, being dispersed among employees. Organizations optimally choose how much to make use of this local information, and the quality of communications among employees. They may opt for an adaptive organizational design which gives employees the flexibility to tailor their actions to the information they alone observe. However, if employees specialize in the tasks in which they enjoy an informational advantage, as was mentioned above communication costs increase because of the need for coordination of specialized tasks. Under these circumstances, delegation with multi-tasking may optimize the trade-offs between the benefits arising from use of local information and communication costs. It follows that organizational designs tend to be of two very different types: either rigid, specialized, and with limited communication among employees, or adaptive, with employees being assigned multiple tasks and intensely communicating between each other.

Fourth, in line with Garicano (2000), let us assume that individuals can be ranked according to the difficulty of the problems they are able to solve, with higher-rank individuals being able to solve all the problems that can be solved by lower-rank ones plus some other more difficult problems. Experts that are able to solve more difficult problems are correspondingly more expensive, but more difficult problems are less likely to occur. Then a pyramidal knowledge hierarchy with a greater number of less skilled individuals at lower levels and fewer more skilled individuals at higher ones allows us to optimally use individuals' expertise (Garicano and Rossi-Hansberg 2006). In a similar setting, Harris and Raviv (2002) show that decentralization of decision-making down the hierarchy (i.e. to middle managers) may be explained by the need to use more effectively the time of higher-rank individuals (i.e. the CEO) who have greater opportunity cost. Conversely, if the value of solving difficult problems (i.e. companywide coordination of activities) increases, then greater centralization follows.

I.3.3　The decentralization of incentive stream

This stream of literature includes a series of rather heterogenous studies that share the common purpose of highlighting the characteristics in terms of individuals' incentives of organizational designs which are hierarchically structured and in which a principal located at the top of the hierarchy (e.g. the top manager of a firm) may delegate decision authority to agents (i.e. division managers).[4] This kind of organizational design is compared with a centralized design where the principal makes all decisions based on the information communicated by agents; agents simply receive instructions and implement the decisions taken by the principal. This literature abstracts from the costs of information processing and transmission in which the information processing stream is interested. Conversely, it focuses attention on the incentive costs that arise with decentralized decision-making. The cost of delegating authority is the principal's *loss of control* over the choice of projects. Thus, loss of control assumes the form of deviation of the firm's action from the objectives of the principal. In fact, agents that are delegated decision authority act in their own self-interest. Hence, they are tempted to hide valuable information in order to pursue objectives that in general are different from those of the principal, and maximize their own utility.

More precisely, most of this literature considers a situation in which agents have private information on their tasks. The principal may hire a middle manager who has no role in production but provides her with informational expertise. The models analyze whether it is desirable for the principal (a) to hire the middle manager or not, and (b) to delegate decision authority to agents or to the middle manager. Therefore, these studies analyze both the depth of the hierarchy and the decentralization of decision authority.

The starting point of this literature is the so-called "Revelation Principle."[5] This principle states that if (i) there are no information processing and communication costs, (ii) the design of complex contracts does not involve any additional cost, (iii) agents do not collude, and (iv) contracts cannot be renegotiated *ex post*, an organizational design with centralized decision-making is always optimal, in the sense that it is not dominated by any organizational design that relies on delegation of decisions. In fact, the outcome obtained by any design of this latter type can be replicated by a centralized one. Then the objective is to identify organizational arrangements that while providing agents with adequate incentives, effectively deal with the loss of control problem and so come as close as possible to the outcome of a centralized design. Note, however, that if the framework of the Revelation Principle applies, decentralization never dominates centralization. So the implicit assumption is made that decentralization is driven by other factors (e.g. information overload problems, communication costs).

Alternatively, the assumptions of the Revelation Principle may not hold. An interesting departure is to assume that agents possess specific knowledge (or local information) which cannot be communicated to the principal in a timely fashion.[6] Then the delegation of decision authority may serve the purpose of inducing agents to use their privately held information. Accordingly, Aghion and Tirole (1997) show that the principal, by giving subordinates formal decision authority over both initiation and ratification of projects on the quality of which she is poorly informed, improves the incentives of agents to search for projects. The associated benefits for the principal can outweigh the costs that arise from the implementation of projects that sometime have limited value to the principal, but provide great private benefits to agents. This is more likely to happen the less informed is the principal and the larger is the extent of the private benefits of the agent. In this situation, delegation is likely to increase both an agent's initiative to acquire information and her participation in the contractual relationship. Conversely, decisions about projects that potentially have a large payoff to the principal and about interdependent projects would be better centralized, as there is a great opportunity cost for the principal if the agent selects a suboptimal project.

Baker *et al.* (1999) depart from this framework in that they assume that the principal always keeps formal authority, as "[she] can restrict the subordinate's actions, overturn his decisions, and even fire him" (p. 56). So the authority which is delegated to the agent is informal. In other words, even though the agent can be given the authority to select and ratify projects with no interference from the principal, this latter keeps the right to renege on her former decision, overrule the agent, and implement a different project. Baker *et al.* rely on a repeated game model and consider two situations, depending on whether the principal has the information necessary to assess the project before it is ratified by the agent or not. In the former situation, decision authority is delegated if the principal values her reputation for delegating authority more than what she would save by overruling an agent's choice of a specific project. In the latter situation it is the threat of the principal retracting the subordinate's authority over future projects that induces the subordinate to abstain from choosing a project which may badly hurt the principal. Then delegation follows. This study again shows that delegation gives agents stronger incentives to search for and develop projects. Nonetheless, with an informed principal, the greater incentive arising from delegation vanishes the more aligned are the agent's and the principal's objectives. Moreover, delegation is more likely if the principal has not much to lose from the agent's decisions. With an uninformed principal, it is a low extreme value of the private benefit that the agent can extract from a project that makes delegation feasible. Lastly, independently of whether the principal is informed or not, a high discount rate decreases the likelihood of delegation.

An interesting variation on this theme is offered by a situation in which even if the agent does not possess any specific knowledge, she has different priors from those of the principal as to the best course of action (see Van den Steen 2006; see also Zabojnik 2002). Under such circumstances, and similarly to what happens in a private information setting, delegation of decision authority has a positive motivational effect if the agent's effort is more useful when the right decision is made. In fact, the agent expects a higher return from her effort when she is in charge of decision-making and can choose the decision that according to her priors is the right one. Nonetheless, delegation poses coordination problems that are greater the more divergent are the principal's and the agent's priors, as each party wants to follow the course of action that she considers best. In contrast to a situation with private benefits, these problems cannot be alleviated through an incentive compensation scheme. In fact, such a scheme, in addition to making the agent care more about coordination, also induces her to behave in accordance with her priors. So disagreement between the agent and the principal engenders a trade-off between motivation and coordination. It follows that delegation will increase in the importance of the agent's effort and decrease in the importance of coordination. This also implies that the principal may delegate decision authority and abstain from overturning the agent's decisions with the aim of "firing the troops," even though she knows that delegation can make decisions worse.

A weakness of this literature is that decisions relating to different aspects of organizational design (e.g. the depth of the hierarchy, delegation of decision authority, use of different work practices and incentive schemes) are often analyzed in isolation. Of course, there are exceptions.[7] Athey and Roberts (2001) explicitly recognize that the design of incentive schemes and the allocation of decision authority are interlinked. They analyze, though in a very specific setting,[8] the trade-off that may arise between motivating agents' effort, which is done best by rewarding agents on precise measures of their effort (i.e. an input measure), and inducing them to take the right decisions, which may require linking their rewards to the total value created (i.e. an output measure). They show that if the need to elicit effort from agents prevails and the compensation scheme relies on a comparative performance evaluation, it may be optimal not to assign decision authority to the best-informed party; in fact, under these circumstances agents have very bad incentives for selection of the right decision (see also Jensen and Meckling 1992). Raith (2005) considers delegation of decision authority to agents in a hidden information setting similar to that of Aghion and Tirole (1997), and contextually analyzes the optimal design of agents' compensation schemes – that is, whether to rely on input- or output-based compensation. A compensation that is commensurate to agents' effort does not give the agent much incentive to use her specific knowledge; conversely, if compensation is closely correlated with the principal's profit, the agent incurs high income risk. The model shows that delegation implies a shift towards an output-based payment scheme. Therefore, the greater the information advantage of the agent and the more valuable is the information she possesses, the more likely is delegation, and the larger is the weight on output in the agent's compensation scheme, even if the agent's effort can be measured quite precisely.

I.3.4   On the dynamics of organizational design

The above approaches consider the costs and benefits of different organizational designs (e.g. more or less hierarchical, more or less decentralized) and highlight factors on which these costs and benefits depend. So they adopt a static approach and provide theoretical predictions as to which organizational design will emerge depending on the contingencies which firms are facing.

Nonetheless, as will be documented in the following chapters of this volume (especially Chapter 4), organizational designs happen to be very resilient (or sticky). So the question arises why are firms so reticent to modify the (supposedly optimal) organizational design they have chosen under certain contingencies when these contingencies have changed? In other words, what explains inertia in organizational design?

Various explanations have been offered by the theoretical literature on firm organization. Behavioralist theorists of organizations (see March and Simon 1958; Cyert and March 1963) point to the bounded rationality of economic agents and the costs involved by decision-making activity under uncertainty to have access to, store, process, and transmit information. As there is no guarantee that a decision to modify the organization may be optimal, and designing a new organization is costly, firms prefer to stay with their current organizational design unless abnormally poor performances trigger change.

The literature on population ecology contends that structural inertia is the outcome of an ecological–evolutionary process: selection tends to favor stable organizations – that is, organizations whose structure is difficult to change (Hannan and Freeman 1984). In comparison with other institutions, business firms enjoy the advantage of a high level of reliability and accountability (i.e. the capacity to collectively produce a product of given quality repeatedly and to document the sequence of decisions and related outcome, see Hannan and Freeman 1984, p. 153). But in order to assure reliability and accountability, a firm's organizational structure needs to be reproducible over time. This is obtained by processes of institutionalization and by the creation of standardized routines, two factors which make firms highly resistant to change.

Evolutionary theories of economic change (see Nelson and Winter 1982) help us to understand why organizational routines may be a source of structural inertia. According to such a stream of literature, routines are the repertoire of a firm's idiosyncratic collective actions; they are built through a cumulative process based on past experience of problem solving activity and involve automatic coordinated responses to specific signals from the environment.[9] So, due their very nature, they can be modified only incrementally and at considerable cost, with this leading to lock-in effects which extend to the firm's entire organizational design.

Two further bodies of theoretical literature are key for understanding the sources of inertia that can hinder changes of organizational design.

On the one hand, the literature concerned with the investment behavior of firms under uncertainty in the framework of real option theory (Dixit and Pindyck 1994) has argued that when an investment decision entails sunk costs and future market conditions are uncertain, there is an additional opportunity cost of implementing the decision which stems from the lost option value of delaying it until new information is available. Any change of a firm's organization design implies sunk costs, and its returns are uncertain by nature. So, it might be optimal for a firm to postpone it until new information is collected.

On the other hand, there are political forces within organizations that may hinder organizational changes (see Milgrom 1988; Milgrom and Roberts 1990a). The reason is that adoption by a firm of a particular organizational design leads to a particular distribution of quasi-rents among firm's employees. Therefore, if the firm is going to change its organizational design, a change which is likely to have considerable distributional implications, individual employees will try to influence the nature of the change so as to protect or augment their own quasi-rents. As such influence activities absorb employees' time and attention, which otherwise could be used in directly productive activities, they engender substantial costs. In order to avoid them, a firm may refrain from implementing organizational changes that would improve productive efficiency, unless failure to do so threatens survival (Schaefer 1998).

1
A New Quantitative Empirical Methodology for the Analysis of Organizational Design and Dynamics

1.1 Introduction

The organization of firms is a complex structure made up of a large number of parts that interact in a non-straightforward way. As was mentioned in the Introduction the business history literature and management and organization studies have developed a well-known classification of organizational structures: U-form, M-form, and lean organization (or J-form) are now standard concepts in the theory of business organizations. Organizational forms defined by these studies are characterized by key elements such as configuration (in particular, depth – i.e. number of levels – and shape – i.e. span of control) of the corporate hierarchy, allocation of authority (centralization), and use of procedures and practices. Every organizational form is associated with a different bundle of these aspects.

Even though we believe that these studies provide interesting insights into the organization of businesses, we depart from this line of research for two main reasons.

First, organizational form is a difficult concept to operationalize, because it involves a great deal of subjectivity. In fact in many (probably most) cases companies use an organizational design which does not completely fit with the above classification of structures. Hence, the assignment of a company to a category of organizational form entails a considerable amount of individual discretion.

Second, the use of the concept of organizational form allows us to analyze the organizational dynamics and its determinants (see Chapter 4), but it is unsuitable for quantitative studies of the single elements upon which these structures are based. In other words, the definition of organizational forms implies a holistic approach to the organization that is not compatible with the quantitative analysis of its single components.

So, even though we share with these studies the same key concepts of business organizations, we depart from this methodology in that we follow a different empirical approach to the study of organizational design and its dynamics.

We build on the pioneer work on organization developed in the 1960s by Derek Pugh and his colleagues at the University of Aston (see Pugh *et al*. 1963, 1968, 1969a, 1969b), and we design a stylized but thorough description of the organization using a vector of *quantitative variables*. These variables operationalize aspects that both the theoretical economic literature on the organization of firms and qualitative studies by management and business history scholars generally consider as key dimensions of organizational design. The use of quantitative variables makes it possible for an organization to be located at a precise point in a multi-dimensional organizational design space. The position on all these dimensions of a particular organization will jointly form a profile of its organizational design. Dynamically, we are thus able to monitor changes in these profiles over a given period of time and thus to assess the evolutionary path of organizational design.

The quantitative approach has a major advantage over classifications of types of organizational structures. In fact,

> there is a very large number of theoretically possible profiles ... Of course many of these theoretical profiles may never appear in reality, and those that are found may fall into clusters of similarly structured organizations. These clusters may well be labeled "types" it being recognized that they have not been postulated a priori but have been evolved with reference to the empirical data.
>
> (Pugh *et al*. 1963)

The emergence of this evidence would act as verification of the empirical content of the theoretical literature.

While there are many interesting aspects of organizational design, we focus attention on four primary dimensions: (i) configuration of corporate hierarchy; (ii) allocation of decision-making (i.e. centralization of decision authority); (iii) procedures (i.e. formal practices that define how workers perform their tasks and incentivize employees); and (iv) changes in these aspects (flexibility).

In so doing, we depart from the organization studies in the Aston group tradition which aimed at developing a comprehensive description of organizational design. For instance, the methodology developed by Pugh and his colleagues was based on the analysis of sixty-four scales of organizational variables for a total of more than 200 variables. This forced scholars that used this methodology to consider samples composed of a relatively small number of organizations,[1] and it represented a serious constraint to a wider diffusion of this methodology in empirical research on organizational design. Conversely, the empirical methodology we are going to illustrate here is more parsimonious and hence more manageable. It considers four dimensions that are characterized by a small set of quantitative variables. Hence it is is suitable to be used in large-scale field analyses.

Each profile of organizational design is thus defined by the following dimensions:

- configuration, as is reflected in the number of levels of the corporate hierarchy and the (average) span of control
- allocation of authority, i.e. the level in the organization responsible for taking a selected number of strategic and operating decisions
- adoption of formal procedures and practices, i.e. innovative work practices (IWPs) and human resource management practices (HRMPs)
- organizational dynamics (flexibility), i.e. how the previous dimensions vary over time.

The remaining of the chapter proceeds as follows. Section 1.2 is devoted to the definition of appropriate measures of these primary dimensions of organizational design. In Section 1.3 we survey the available evidence on structural organizational variables (i.e. configuration and allocation of decision authority) and their evolution over time; we also describe the international diffusion of IWPs and HRMPs. In so doing we also provide a practical application of the proposed empirical methodology. Some summarizing remarks in Section 1.4 conclude the chapter.

1.2 Measures of organizational design

1.2.1 Structural organizational variables: configuration and centralization[2]

Organizational design is characterized by some key structural aspects. In particular, we consider here a bundle of structural organizational variables (SOVs) which provide detailed information on two primary dimensions: configuration (i.e. the depth and shape of the corporate hierarchy) and the allocation of decision-making power (i.e. centralization). The next two subsections are devoted to the presentation of these variables.

1.2.1.1   Configuration: measures of corporate hierarchy

Every organization has an authority structure, a system of relationships between positions and jobs described in terms of the authority of superiors and the responsibility of subordinates. This conceptualization is commonly expressed in the form of an *organization chart*. The configuration of this structure – that is, its depth and shape – may be compared in different organizations (Pugh *et al.* 1963).

The first aspect of interest in the configuration of an organization is its *depth* (also called its "vertical span of control" by the Aston group). In fact, since the seminal work of Williamson (1967) many theoretical papers (see, for instance, Keren and Levhary 1979, 1983, 1989; Rosen 1982; Radner 1993; Qian 1994) have described a firm's organization by its number of hierarchical levels. Thus we define the variable *Level* as the number of hierarchical levels of organizations.

Of course, the minimum of *Level* is two, corresponding to the situation in which an organization comprises only two levels (e.g. workers and owner–manager/top manager). *Level* is a measure of organization complexity. On the one hand, firms face problems of "loss of control" in expanding organizational depth (Williamson 1967). In fact, the reliance of hierarchical organizations on serial reproduction for their functioning exposes them to serious distortions in the transmission of information (Keren and Levhari 1979, 1983, 1989) and implementation delays (Radner 1993; Van Zandt 1999b). Hence, bounded rationality within organizations should impose a severe limitation on a hierarchy's depth. On the other hand, the corporate hierarchy is a source of economies of scale in gathering and elaborating new information (Chandler 1962, 1977; Radner 1993). Indeed, the purpose of the hierarchy is to capture scale and scope economies within and among functions through planning and coordination.

The second notion of configuration refers to the *shape* of organizations. While the number of hierarchical levels is a straightforward variable to define, the span of control is trickier. In general, the span of control is, for each tier of a hierarchy, the number of subordinates under the same superior. However, information about employees' distribution among levels is often unavailable or very expensive to gather.[3] So, we derive a proxy, called *Span*, which is easy to calculate and involves a small set of information (i.e. the number of employees and *Level*). *Span* is the "average span of control" defined as the number that, given the number of employees *n* and the number of hierarchical levels (*Level*), satisfies the following equation:[4]

$$n = 1 + Span + Span^2 + \dots + Span^{Level-1}$$

The (static) choice of the span of control again depends upon the "loss of control" phenomenon. In a context where employees are vertically related, the more subordinates a superior monitors (greater span of control), the smaller the probability of the subordinate being checked (Calvo and Wellisz 1978, 1979; Rosen 1982; Qian 1994). Hence a greater span of control will raise the likelihood of subordinates' shirking. However, a lower value of the span of control, given the number of employees, implies a higher number of hierarchical levels, with the related disadvantages that were mentioned earlier.

To sum up, we claim that organizations can be viewed as complex hierarchical structures. A robust way to analyze them quantitatively is to look at their configuration, that is primarily defined by the number of hierarchical tiers (the depth of the hierarchy) and the span of control (the shape of the hierarchy). We expect to find static and dynamic regularities in the values taken by such variables. Before doing so, we introduce other indices that measure the allocation of decision authority within business organizations.

1.2.1.2 Centralization: measures of the allocation of decision authority

Since Marschak and Radner's (1972) seminal contribution, the term "organizational design" has been employed to characterize the key elements of organizations within a decision-making framework. Even though there is more to organizational design than just centralization and decentralization, it is indisputable that authority relations are a key aspect of business organizations. Centralization (and decentralization) concerns the locus of the authority to make decisions affecting the organization. We may therefore conceive of a corporate hierarchy comprising various tiers of decision-making. The power to make strategic and operating decisions is not necessarily concentrated at the pinnacle of the hierarchy, but may be diffused throughout the firm.

In the organization literature two types of authority have been recognized: formal (or institutional) authority and real (or personal) authority. Both formal and real authority may be delegated to a greater or lesser extent.

In order to analyze the allocation of formal and real decision-making power we have adopted a rather stylized, yet meaningful, description of the decision-making structure relating to strategic and operating decisions (shown in Figures 1.1a and 1.1b, respectively), which is instrumental to obtaining data that are comparable across business organizations. Note that the focus of the analysis is a generic "organizational unit" (or unit) which can be either an entire company or a smaller part (e.g. plant, factory, shop, laboratory) of a bigger (multi-unit) organization.

In this way, organizations can be characterized by the degree of centralization of decision authority that depends on the level at which decisions are taken. As concerns strategic decisions, the highest degree of decentralization corresponds to the situation in which the levels under the manager of the organizational unit are responsible for taking decisions (level 1). Going up the hierarchy, we find situations in which the manager of the unit is autonomously in charge of the firm's strategic decisions (level 2). Otherwise her power may be limited by superiors' supervision (level 3), or she might be entitled only to make proposals (level 4). Finally, the highest degree of centralization is the case in which hierarchical levels higher than the manager of the unit (for example, the owner–manager in a small owner-managed firm, or a higher rank salaried manager in a unit

Figure 1.1a   Decision-making structure: strategic decisions

Notes
IL: intermediate levels (such as workers/clerks, middle managers).
MU: manager of the organizational unit (e.g. firm, plant, factory, shop) autonomously (i.e. formal and real authority to the MU).
MU + AUT: situations in which the manager of the organizational unit needs a formal authorization before taking a decision (real authority to the MU, formal authority to his superior).
MU's PROP: situations in which the manager of the unit can only propose but not decide autonomously.
HL: higher levels (i.e. a corporate superior of the MU).

Figure 1.1b   Decision-making structure: operating decisions

Notes
LL: lower levels (e.g. workers, clerks).
MM: middle managers (i.e. levels between lower levels and the manager of the unit).
MU: manager of the organizational unit (e.g. firm, plant, factory, shop).

owned by a multi-unit public firm) take strategic decisions. It is worth noticing that this classification of the decision-making process allows us not only to envisage the allocation of power within the corporate hierarchy but also to investigate situations in which formal and real authority is split between two different tiers (the manager of the unit, on the one hand, and his superior, on the other) as in the case of level 3 (for a discussion, see Chapter 2).

As for operating decisions, a similar distinction can be made between centralized units, where decision-making power is concentrated in the manager of the unit, and decentralized ones, where responsibility is delegated to lower hierarchical levels (e.g. workers, clerks).

Having defined this framework, we present three different measures of the decision-making structure of organizations. We claim that they give an exhaustive and comprehensive picture, both statically and dynamically, of the allocation of power (Sah and Stiglitz 1986, 1988; Aghion and Tirole 1995, 1997).

Data on the decision-making structure are multivariate categorical ranked data. Moreover, it is very likely that data relating to different decisions are highly correlated. Our main objective is to describe the main structural features of the allocation of decision-making power in terms of a small number of variables. In order to do this one can use principal component analysis (PCA), a fairly standard approach in situations such as these. Thus, we have defined for organization *j* a measure of the degree of *centralization of decision-making* (*DC*), in the following way:

$$DC(j) = \sum_{i=1}^{I} a_{1i}\, x_i(j)$$

where *I* is the number of (strategic or operating) decisions taken into consideration, a_{1i} ($i = 1,..,I$) are the *I* coordinates of the first component of a PCA on decision variables, and $x_i(j)$ ($i = 1,..,I$) are the values of the decision variables once linearly ranked (recall that for the cases described above such variables range from 1, maximum decentralization, to 5, maximum centralization, for strategic decisions, see Figure 1.1a, and from 1 to 3 for operating decisions, see Figure 1.1b). Thus *DC* will be high if decision-making is highly centralized, and low in decentralized organizations.

In addition, one can calculate, for organization j, the number, $ND_k(j)$, of decisions taken by each hierarchical level k. That is:

$$ND_k(j) = \sum_{i=1}^{I} D_i^k(j) \quad k = 1, \cdots, K,$$

$$\text{with: } D_i^k(j) = \begin{cases} 1 & \text{if } x_i(j) = k, \\ 0 & \text{otherwise.} \end{cases}$$

where $D_i^k(j)$, is a dummy variable that equals one when decision i is taken by level k (namely if $x_i(j) = k$) and is zero if it is taken by another level, and K is the total number of hierarchical levels considered (in earlier framework $K = 5$ for strategic decisions, and $K = 3$ for operating decisions). Hence, for each organization j, $ND(j)$ is a vector of K discrete coordinates, that range between zero (no decision is taken at that level) and I (all decisions are taken at that level).

Unlike the previous measure, *ND* captures, besides the degree of centralization, the distribution of authority within the hierarchy. Whereas from *DC* we know the average level of centralization of decision-making activity, from *ND* we can distinguish situations in which decision-making is concentrated at high, middle, or even low hierarchical levels from cases in which it is more evenly distributed.

Lastly, we have defined a measure of the degree of *concentration of decision-making power*. To do so, we have followed three steps. First, since the levels described earlier represent not only hierarchical levels but also ways in which a level takes the decision (in previous framework levels 3 and 4), we have aggregated them in to G groups corresponding actual tiers (e.g. lower levels and middle management – level 1 – manager of the unit – level 2 and 3 – and higher levels – level 4 and 5). Second, we have used Euclidean distance as a measure of decision concentration. That is, for organization j,

$$Conc(j) = (y_{1j}^2 + y_{2j}^2 + \cdots + y_{Gj}^2)^{1/2}$$

where y_{ij} is the number of (strategic or operating) decisions, out of the I considered, taken by group i. Clearly, *Conc* reaches its maximum when all decision-making is concentrated at one level. Third, we have standardized *Conc* in the following way,

$$Std\_Conc(j) = \frac{Conc(j) - \min(Conc)}{\max(Conc) - \min(Conc)}$$

Notice that $0 \leq Std\_Conc \leq 1$, and that higher values represent a higher concentration of decision authority. If $Std\_Conc = 1$, then all decisions are concentrated at one tier.

1.2.2 Organizational practices

Organizational practices that indicate how workers perform their tasks (e.g. in a group or in isolation) and which kind of incentives they are provided with are an essential component of organizational design. Moreover, there is general agreement in the literature that the new model of work organization (i.e. the lean type of organization, see Box I.4 in the Introduction) that became increasingly popular among firms in the last thirty years is based on organizational practices which have different aims and are inspired by different principles than those to which firms previously adhered. Unfortunately, this agreement largely vanishes when one has to determine which individual practices should be included in this new organizational model and how they can be assigned to the IWP and HRMP categories. In fact, there is no unambiguous and generally accepted way of defining IWPs and HRMPs (Becker and Gerhart 1996). On the one hand, there are considerable ambiguities as to the exact meaning and characteristics of such practices (for a discussion of the empirical consequences of this issue, see Section 1.3.3). On the other hand, there is no clear distinction between the two categories: authors often use the term "IWPs" to refer also to supporting HRMPs relating to incentive-based compensation schemes, training, promotion, recruitment, and dismissal practices (see, for instance, Huselid 1995; Ichniowski and Shaw 1995; Ichniowski *et al.* 1997, Cully *et al.* 1998). In fact, it is claimed that work practices that are designed to take advantage of the capabilities of individual workers will be ineffective without, and so need to be used in conjunction with the HRMPs that insure a proper skill level of, and adequate commitment from, the workforce.

The above-mentioned definitional differences have unpleasant consequences. The one of greatest concern for the purpose of this book is that in spite of the existence of numerous surveys in different countries that have documented the diffusion of IWPs and HRMPs (see again Section 1.3.3) and of several studies that have analyzed the determinants of their adoption (see Chapter 4) and have tried to assess their effects on firm performance (see Chapter 5), the results of these studies are difficult to compare.

In this work we will adopt a rather restrictive definition of organizational practices (for a similar approach see, for instance, Pil and MacDuffie 1996). As was mentioned earlier, the goal is to concentrate only on a manageable set of variables which are key in the definition of organizational design, rather than to provide a detailed account of every single element of business organizations.

Following this approach, we will concentrate attention exclusively on IWPs that directly modify how workers perform their tasks. Accordingly, we will consider the following practices:

- self-managed teams (SMT)
- quality circles (QC)
- job rotation
- total quality management (TQM).

As for HRMPs, which are here considered in a separate category, the emphasis will be on the use of individual and team incentive schemes, more precisely on:

- high-powered compensation schemes for workers, namely non-traditional individual incentive schemes that also consider qualitative aspects of workers' output (i.e. pay for knowledge and skills)
- profit-sharing arrangements.

1.3   International evidence on organizational design and its dynamics

1.3.1   Evidence on structural organizational variables

1.3.1.1   A brief survey of the empirical literature

Quite surprisingly, the empirical literature on organizational design has so far provided very limited large-scale evidence on structural organizational variables and their evolution over time. Moreover, this evidence which will be analyzed below in detail, is mostly confined to large- and medium-sized firms. Altogether, it supports the view that in the last twenty years these firms have undergone a *flattening* process, with a reduction of the depth of the organization measured by the number of hierarchical levels and an associated increase of the span of control. In particular, the number of first-level managers who directly report to firm's CEO has increased. This process has been accompanied by the *decentralization* of decision authority down the corporate pyramid. In other words, several middle manager positions have been eliminated in large firms, with the remaining ones being empowered with greater authority over strategic decisions. In addition, operating decisions have been increasingly delegated to low levels on the corporate ladder.

Let us now analyze in greater detail the available evidence on this process relating respectively to US and European firms.[5] The key evidence on this issue is synthesized in Table 1.1.

Evidence on US firms

Evidence on structural characteristics of the organizational design of US firms and their evolution over time is provided by Rajan and Wulf (2006). They illustrated data on a panel composed of more than 300 US public firms that were observed over the years 1986–99. The data were collected from different waves of a confidential compensation survey conducted by Hewitt and Associates, a leading human resources consulting firm. While the panel is unbalanced, out of these firms fifty-one are observed over the entire fourteen-year period. Because of the very nature of this data source, the typical firm included in the panel is a large mature stable company.

The authors considered the following structural organizational variables:

- the *depth* of the corporate hierarchy. This was measured by the number of hierarchical levels between the CEO and divisional managers. In turn, a division is defined as the lowest level of profit center responsibility for a business unit that engineers, manufactures, and sells its own products
- the *span of control* of the CEO – that is, the number of managers that directly report to the CEO
- the number of divisional managers that are designated as "*officers*" in firms' official documents. This is regarded as a proxy of the delegation of decision authority down the corporate hierarchy (that is, to division managers).

The evidence provided in Rajan and Wulf (2006) clearly documents the flattening process mentioned above. If one considers the whole sample, the average depth of the corporate hierarchy was 1.49 in 1986,

Table 1.1 Evolution of structural organizational variables, US and Europe

	Depth of the organization		Span of control of the CEO		Decentralization of strategic decisions (% of firms)		Decentralization of operating decisions (% of firms)	
	whole sample	balanced sample (51 firms)	whole sample	balanced sample (51 firms)	none	large	none	large
US firms[a]								
1986	1.49	1.58	4.46	4.39				
1999	1.09	1.15	6.70	7.16				
European firms[b]								
1992	3.60				40.91	17.97	14.22	29.62
1996	3.32				10.29	22.58	2.31	52.31

Notes
[a] See Rajan and Wulf (2006).
[b] See Ruigrok et al. (1999), Whittington et al. (1999).

while the average value of the span of control of the CEO was 4.46. In 1999 these figures were 1.09 and 6.70, respectively. Changes are even more apparent if one focuses attention on the balanced panel of fifty-one firms. In this case, the span of control went up from 4.39 to 7.16, an increase of 63%. The depth of the hierarchy diminished from 1.58 to 1.15. The authors also showed that divisional managers have been assigned greater decision authority: the probability of a division manager being designated as an officer of the firm has increased significantly over time.

Wang (2006) provided additional evidence on changes of organizational depth over time for a very large sample composed of 10,024 public firms and 59,586 privately held firms with at least $10 million in revenues located in the US and observed over the period 1993–2003. Data were provided by the Directories of Corporate Affiliations. The strength of this data set is the inclusion of a large number of firms of smaller size, especially privately held firms. The number of hierarchical levels counts the reporting levels between the corporate headquarter (i.e. the top of a firm's managerial hierarchy) and the lowest level of subunits within the firm, where a subunit is defined as any legal unit of the firm including subsidiaries, divisions, branches, and joint ventures (JVs). This definition is quite close to that used by Rajan and Wulf (2006).

Quite interestingly, the distribution of the number of hierarchical levels was found to differ according to the ownership status of sample firms. In particular, public firms exhibited greater depth than privately held ones, with only 31% of public firms having one hierarchical level as opposed to 71% of private firms. Conversely about 20% of public firms had three or more hierarchical levels; this percentage was only 2.5% for private firms. As to changes over time, unfortunately the data provided by this study do not allow us to compare the values of organizational depth at the beginning and at the end of the observation period. However, the data do indicate that changes of depth are sporadic; they relate to only 5.2% of the firm–year observations under scrutiny. Public firms were considerably more likely than privately held ones to change the number of hierarchical levels in either direction (9% of changes as opposed to only 3.8%). Nonetheless, quite surprisingly there was no evidence of the flattening of the managerial hierarchy highlighted by Rajan and Wulf (2006); so one may wonder whether this phenomenon is confined to larger firms.

Evidence on European firms

Ruigrok *et al.* (1999) and Whittington *et al.* (1999) illustrated the results of a survey conducted in Western Europe in 1997 as part of the INNFORM project. The survey involved more than 3,500 independent domestically owned large- and medium-sized European firms (i.e. number of employees greater than 500), out of which the greatest share was located in the UK. A questionnaire was mailed to the CEO of these firms; unfortunately, the response rate was rather low (13%): out of the respondent firms, more than 40% were located in the UK. The survey analyzed changes in the structure of the organization of firms between 1992 and 1996, and considered the following aspects:

- the depth of the hierarchy, measured by the number of levels between the CEO and the lowest manager with profit responsibility
- the extent of the decentralization of strategic and operating decisions to subunit (i.e. division) managers.[6]

Again, evidence was provided of both the flattening of firms' hierarchy and the decentralization of decision authority over the observation period. The average depth of the organization decreased from 3.60 to 3.32, with 29.8% of companies having eliminated some hierarchical levels.[7] As to operating decisions, the absence of any decentralization of authority to subunit managers was a rarity in 1996: it was mentioned only by 2.3% of sample firms. In fact, the majority of firms (52.3%) stated that decentralization of these decisions was large. The corresponding figures in 1992 were 14.2% and 29.6%. Not surprisingly, strategic decisions were far more centralized: in 1996, a large degree of delegation of these decisions to subunit managers was typical of only 18.0% of firms, while in 22.6% of firms strategic decisions were completely centralized in the CEO's hands. Nonetheless, decentralization of authority has again occurred in the observation period. In fact, in 1992 firms in the "no decentralization" and "large decentralization" categories were 40.9% and 10.3% of the sample, respectively.

1.3.2   Evidence on structural organizational variables based on the new empirical methodology

In this section we synthesize the evidence on structural organizational variables provided by Colombo and Delmastro (1999). This study used the indicators that were described in Section 1.2.1. It analyzed a data set composed of 438 Italian manufacturing plants. Data were provided by a survey conducted in 1997. The details of the empirical analysis and of the data set are reported in the Appendix of this volume, to which the interested reader should refer.

For every organizational unit taken into consideration, data were collected on the "present organization," where "present" refers to the time of the field analysis (i.e. 1997). Moreover, we know whether sample units changed their organizations in the period 1975–97 meaning that they changed one of the SOVs under scrutiny. If the answer is affirmative we have also information on the "previous organization." If a unit did not change its structure, then the present and previous organizations coincide.

1.3.2.1   Evidence on organizational depth and shape*[8]

Table 1.2 shows descriptive statistics of the variable *Level* (for a definition see Section 1.2.1.1). For each category of plant ordered by the number of hierarchical levels, columns (1) and (2) describe the sample distribution, and column (3) reports average plant size measured by the number of employees; in column (4) we present the results of *t*-tests of the differences in average plant size between *Level* classes. Columns (5)–(8) do the same for the previous organization. The data presented in Table 1.2 provide interesting initial evidence on the organizational depth of business organizations.

First, the sample distribution is concentrated around three and four hierarchical levels. Taken together they account for 82% and 74% of the sample plants for the present and previous organizations, respectively. Second, there is a strong evidence of a positive relation between the number of hierarchical tiers and plant size (for an econometric study on this and other relations, see Chapter 3). In particular, almost all differences of plant size averages between consecutive *Level* categories are statistically significant at conventional levels. More interestingly, the sample mean of *Level* for the present organization does not significantly differ from that for the previous organization, even if a χ^2 test shows that the null hypothesis that the distributions by *Level* classes of the present and previous organizations do not significantly differ is rejected at 1%. This is the result of two opposite processes. On the one hand, the number of plants that adopt a two-level hierarchy has diminished: they have evolved towards more complex structures. On the other hand, very articulated organizations, with five and six levels, have turned to less complex

Table 1.2   Number of hierarchical levels (*Level*) and plant size, distribution, and tests

Level	Present organization[a]				Previous organization[b]			
	no. of obs.	%	average plant size	t-tests[c]	no. of obs.	%	average plant size	t-tests[c]
2	29	6.6	34.4	–	44	10.0	43.9	–
3	233	53.2	121.0	6.26[d]	217	49.5	104.6	4.32[d]
4	126	28.8	217.1	3.77[d]	107	24.4	238.5	4.43[d]
5	40	9.1	569.4	2.51[e]	43	9.8	567.3	2.94[d]
6	10	2.3	623.4	0.21	27	6.2	1023.5	1.53
Total	438	100.0	195.3	–	438	100.0	233.3	–

Notes

[a] Plant size is defined as the number of employees in 1997.

[b] Plant size is defined as the number of employees in 1989.

[c] H_0: $Size_j = Size_{j-1}$, $j = 3,4,5,6$, with $Size_j$ being the average no. of employees of plants having a j-level hierarchy.

[d] Difference in average plant size between the *Level* class and the previous one significant at 1%.

[e] Difference in average plant size between the *Level* class and the previous one significant at 5%.

architectures. To gain further insights into such phenomena we need less aggregated data.

Table 1.3 distinguishes three categories of plants: small (number of employees smaller than 100), medium (between 100 and 500), and large plants (more than 500 employees). As is shown in Table 1.3, small units have become marginally more articulated over time, with a decreasing share of small plants with two tiers out of the total of small plants (from 15.3% to 11.3%) and an increasing percentage of those with a number of tiers between three and five (from 83.2% to 88.3%). Medium-sized plants have instead adopted organizations characterized by three and four tiers, with a decreasing share of five and six tiers (from 24% to 15.3%). Lastly, large plants have drastically simplified their organizational design. The percentage of large plants with six tiers has decreased from 31.9% to 8.8%, while the percentage of those with three tiers has risen from 10.6% to 26.5%. In order to evaluate the statistical robustness of changes of the distributions of *Level* for the three plant-size categories, we computed χ^2 tests. Whereas the distribution by *Level* classes does not change substantially in the period under investigation for small plants, the same does not hold true for medium- and large-sized plants. In fact, for the latter

Table 1.3 Number of hierarchical levels (*Level*), distribution by plant categories

| Level | No. of employees < 100 | | | | No. of employees: 100–500 | | | | No. of employees >500 | | | |
| | Present org.[a] | | Previous org.[b] | | Present org.[a] | | Previous org.[b] | | Present org.[a] | | Previous org.[b] | |
	obs.	%	obs.	%	obs.	%	obs.	%	obs.	%	obs.	%
2	28	11.3	40	15.3	1	0.6	4	3.1	0	0.0	0	0.0
3	160	64.9	163	62.2	64	40.8	49	38.0	9	26.5	5	10.6
4	48	19.4	49	18.7	68	43.3	45	34.9	10	29.4	13	27.7
5	10	4.0	6	2.3	18	11.5	23	17.8	12	35.3	14	29.8
6	1	0.4	4	1.5	6	3.8	8	6.2	3	8.8	15	31.9
Total	247	100.0	262	100.0	157	100.0	129	100.0	34	100.0	47	100.0

Notes
[a] Plant size is defined as the number of employees in 1997.
[b] Plant size is defined as the number of employees in 1989.

two categories the null hypothesis that the distributions by *Level* classes of the present and previous organizations do not significantly differ is rejected at conventional levels.[9]

For a thorough analysis of the determinants of such dynamic phenomena, see Chapter 4. At this stage of the analysis, some preliminary remarks are in order. First, it is worth emphasizing that our sample does not include plants set up after 1986. Hence, as far as small plants are concerned, the data presented in Table 1.3 might be explained by the aging of the population of small plants – that is, by the process of consolidation of surviving small units. The lower number of hierarchical levels of large plants in the 1990s is partially a consequence of the downsizing of large organizations: the average number of employees of plants with more than 500 employees decreased between 1989 and 1997 from 1,277 to 1,143. However, in accordance with the qualitative evidence provided by the managerial literature (see, for instance, Drucker 1988) and the studies illustrated in Section 1.3.1, it probably also reflects the adoption by large units of a flatter hierarchical structure, with a lower number of intermediate levels.

To study organizational dynamics further we have computed transition probabilities, where each state is defined by the value of the variable *Level*. In other words p_{ij} is the probability that a plant characterized by an *i-level* hierarchy turns its organization to a *j-layered* design. Results are presented in Table 1.4. The first robust result is the existence of very strong inertial forces on organization. The probabilities of maintaining a stable organizational design over time are in general greater than those of changing it. Indeed, 63% of sample

Table 1.4   Transition probabilities (p_{ij}), number of hierarchical levels (*Level*)

No. of levels of the previous organization	No. of levels of the present organization				
	2	3	4	5	6
2	0.57	0.32	0.07	0.04	0.00
3	0.01	0.79	0.17	0.03	0.00
4	0.01	0.36	0.57	0.06	0.00
5	0.00	0.21	0.44	0.28	0.07
6	0.00	0.00	0.26	0.48	0.26

plants did not change the number of hierarchical tiers in the period under scrutiny. Moreover, organizational dynamics seems to be characterized by a process of marginal adaptation instead of radical modification. One-level changes prevail with respect to more radical ones. Lastly, more complex structures characterized by a higher number of tiers modified their organizational design more often and more radically than simple two- and three-level organizations. In particular, there are only two cases in which the likelihood of a two-level reduction is significantly greater than zero: starting from an organization comprising five or six tiers this probability equals 0.21 and 0.26, respectively. Such data confirm a tendency within the manufacturing industry towards the simplification of very articulated hierarchies, partly, as was said earlier, driven by a reduction in the average number of employees.

Turning now to the findings regarding span of control, Table 1.5 presents means and *t*-tests for the *Span* variable (for a definition, see again Section 1.2.1.1). In aggregate, the average span of control has decreased over time. In the old organization each manager had more than ten subordinates on average. More recently plants tended to organize their internal design by reducing the average number of subordinates under one manager to fewer than nine, with the difference being significant at 5%. Moreover, as to both the present and the previous organizations, small plants have a value of *Span* (7.89 and 9.77) lower than the average (8.72 and 10.23). The opposite applies to medium-sized plants, which have a number of subordinates under each manager (9.21 and 11.69, respectively) above the average value. Lastly, large plants have the highest value of *Span* in the 1990s (12.5), while they have the lowest value as regards the previous organization (8.7).

Table 1.5   Span of control (*Span*), means, and tests

Plant categories	Present organization[a]	Previous organization[b]	Present organization[b]	t-tests for matched pairs[c]
Total	8.72	10.23	8.72	−2.10[f]
Small plants (no. of employees < 100)	7.89	9.77	7.86	−3.02[e]
Medium plants (no. of employees 100–500)	9.21	11.69	9.33	−1.18
Large plants (no. of employees > 500)	12.51	8.74	11.20	2.29[f]
t-tests between plant categories[d]				
small vs. medium	−1.35	−0.94		
small vs. large	−2.42[f]	0.70		
medium vs. large	−1.70	1.32		

Notes
[a] Plant size is defined as the number of employees in 1997.
[b] Plant size is defined as the number of employees in 1989.
[c] H_0: *Span(present)* = *Span(previous)*, with *Span (present)* and *Span (previous)* being the average span of control for the present and the previous organizations respectively.
[d] H_0: $Span_j = Span_i$, $i \neq j$, with $Span_j$ being the average span of control of plants having fewer than 100 employees (small), between 100 and 500 employees (medium), and more than 500 employees (large).
[e] Significant at 1%.
[f] Significant at 5%.

The *t*-tests show that the difference between the span of large- and small-sized plants is significant at 5%, while other differences are not significant at conventional levels.

Again, we observe two very different dynamics. Small- and medium-sized plants reduced the average number of subordinates. In particular, if one considers plants which in 1989 had fewer than 100 employees, a *t*-test for matched pairs shows that the reduction of *Span* is significant at the 1% level. The evolution of the organization of large plants followed an opposite pattern. They increased the span of control, with the difference in the value of *Span* between the previous and present organizations for plants which in 1989 had more than 500 employees being significant at the 5% level. These results provide additional evidence of the adoption by large units of a leaner type of organization.

1.3.2.2   Evidence on the allocation of authority *[10]

Strategic decisions

Table 1.6 presents results for the degree of centralization of decision-making activities (*DC*, see Section 1.2.1.2 for a definition). In the 1980s and 1990s plants decentralized decision-making activities. This process of downward delegation of strategic decisions led to a statistically significant (at the 1% level) decrease in the value of *DC*.

Again we can distinguish plants according to their size. Decision-making in small plants is more centralized than in medium and large units. This holds true as regards both the present and previous organizations, with most differences being statistically significant (or almost significant) at conventional levels. When ownership and control are not separated as is often the case for small enterprises, strategic decisions are mostly taken at the top tier (namely, by the owner–manager).[11] Conversely

> in large organizations, only a small fraction of the available information will be brought to bear on any single decision ... Combining this observation with the fact that individual decision-makers are limited in their capacities for information processing, one is led to the inevitability of decentralized decision-making in which different decisions – or groups of decisions – are made by different decision-makers on the basis of different information.
>
> (Radner 1996)

Moreover, organizational dynamics turn out to depend again upon the size of organizational units (see again Table 1.6). Besides being centralized, small plants have partially delegated strategic decisions down the corporate hierarchy. The results of *t*-tests for matched pairs show that for plants that had fewer than 100 employees in 1989, the difference between the values of *DC* for the present and the previous organizations is statistically significant at the 5% level. A similar dynamic pattern applies to medium-sized plants, which have significantly (at the 10% level) decentralized decision-making activities, starting from values of *DC* around the mean and becoming the most decentralized plant class. In contrast, for large plants, the null hypothesis that the values of *DC* for previous and current organizations do not significantly differ cannot be rejected at conventional levels.

In order to gain further insights into organizational dynamics, we have computed the probabilities of transition, where each state is defined

Table 1.6   Degree of centralization (*DC*) of strategic decisions, means, and tests

Plant categories	Present organization[a]	Previous organization[b]	Present organization[b]	t-tests for matched pairs[c]
Total	–0.12	0.12	–0.12	3.08[e]
Small plants (no. of employees <100)	0.13	0.23	0.02	2.20[f]
Medium plants (no. of employees 100–500)	–0.45	0.04	–0.21	1.87[g]
Large plants (no. of employees > 500)	–0.31	–0.36	–0.59	1.13
t-tests between plant categories[d]				
Small vs. medium	2.82[e]	0.86		
Small vs. large	1.60	2.00[f]		
Medium vs. large	–0.54	1.34		

Notes
[a] Plant size is defined as the number of employees in 1997.
[b] Plant size is defined as the number of employees in 1989.
[c] H_0: *DC(present) = DC(previous)*, with *DC (present)* and *DC (previous)* being the average degree of centralization for the present and the previous organizations respectively.
[d] H_0: $DC_j = DC_i$, $i \neq j$, with DC_j being the average degree of centralization of plants having fewer than 100 employees (small), between 100 and 500 employees (medium), and more than 500 employees (large).
[e] Significant at 1%.
[f] Significant at 5%.
[g] Significant at 10%.

according to the value of the degree of centralization. In particular, we have divided plants in three categories: centralized, average, and decentralized. We have then calculated the transition probabilities from one category to another. Results are summarized in Table 1.7. We can infer that the allocation of decision-making power tends to be pretty stable over time: structural inertia again seems to dominate organizational evolution. In addition, changes are incremental rather than being radical. Indeed, the probabilities of changing the decision-making structure starting from either a centralized or a decentralized organization and turning to an average architecture are higher than those of adopting either a decentralized or a centralized organization (0.20 versus 0.11, and 0.16 versus 0.04, respectively).

Moreover, in contrast to the suggestion by Hannan and Freeman (1984), the level of structural inertia does not increase with size. In

Table 1.7   Transition probabilities (p_{ij}), DC of strategic decisions

Previous organization	Present organization		
	centralized	average	decentralized
Centralized	0.69	0.20	0.11
Average	0.06	0.81	0.13
Decentralized	0.04	0.16	0.80

particular, for small and large plants, inertia is much more pronounced than for medium-sized plants. In fact, 63.9% of small plants and 64.7% of large plants did not change any decision level for each of the strategic decisions considered, while the same percentage was 50.9% for medium-sized plants. For small units, the unwillingness of owner-managers to delegate responsibility is likely to be a main cause of organizational stability. Conversely, for large plants complexity of agent relations might undermine a firm's stimulus towards changes. Organizational inertia thus appears to be a bell-shaped function of size. In any case, the allocation of authority is remarkably stable over time independently of size.

The analysis so far has considered the aggregate degree of centralization. How is authority allocated among hierarchical levels? The number of decisions taken by each tier (*ND*, see Section 1.2.1.2) helps us analyze this issue. Table 1.8 presents results relating to the *ND* variable for the present and previous organizations. Intermediate levels (including workers and supervisors) are totally excluded from plant strategic decision-making. There exists some minor diversity for plants of different size, but overall intermediate levels make almost no decisions. The plant manager takes, either independently or subject to the superior's ultimate control (levels 2 and 3), nearly two decisions, its authority changing little over time. Situations in which the plant manager and higher levels coordinate through a sharing of decision-making (level 4) are now more likely. Conversely, authority of higher-level management (level 5) is decreasing.

Another interesting aspect concerns the relation between power allocation and size. From Table 1.8, it is evident that in small plants higher levels (very often the owner–manager) take a considerably higher number of strategic decisions than the same levels in medium and large units.[12] This result has a straightforward interpretation: in small units, ownership and actual control tend often to coincide (i.e. formal authority – the right to decide – and real authority – the effective

Table 1.8 Number of strategic decisions (*ND*) taken by each hierarchical level[a]

Levels	Total	Plant categories, number of employees		
		<100	100–500	>500
Present organization[b]				
1 *Intermediate levels*	0.12	0.08	0.17	0.21
2 *Plant manager (PM)*	0.98	1.14	0.81	0.59
3 *PM + authorization*	1.48	1.19	1.88	1.76
4 *PM's proposals*	2.18	1.83	2.57	2.94
5 *Higher levels*	1.24	1.76	0.57	0.50
Previous organization[c]				
1 *Intermediate levels*	0.10	0.08	0.09	0.21
2 *Plant manager (PM)*	1.08	1.26	0.77	0.91
3 *PM + authorization*	1.18	1.00	1.42	1.50
4 *PM's proposals*	1.95	1.51	2.60	2.60
5 *Higher levels*	1.69	2.15	1.12	0.78

Notes
[a] The sum for each column equals 6, the number of strategic decisions considered.
[b] Plant size is defined as the number of employees in 1997.
[c] Plant size is defined as the number of employees in 1989.

control over decisions – are concentrated at the owner-manager level; see Chapter 2).

Finally, we have computed the standardized degree of concentration of decision-making (*Std_conc*, see again Section 1.2.1.2). Our main objective was to investigate whether firms tend to diffuse authority in order to exploit specialized managerial capabilities, or alternatively concentrate decision-making at a particular hierarchical level so as to avoid coordination problems. From Table 1.9 we derive that strategic decisions are highly concentrated. Differences between the value of *Std_conc* of small units and those of both medium and large plants are statistically significant at 1%, for both the present and previous organizations, showing that strategic decision-making is considerably more concentrated for the former units than for the latter ones.

Operating decisions
The analysis of operating decisions is based on indices analogous to those used for strategic decisions. The results are synthesized in Tables 1.10–1.13. Overall, they clearly support the view that in the period under consideration organizational units, especially of medium and large size, increasingly adopted a leaner pattern of structure.

Table 1.9 Degree of concentration (*Std_Conc*) of strategic decisions, means, and tests

Plant categories	Present organization[a]	Previous organization[b]	Present organization[b]	t-tests for matched pairs[c]
Total	0.89	0.91	0.89	3.90[e]
Small plants (no. of employees < 100)	0.92	0.94	0.92	3.23[e]
Medium plants (no. of employees 100–500)	0.86	0.89	0.87	2.01[f]
Large plants (no. of employees > 500)	0.82	0.85	0.83	1.04
t-tests between plant categories[d]				
Small vs. medium	4.88[e]	3.45[e]		
Small vs. large	4.28[e]	3.93[e]		
Medium vs. large	1.57	1.66		

Notes
[a] Plant size is defined as the number of employees in 1997.
[b] Plant size is defined as the number of employees in 1989.
[c] H_0: *Std_Conc(present)* = *Std_Conc(previous)*, with *Std_Conc (present)* and *Std_Conc (previous)* being the average degree of concentration for the present and the previous organizations, respectively.
[d] H_0: $Std\_Conc_j = Std\_Conc_i$, $i \neq j$, with Std_Conc_j being the average degree of concentration of plants having fewer than 100 employees (small), between 100 and 500 employees (medium), and more than 500 employees (large).
[e] Significant at 1%.
[f] Significant at 5%.

As is apparent from Table 1.10, operating decisions have been significantly decentralized over time for all categories of plants. The average value of *DC* has decreased from 0.13 to –0.13. Small (from 0.34 to 0.16), medium (from –0.09 to –0.46), and large plants (from –0.45 to –0.84) have all delegated operating decisions down the corporate hierarchy; the differences between the values of *DC* for the previous and the current organizations are significant at conventional levels (see the *t*-tests for matched pairs). In particular, intermediate levels between the plant manager and line workers are increasingly important for the implementation of operating decisions. The *ND* variable (see Table 1.12) shows that on average these hierarchical levels take three operating decisions out of five, while the plant manager takes most of the remaining two. Authority has shifted marginally also towards line workers, especially in large plants, but they still do not have any significant role.

Table 1.10 Degree of centralization (*DC*) of operating decisions, means, and tests

Plant categories	Present organization[a]	Previous organization[b]	Present organization[b]	t-tests for matched pairs[c]
Total	−0.13	0.13	−0.13	3.98[e]
Small plants (no. of employees < 100)	0.15	0.34	0.16	2.23[f]
Medium plants (no. of employees 100–500)	−0.45	−0.09	−0.46	2.82[e]
Large plants (no. of employees > 500)	−0.63	−0.45	−0.84	2.08[f]
t-tests between plant categories[d]				
Small vs. medium	4.17[e]	2.68[e]		
Small vs. large	3.37[e]	4.05[e]		
Medium vs. large	0.73	1.72[g]		

Notes
[a] Plant size is defined as the number of employees in 1997.
[b] Plant size is defined as the number of employees in 1989.
[c] H_0: *DC (present) = DC (previous)*, with *DC (present)* and *DC (previous)* being the average degree of centralization for the present and the previous organizations, respectively.
[d] H_0: $DC_j = DC_i$, $i \neq j$, with DC_j being the average degree of centralization of plants having fewer than 100 employees (small), between 100 and 500 employees (medium), and more than 500 employees (large).
[e] Significant at 1%.
[f] Significant at 5%.
[g] Significant at 10%.

Table 1.11 Transition probabilities (p_{ij}), *DC* of operating decisions

Previous organization	Present organization		
	centralized	average	decentralized
Centralized	0.70	0.18	0.12
Average	0.10	0.79	0.11
Decentralized	0.08	0.14	0.78

The evolution of the distribution of authority of operating decisions (Table 1.11) shows that structural inertia again dominates organizational dynamic behavior. More than 75% of plants do not change class of *DC*, with medium-sized units being the more inclined towards change. Thus, the allocation of operating decisions is quite stable over time, but when changes do occur they tend to be towards a more decentralized organization.

Table 1.12 Number of operating decisions (*ND*) taken by each hierarchical level[a]

Levels	Total	Plant categories, number of employees		
		<100	100–500	>500
Present organization[b]				
1 *Lline workers*	0.25	0.21	0.30	0.32
2 *Intermediate levels*	3.07	2.84	3.32	3.56
3 *Plant manager*	1.68	1.95	1.38	1.12
Previous organization[c]				
1 *Line workers*	0.15	0.14	0.19	0.13
2 *Intermediate levels*	2.98	2.78	3.12	3.72
3 *Plant manager*	1.87	2.08	1.69	1.15

Notes
[a] The sum for each column equals 5, the number of operating decisions considered.
[b] Plant size is defined as the number of employees in 1997.
[c] Plant size is defined as the number of employees in 1989.

Table 1.13 Degree of concentration (*Std_Conc*) of operating decisions, means, and tests

Plant categories	Present organization[a]	Previous organization[b]	Present organization[b]	t-tests for matched pairs[c]
Total	0.51	0.59	0.51	5.67[e]
Small plants (*no. of employees < 100*)	0.52	0.61	0.52	5.26[e]
Medium plants (*no. of employees 100–500*)	0.49	0.52	0.47	2.35[f]
Large plants (*no. of employees > 500*)	0.55	0.63	0.60	0.94
	t-tests between plant categories[d]			
Small vs. medium	1.23	2.65[e]		
Small vs. large	–0.40	–0.43		
Medium vs. large	–0.97	−2.00[f]		

Notes
[a] Plant size is defined as the number of employees in 1997.
[b] Plant size is defined as the number of employees in 1989.
[c] H_0: *Std_Conc(present) = Std_Conc(previous)*, with *Std_Conc (present)* and *Std_Conc (previous)* being the average degree of concentration for the present and the previous organizations respectively.
[d] H_0: *Std_Conc$_j$ = Std_Conc$_i$, i≠j*, with *Std_Conc$_j$* being the average degree of concentration of plants having fewer than 100 employees (small), between 100 and 500 employees (medium), and more than 500 employees (large).
[e] Significant at 1%.
[f] Significant at 5%.

The size of organizational units influences the allocation of decision-making activities even for operating decisions. Small plants are the most centralized, and the differences in the degree of centralization between this category and medium- and large-sized plants for both the previous and the current organizations are statistically significant at 1% (see the *t*-tests between plant categories in Table 1.10). Moreover, small plants tend to distribute responsibility between intermediate levels and the plant manager quite evenly, while large plants concentrate authority at intermediate levels (see Table 1.12). Lastly, Table 1.13 shows that operating decisions are more diffused within hierarchies than are strategic ones; the average value of *Std_Conc* for current organizations is 0.51, significantly lower than 0.89, the standardized degree of concentration of strategic decisions. In addition, in the 1990s differences between plant categories are not statistically significant, whereas the previous organization decision-making in small and large plants was considerably more concentrated than in medium-sized plants, with *t*-tests being significant at conventional levels. Even more interestingly, in the 1980s and 1990s the level of concentration substantially decreased for all categories of plants; the *t*-tests for matched pairs presented in Table 1.13 reveal that such changes are statistically significant save for large units.

1.3.2.3 A synthesis

We have applied the empirical methodology developed in Section 1.2.1 to a sample of Italian manufacturing plants (which are the organizational units under investigation).

The data illustrate some rather interesting findings on key dimensions of organizational design and its dynamics: configuration, centralization, and flexibility. First, organizational depth increases with size, and this relation is concave (i.e. a marginal increase in the size of the unit determines a positive, but decreasing, rise in the organizational depth; more will be said on this aspect in Chapter 3). Nonetheless, the span of control also increases with size. This result may be explained by the attempt of organizations to limit the increase of hierarchical levels when the number of employees gets higher.

Second, as to strategic decisions authority is overall concentrated at either the level of the manager of the organizational unit or at higher levels. However, it transpires that in small organizations higher levels (very often the owner-manager of a single-unit firm) take a considerably higher number of strategic decisions than the corresponding levels in medium and large organizations. In particular, small units tend to have the highest degrees of both concentration and centralization of decision-making power. Medium and large units diffuse authority slightly more; they also partially delegate strategic decision-making down the corporate hierarchy. In this respect, coordination seems to play a more important role than the exploitation of local specialized capabilities. These results hold true for both strategic and operating decisions. As to operating decisions, centralization again is higher for small units than for medium- and large-sized ones. However, in all size categories intermediate levels take a larger number of decisions than either line workers or plant managers.

As to organizational dynamics (flexibility), this involves the determination of changes in each particular organizational unit over the observed period of time (the 1980s and 1990s). Two main factors can be distinguished: the amount and the speed of change. Empirical results show the existence of very strong inertial forces on organizations. Further, change in organizational design, when it occurs, is not radical and follows incremental adjustments. In sum, organizational dynamics follow an inertial process (i.e. very slow speed) with marginal modifications (i.e. modest amounts of change).

Moreover, the empirical evidence shows a process in which during the 1980s and 1990s organizational depth on average remained unchanged. Nonetheless, organizational dynamics crucially depend on the size of the organizational unit. Small organizations have adopted more articulated structures characterized by a lower span of control. Medium-sized units have changed their internal structure from either very complex or very simple organizations to three- and four-level hierarchies. In addition, they have also been decreasing their span. Lastly, large units, starting from rather bureaucratic organizations, have chosen flatter structures characterized by a lower number of managerial levels (i.e. delayering) and a higher span of control.

There is no evidence of a radical shift towards multi-leader structures (especially for strategic activities), as predicted by some theory (Lindbeck and Snower 1996), even though organizations, independently of their size, have been characterized by a significant process of delegation of authority over both strategic and operating decisions.

1.3.3 Evidence on the use of organizational practices

Several national surveys have analyzed the diffusion of IWPs and HRMPs in different countries including Canada, Denmark, France, Germany, Italy, the UK, and the US. In spite of the interest of the results of these studies, cross-country comparisons remain a rather difficult undertaking. First of all, the definitional ambiguities illustrated in Section 1.2.2 led different studies to focus on different sets of practices; therefore, data on diffusion rates in all the above-mentioned countries are not available for all the organizational practices in which we are interested. Second, there is heterogeneity across studies in the industries and firm-size classes that are the target of the surveys. Third, some studies simply considered adopters of a given practice independently of the share of the firm's (or plant's) employees that are involved in its use (that is, using the terminology of the innovation diffusion literature, they did not take care of intra-firm diffusion), while others focused on heavy adopters, defined as firms where a practice is used by a sizable portion of employees (typically, 50% or more). Fourth, and even more important, contrary to what happens with technological innovations, translation from one language to the other creates additional ambiguities as to the meaning and characteristics of some practices.[13] For all these reasons, the results of the different surveys need to be compared with extreme caution.[14] They are illustrated in Table 1.14, while in Table 1.15 we report the characteristics of the underlying data sets.

In spite of all these methodological problems, the results of these surveys are very interesting and highlight some common stylized facts. First of all, they clearly document that, with the exception of Canada and Denmark, IWPs and HRMPs were quite widespread at the end of the 1990s, with most of them being used by a share of surveyed firms (or plants) ranging between 40% and 60% depending on the specific practice. Second, where longitudinal data are available, they suggest that diffusion took place to a large extent during the 1990s; in fact, diffusion levels at the beginning of the 1990s or at the end of the 1980s were considerably lower than at the end of the 1990s. In other words, the evidence provided by Table 1.14 indicates that during the 1990s and thereafter firms in advanced countries increasingly abandoned traditional organizational practices and switched to a new organizational design characterized by a bundle of new practices (Ichniowski and Shaw 2003) that promised to substantially increase productivity by taking advantage of the skills and creativity of the workforce. Third, there are large differences in the use of organizational practices, with individual pay schemes being poorly diffused, and job rotation, teams, and profit-sharing quite widespread.

Table 1.14 Use of IWPs and HRMPs: international evidence

Study	Indicator	Country–Year	IWPs				HRMPs	
			job rotation	SMT	QC	TQM	incentive pay schemes (pay for skills and knowledge)	profit-sharing
Osterman (2000)	% of heavy adopters: establishments with 50% or more of core employees involved	US 1997	55.5	38.4	57.7	57.2		
Osterman (1994)	% of adopters (in manufacturing)	US 1992	43.4 (55.6)	54.5 (50.1)	40.8 (45.6)	33.5 (44.9)		
	% of heavy adopters (in manufacturing)	US 1992	26.6 (37.4)	40.5 (32.3)	27.4 (29.7)	24.5 (32.1)		
	Estimated adoption rates five years before survey	US 1987	16.5	27.5	8.8	7.0		
Gittleman et al. (1998)	% of adopters among establishments with 50 employees or more	US 1993	12.6 (24.2)	14.2 (32.0)	4.8 (15.8)	21.4 (46.0)	11.2 (12.2)	30.4 (40.9)
Workplace and Employee Survey, Statistics Canada	% of adopters	Canada 2001	18.5	8.7	22.1	(b)		
Forth and Millward (2004)	% of adopters among establishments with 25 employees or more: establishments with 60% or more of employees in the largest occupational group involved	UK 1997–8	28[a]	51	30			

Study	Country/Year						
Cully et al. (1998)	% of adopters among establishments with 25 employees or more	UK 1997–8		65^b	42	11	30
Bauer (2003)	% of establishments having adopted the practice in the 1993–5 period	Germany 1995		25			
Greenan and Mairesse (1999, 2002, 2004)	% of adopters among manufacturing plants with 50 employees or more	France 1997		31^c	28^c	35	
Colombo et al. (2007)	% of adopters in the metalworking industry	Italy 1996	60.5	37.2^d	37.2^d	34.0	32.6	73.7
		Italy 1990	43.8	11.9^d	11.9^d	12.8	22.8	41.8
Eriksson (2003)	% of adopters among private sector firms with 20 employees or more; salaried employees/ hourly paid workers	Denmark 1999	6.2/17.4	26.5/21.8	3.7/3.4	8.3/4.1	10/17	8/6

Notes

a 60% of employees in the largest occupational group are formally trained to be able to do jobs other than their own.

b Most employees work in formally designated teams.

c At least 10% of a plant's workforce is involved in the work practice.

d QC and/or quality teams.

e Team bonuses.

Table 1.15 Use of IWPs and HRMPs: international data sets

Study	Characteristics of data sets
Osterman (2000)	National Survey of Establishment, 1997. Establishments with 50 or more employees. Non-profit organizations and agricultural establishments are not considered. Sample stratified by size: 462 establishments interviewed in 1992 (representative of the 1992 population) + 221 new establishments = 683 establishments. Information on workplace organization only for "core" employees.
Osterman (1994)	National Survey of Establishment, 1992. Establishments with 50 or more employees. Non-profit organizations and agricultural establishments are not considered. Sample stratified by size: 875 establishments (out of which 694 usable questionnaires). Information on workplace organization only for "core" employees.
Gittleman *et al.* (1998)	1993 Survey of employer-provided training (SEPT93), Bureau of labor statistics. Private non-agricultural plants. Sample stratified by industry and size: 5,987 establishments.
Workplace and Employee Survey, Statistics Canada	Workplace and Employee Survey, 1999 and 2001: 6,351 workplaces. Representative of all (701,123) workplaces with at least 1 paid employee. Sample stratified by size, industry, and location.
Cully *et al.* (1998)[a]	1998 Workplace Employee Relations Survey (WERS 98). Establishments with 10 or more employees in all sectors: 1,926 establishments. Weighted results, representative of establishments with 25 or more employees.
Bauer (2003)	IAB Establishment Panel & Employment Statistics Register. Establishments in the agricultural and mining sectors, non-profit firms, banks, and insurance companies are not considered. Establishments that participated in the survey in 1993 and 1995 (1,128) or in 1993 and 1997 (772). Results of the survey in 1995. Data on organizational changes in the previous two years (1993–5).
Colombo *et al.* (2007)	National survey of metalworking establishments, 1997: 438 establishments with 10 or more employees in operations in 1986.
Greenan and Mairesse (1999, 2002, 2004)	*Changements Organisationnels et Informatisation* (COI) survey, 1997. Questionnaire to a representative sample of about 4,000 manufacturing firms with 50 or more employees. 82% response rate (3,286 firms). Results relating to 1997 and changes from 1994.
Eriksson (2003)	Survey administered in 1999 by Statistics Denmark to 3,200 private sector firms with 20 employees or more: 1,605 observations.

Notes
[a] The 2004 WERS data were not public when the book was completed. See Kersley *et al.* (2006).

1.4 Concluding remarks

There is large and growing interest among both scholars and practitioners on the organizational design of firms, its determinants and its evolution over time. However, conceptual models are based on very little data and limited stylized facts. This seriously limits theory-building exercises in this domain.

In our view, the study of organizational design can no longer be confined to *a priori* postulations and qualitative case studies. In fact, there is a need for large-scale quantitative studies on representative samples of business organizations that resort to econometric and statistical techniques. The results of these studies play a fundamental role for the validation or confutation of theoretical hypotheses. In turn, this requires the identification of a *limited number of key aspects* of organizational design that are suitable to be measured through quantitative indicators. This is precisely the main weakness of the empirical work that was carried out in the 1960s by the Aston group; this weakness prevented a widespread application of the innovative measurement approach proposed by these scholars. In fact, this approach suffered from a lack of synthesis: as a large number of organizational variables were considered with the aim of obtaining a precise description of organizational design, the application of this approach was confined to small samples of organizations.

So in this chapter we have focused attention on a limited number of primary dimensions of organizational design: configuration (depth and shape of the management hierarchy), allocation of authority (centralization), formal procedures and practices, and organizational dynamics (flexibility). The empirical methodology described in this chapter provides a more parsimonious and more manageable description of organizational design than earlier attempts. We focus on dimensions that can be measured through indicators that are suitable to be used in large-scale quantitative studies and explain most of variability, among firms' organizations. Finally, our methodology is theoretically driven so that we can test theoretical predictions and indicate further lines of research.

We have first synthesized the evidence provided on (some of) these dimensions by previous large-scale empirical studies. This evidence is rather scarce, especially as regards structural organizational variables (i.e. configuration and centralization). Then we have applied our multi-dimensional measurement approach to the analysis of the organizational design of a large sample of Italian manufacturing establishments that have been observed for a long period of time (i.e. twenty years).

Altogether, this chapter provides some interesting stylized facts on organizational design, which can be synthesized as follows.

- The depth of business organizations measured by the number of hierarchical levels increases with their size, measured by the number of employees, though at a decreasing rate, as was highlighted by the empirical studies of the 1960s and 1970s (see Chapter 3).
- In small firms, decision authority is far more centralized at the top of the corporate hierarchy than in their larger counterparts. This applies to both strategic and operating decisions.
- In all organizations, strategic decisions generally are more centralized than operating ones.
- Organizational dynamics is characterized by structural inertia[15]; moreover, organizational change when occurs is incremental rather than radical.
- Since the 1980s the number of hierarchical levels of large organizations decreased, a phenomenon usually referred to as delayering, with the elimination of layers of middle managers. Nonetheless, there is no evidence that this phenomenon extends to smaller organizations.
- Conversely, we have clearly shown that in the same period, and independently of their size, business organizations increasingly decentralized authority over strategic and operating decisions down the corporate hierarchy.
- Similarly, new IWPs such as job rotation, SMT, QC, TQM, and new HRMPs, especially those connected with incentive-based compensation schemes, have been rapidly diffusing among business organizations.

Of course, the question arises as to the determinants of these phenomena and the impact of organizational design on firm performance. In Chapters 2–5 we will address these questions. In particular, we will first report existing international evidence on these aspects based on quantitative empirical studies. We will then illustrate the results of the estimates of econometric models that rely on the measurement approach described in this chapter.

2
The Determinants of the Allocation of Decision Authority

2.1. Introduction

Economists and management scholars are increasingly concerned with the determinants of the allocation of decision-making power in firms. As was noted in the Introduction, a rich stream of theoretical papers inspired by different modeling approaches has recently addressed this issue.

In spite of the fact that the delegation of decision authority has been a hot issue in the organization literature since the studies of the Aston group in the 1960s (see Pugh *et al.* 1963, 1968, 1969b), the empirical evidence is, however, rather fragmented and findings generally rely upon personal experience and anecdotal evidence. Quite surprisingly, large-scale quantitative studies are relatively rare and with few exceptions, they do not provide a direct test of the hypotheses set out by theoretical studies. As was argued in Chapter 1, one of the most important reasons is the lack of a quantitative empirical methodology that is both manageable in practice and suitable to studies that rely on econometric techniques.

The objective of this chapter is to make an attempt to systematize the available quantitative evidence on the determinants of the allocation of decision authority in business organizations, and to highlight which theoretical predictions are supported by robust empirical findings. For this purpose, we also show how use of the indicators of the centralization of the (strategic) decision-making process that were described in Chapter 1 can contribute to advance our knowledge of the determinants of this important aspect of organizational design.

The chapter proceeds as follows. We first present in Section 2.2 a general conceptual framework aimed at highlighting the factors that influence the benefits and costs that business organizations obtain from the decentralization of decision-making; for this purpose we combine and distillate arguments set out by different streams of the economic theoretical literature on organizational design, namely the information processing, the decentralization of incentives, and the transaction cost economics streams of literature. This framework is then used to highlight the determinants of the relative allocation of decision power in business organizations between an agent (i.e. a line worker, a supervisor, or a middle manager) and her corporate superior. In Section 2.3, we survey the findings of previous quantitative empirical studies on this issue. Then, in Section 2.4 we present a new econometric test of the determinants of the delegation of decision authority in business organizations based on the indicators and the data set that have been described in Chapter 1. Some summarizing remarks in Section 2.5 concludes the chapter.

2.2 A conceptual framework of the determinants of the allocation of decision authority

2.2.1 The benefits and costs of delegation of decision authority

In this section we consider the benefits that a firm will obtain, and the costs it will incur, if decision authority is delegated down the hierarchical pyramid (i.e. from top managers to middle managers, from middle managers to supervisors, and from them to line workers). In so doing we will combine insights provided by different streams of the theoretical literature on the economics of organizational design, namely the information processing stream (see Radner 1992; Van Zandt 1999a; see also Harris and Raviv 2002; Dessein and Santos 2006), the decentralization of incentive stream (Laffont and Martimort 1997; Poitevin 2000; Mookherjee 2006; see also Aghion and Tirole 1997; Baker *et al.* 1999; Hart and Moore 2005; Raith 2005), and the transaction cost economics stream (Williamson 1975; Dow 1987; Menard 1997).

2.2.1.1 *The benefits of delegation*

The information processing stream contends that hierarchical organizations that centralize the decision-making function suffer from organizational failures. A primary source of these failures consists in the leaks that arise in transmitting information from the top to the bottom of the hierarchy. The strategies defined by the superior (i.e. the firm's top management) might differ from those implemented by subordinates simply because of inefficiencies in intra-firm communication (Keren and

Levhari 1979, 1983, 1989). In addition, even if orders given by top managers are closely followed by the agents in charge of their implementation, they may fail to produce the expected benefits because of implementation delays. This is especially worrisome when environmental conditions change rapidly, as even decisions made at time t by a perfectly informed and fully rational decision-maker who sits at the top of the hierarchical pyramid may have become obsolete, and thus far from optimal, by time $t + k$ when they are put in place by individuals situated at the bottom of the pyramid. Decentralization reduces delays because it allows tasks to be performed concurrently (Radner 1993; Van Zandt 1999b).

Even if environmental conditions are quite stable, the capacity of each individual decision-maker to acquire and process information is limited and her screening ability is not perfect. This may create inefficiencies if decision-making authority is concentrated at the top of the corporate pyramid. In fact, suppose that in each time period a firm faces N decisions; for instance, it must select one or more out of N possible projects of m types. Because of information gathering and processing constraints, centralized organizations are forced to select a relatively lower number of projects than decentralized ones. Decentralization then emerges as an efficient arrangement in situations where projects are on average of a good type (Sah and Stiglitz 1986, 1988). In addition, centralization of decision-making leads to a more intensive use of the expertise of higher-rank managers; if the opportunity cost of their time is high, this may create inefficiencies (Harris and Raviv 2002).

A further source of inefficiencies of centralization of decision authority arises from the fact that the tasks that need to be performed by an organization, and so the nature of the decisions that need to be made, are heterogenous, agents within organizations possess different information sets, and there are increasing returns from task specialization (Bolton and Dewatripont 1994). Decentralization permits agents to specialize in different types of tasks and to assign to them responsibility for decisions in which they enjoy an information advantage. In other words, by delegating decision-making to the agent who has the best information relating to a given decision firms can fully exploit economies arising from local capabilities and specialization of tasks (Geanakoplos and Milgrom 1991).

Moreover, in a "knowledge hierarchy" routine problems can be delegated to low-level less skilled workers, while increasingly diffcult problems, that are encountered less frequently, can be assigned to higher-rank, more skilled problem solvers, who specialize in giving instructions to lower-rank individuals (Garicano 2000). In a hierarchy like this, a decrease of communication costs leads to greater centralization of decisions (Garicano and Rossi-Hansberg 2006).

A similar claim that decision-making authority must be assigned to the most informed agent, though based on a different argument, is made by the decentralization of incentive literature. Aghion and Tirole (1997) consider a situation in which an agent is assigned the task of selecting and implementing one out of N projects, even though the principal keeps the right to overrule her decisions (that is, formal authority remains with the principal). Projects differ in both the (non-contractible) monetary gains for the principal and the private benefits they provide to the agent. Under such circumstances, it is shown that the transfer of decision authority to the agent depends positively on the information advantage she enjoys with respect to the principal (see also Baker *et al.* 1999; Raith 2005). In fact, in Aghion and Tirole's (1997) model, if the parties are uninformed they incur the risk of selecting a project with a negative payoff (i.e. negative monetary gains for the principal and negative private benefits for the agent). Therefore, the less informed the principal, the more likely that she optimally rubber-stamps the agent's proposal. Delegating authority to the agent is also beneficial for the principal whenever the extent of the private benefits that the agent can extract from the exercise of decision-making power is large. In this situation, delegation is likely to increase both agent's initiative to acquire information and her participation in the contractual relationship.

2.2.1.2   The costs of delegation

The cost of authority delegation is the principal's loss of control over the choice of strategies. Loss of control assumes the form of a deviation of the firm's action from the objectives of the principal. This deviation will be greater the less aligned are the principal's and agent's interests. Under such circumstances, decisions about projects that possibly involve a large payoff to the principal and decisions about interdependent projects would be better centralized, as there is a great opportunity cost for the principal if the agent selects a suboptimal project (see again Aghion and Tirole 1997; see also Hart and Moore 2005). Even if one neglects problems arising from incentive misalignment, delegation of authority to agents may prevent the benefits of coordination of interdependent activities being reaped, due to agents' lack of expertise in these matters (Harris and Raviv 2002).

Moreover, it is argued by transaction cost economics that individuals may be prone to a conduct inspired by the aim of seeking their own self-interest even with guile (Williamson, 1975, p. 26). This applies to individuals at all levels of the corporate hierarchy and it has important implications for the allocation of decision-making power. On the one hand, it is natural in a context of asymmetric information and incomplete contracts that an agent is tempted to hide valuable information in order to pursue objectives that are different from those of her superior, and maximize her own utility to the detriment of that of the superior. Therefore, if monitoring agents' behavior is difficult and there is room for agents' opportunistic behavior, centralization of decision-making will follow.[1] On the other hand, the principal, if she keeps decision authority, may leverage it to make decisions that renege on previously agreed contractual obligations. Therefore, the cost for the principal of delegating decision authority downward the corporate hierarchy also includes the opportunity cost of renouncing the right to indulge in opportunistic behavior to the detriment of subordinates (see Dow 1987, pp. 20–22). A similar reasoning applies to decisions that reduce the bargaining power of subordinates. If decision authority is delegated, these decisions will never be made.[2]

To sum up, there are several factors that influence the benefits and costs of delegating decision authority. The benefits include:

- the increase of agents' initiative and participation associated with the opportunity to capture the private benefits of decisions
- the exploitation of agents' specific competencies and information advantage
- the avoidance of leaks in information transmission and overload in information processing
- the timely implementation of decisions.

Conversely, the costs to the principal of delegation include:

- the principal's loss of control and the associated increase of monitoring costs
- the reduction of the room for strategic maneuvering on the part of the principal, to the detriment of agents.

These benefits and costs make delegation more or less profitable, hence more or less likely.

2.2.2   The determinants of the delegation of decision authority

In this section we are interested in the factors that, in accordance with the conceptual framework that has just been illustrated, are likely to influence the relative allocation of decision power in business organizations between an agent (e.g. a line worker, a supervisor, or a middle manager) and her corporate superior. Such factors relate to: (i) the characteristics of firms; (ii) the characteristics of firms' business environment, and (iii) the nature of the decisions at hand. They can be grouped into three families:

- factors that make centralization of decisions *ineffective*, thus favoring decentralization
- factors that make coordination and centralized control of decisions *effective*, thus hindering decentralization
- factors that increase the ability of firms to *decentralize decisions*, thus favoring decentralization.

First of all, there are factors that *increase the need to delegate authority to subordinates* as they make the *centralization of decisions relatively ineffective*. These include factors limiting the flow of information within the firm and factors making local knowledge or a quick response important.

Among these factors, the *size* and the *organizational complexity of firms* play a prominent role, an argument that dates back to Weber's (1946) study of bureaucracy. By generating overload of information within a firm, the firm's size and complexity increase the principal's marginal disutility of getting informed, and press her to leave decision-making power to subordinates. The greater opportunity cost of the time of higher rank managers in greater, more complex organizations reinforces this tendency (Harris and Raviv 2002). In addition, while being closer to the firm's operations, subordinates enjoy an information advantage that is greater (i) the more diversified are the businesses the firm is in and the activities composing the firm's value chain, and so the more diversified the nature of the decisions that need to be made; and (ii) the more heterogenous is the business environment and the closer is the firm to the technological frontier, as in these situations the principal cannot rely on the information provided by the decisions taken by similar firms (Acemoglu *et al.* 2006).

Agents' local knowledge is especially important for *operating decisions* which become routinized over time. In fact, because of learning-by-doing agents develop specific knowledge in performing their tasks that cannot be replicated by the principal and renders their decisions more effective than those of the principal. According to this argument, operating decisions will de delegated down the corporate hierarchy, while strategic non-recurrent decisions will be kept at the top of the pyramid.

In addition, prompt implementation is more valuable for a firm the more urgent is a decision. Therefore, the *urgency* of decisions should favor assignment of authority to downward levels of the corporate hierarchy (Keren and Levhari 1989; Radner 1993).[3] Aghion and Tirole (1997) analyze the effect of urgency in an extension of their basic model; they conclude that "the principal is more likely to rubber-stamp, the more urgent the decision" (p. 26). The reason is that for any level of principal's effort, urgency in decision-making results in an increase of her marginal disutility: the more she oversees, the slower the decision-making process, the lower the returns from implementing the selected project.[4] Accordingly, whenever a firm's organization is shaped by the desire to reduce time to market and assure quick response to external stimuli, we expect responsibility for decision-making to be quite decentralized. For example, this occurs when a firm adopts a just-in-time (JIT) model to organize production and logistics. It may also occur when a firm operates in a rapidly changing business environment, one where there is high technological turbulence or increased competitive pressures (e.g. from new international competitors).

Aghion and Tirole (1997) also show that the need to delegate authority to subordinates is higher for *decisions that involve large private benefits for the agent*. These include, for instance, decisions relating to the management of a firm's workforce. In fact, centralization of this type of decision may hamper the personal leadership of middle managers and supervisors over subordinates, and negatively affect personal relationships with them.

Nevertheless, one has to recognize that the information advantage of subordinates on local matters, the overload generated by centralized processing of information, and the leaks and delays of transmitting orders down the corporate hierarchy can be reduced through use of *advanced information and communication technologies* (ICTs). Indeed, the costs of using information[5] and of communicating[6] have been altered by recent technological advancements. Innovations in ICTs decrease the costs that both the principal and subordinates incurs in getting informed on issues relevant to the firm's operations. With all else equal, assignment of decision authority to subordinates could be less frequent (Aghion and Tirole 1997) or more frequent (Garicano and Rossi-Hansberg 2006), depending on which effect prevails. The costs of processing information and the inefficiencies of communicating orders down the corporate hierarchy are also reduced. This should reinforce the tendency to centralization of decisions, consistent with the arguments highlighted by the information processing literature (Keren and Lehvari 1979, 1983; Radner 1993; Garicano and Rossi-Hansberg 2006).[7] Note however that as will be explained below, use of ICTs within organizations may have other effects, of opposed sign, on the allocation of decision authority, as it also improves the principal's monitoring capabilities and her ability to coordinate the decisions made by peripheral units.

Second, there are factors that *hinder decentralization* because they make *coordination and centralized control of operations valuable*. This set of factors is mostly relevant for multi-unit firms. A firm's *ownership status* is likely to affect the organization of decision-making within the firm. Within multi-unit firms investment and pricing policies, for example, may need to be coordinated in order to properly exploit economies of scale (e.g. in purchasing equipment) or avoid counter-productive internal competition (i.e. cannibalization between different products or services). Hence, in these matters locally optimal decisions are less likely to be also optimal for the firm as a whole, as there are externalities on other units of the same firm. In other words, under these circumstances there is a large gain to coordination of decisions, and this favors centralization (Harris and Raviv 2002; Hart and Moore 2005). With all else equal, centralization of these strategic decisions is more likely in a multi-unit firm than in a single-unit one. In turn, this creates indirect incentives to greater centralization of operating decisions upward the corporate hierarchy.[8]

Nonetheless, it is crucial to emphasize that the impact of a firm's ownership status upon the organization of decision-making may be moderated by other variables which influence the costs for the principal (i.e. the top management of a multi-unit firm) of collecting and transmitting information relevant to the coordination of operations, of checking agents' behavior (i.e. decisions made by heads of subsidiaries), and of designing and implementing high-powered incentive schemes capable of inducing agents to pursue companywide objectives. In particular, such argument applies to the adoption of ICTs. Child (1984) argued that ICTs facilitated the delegation of decision authority in multi-unit organizations by linking each unit in a common network and allowing peripheral decision-makers (and their bosses) to be immediately aware of the wider consequences of their decisions. Hence, we should expect the adoption of ICTs to reduce the pressure to centralize decision authority in multi-unit organizations.

More generally, coordination is important independently of ownership status whenever decisions involve considerable financial resources. This argument applies, for instance, to decisions such as increasing research and development (R&D) expenses rather than the advertising budget, or of expanding production capacity rather than acquiring a competitor. In fact, competition within the firm between agents that are assigned different tasks for the use of fixed corporate resources may absorb their time and energy, to the detriment of the firm's performance. In particular, we should expect the *externality* argument to have a greater influence on strategic decisions than on operating ones and, among strategic decisions, on decisions that concern capital rather than labor.

Finally, as is argued by transaction cost economics, whenever the principal is in a position to indulge in opportunistic behavior to the detriment of subordinates the most obvious way to take advantage of this position is to centralize decisions. For instance, when there are *imperfections in the labor market*, subordinates have to incur substantial costs to find alternative employment opportunities. These switching costs boost the bargaining power of the principal, and create a situation which makes decentralization more costly to the principal, and thus less likely.

Third, the observed degree of decentralization is also crucially influenced by *a firm's ability to decentralize*. This in turn depends on the ability of the principal to observe the behavior of subordinates. Alternatively, even if there are substantial *ex post* information asymmetries between the principal and her subordinates, decentralization of decision-making may still be possible if efficient incentive schemes can be designed, thus realigning the objectives of subordinates with those of the principal. Conversely, suppose that the principal fears that subordinates will be in the position to indulge in opportunistic behavior if they are endowed with decision-making power; then centralization of decision authority follows. This means that any factor that (i) increases the observability of the decisions made by subordinates, (ii) makes available better performance indicators to which subordinates' compensation can be tied, thus rendering monitoring easier for the corporate superior, or (iii) otherwise reduces the room for opportunism on the part of subordinates, should translate into greater decentralization.

Three such factors are worth being mentioned here. First, as was mentioned above, *adoption of ICTs* considerably increases the monitoring capabilities of the principal and makes subordinates' decisions more transparent (Hubbard 2000). In turn, this allows greater delegation of decision authority to lower levels. Second, *multi-unit firms* should be better able to design effective incentives schemes as they can rely on some forms of yardstick competition. This type of monitoring is especially effective if the different units have similar product lines (i.e. for non-diversified multi-unit firms). So, with all else equal (in particular, the need for greater coordination in a multi-unit setting, see above), multi-unit firms with homogenous product lines should adopt a more decentralized organization than other firms. Third, the ability of the principal to observe and evaluate the behavior of subordinates increases with her *tenure*, as experience is very helpful in these matters. The *firm's age* is

Table 2.1 Determinants of the decentralization of decision authority in business organizations

Factors	Increased need for delegation	Increased need for coordination	Greater ability to delegate	Net effect
Firm-specific				
Complexity of the organization (e.g. size)	+			+
Use of advanced ICTs	−		+	?
Use of advanced ICTs × Complexity of the organization	−			−
Ownership status: Multi-unit organization	+	−	+[a]	?
Use of advanced ICTs × Multi-unit organization	−	+		?
Subcontractor		−		−
Capital intensity of production process				−
Tenure of managers			+	+
Firm age			+	+ +
Proximity to the technological frontier	+			+
Decision-specific				
Strategic decisions		−		−
Operating decisions	+			+ +
Labor decisions	+			+
Capital decisions		−		−
Environment-specific				
Urgency of decisions	+			+ +
Heterogeneity of firms	+			+ +
Competition	+		+	+ +
High switching costs for labor		−		−

Notes
+ Predicted positive effect on decentralization.
− Predicted negative effect on decentralization.
? Ambiguous predictions.
[a] With homogeneous product lines in different sites.

likely to have a similar effect, as decisions becomes more routinized over time and so easier to control. Again, more delegation should follow.

The predictions relating to the determinants of the decentralization of decision authority in business organizations based on the theoretical arguments illustrated above are synthesized in Table 2.1. As a final remark, it is important to emphasize that some of the variables mentioned in Table 2.1 (e.g. firm size) have an unequivocal effect on the delegation of decision authority to subordinates. Conversely, other variables (e.g. ownership status, use of advanced ICTs) are likely to have different effects, of an opposed nature. So determining which effect prevails is a matter of empirical testing.[9]

2.3 Empirical evidence on the determinants of the allocation of decision authority

Even though the decentralization of decision authority and its determinants have captured the attention of scholars since the 1960s, quite surprisingly there are relatively few quantitative studies in this field that consider large samples of business organizations. The aim of this section is to survey this literature.

2.3.1 The work of the Aston group

Attempts to collect large-scale empirical evidence on the allocation of decision authority originate from the work carried out in the UK by the Aston group on the measurement and explanation of organizational structures (Pugh *et al.* 1968b, 1969; Hickson *et al.* 1969).[10] This approach assumed that one dimension of the organizational structure was primarily shaped by the other dimensions of the context in which organizations operated. Accordingly, Pugh and his colleagues concentrated attention on the effects on delegation of decisions of contextual variables such as the size and ownership status of organizations, and the technologies in use.

More precisely, Pugh *et al.* (1968) considered fifty-two organizations located in the Birmingham area; out of these forty-six were a random sample stratified by size and industry of the 293 organizations in the area that at the time of the survey (i.e. in the early 1960s) had more than 250 employees. The organizations under scrutiny were as diverse as "firms making motor cars and chocolate bars, municipal departments repairing roads and teaching arithmetic, large retail stores, small insurance companies, and so on" (Pugh *et al.* 1968). In line with the philosophy examined in Chapter 1, several "objective" organizational variables were measured, including aspects relating to the centralization of decision authority in organizations and their configuration.[11] As to the allocation of decision-making, the level in the hierarchy to which decision power was formally assigned was determined for thirty-seven recurrent decisions covering a range of activities.[12] Scores were obtained for each decision from 5 when a decision was taken outside the organization (e.g. at the head office level) to 0 when it was taken at the operation level; these scores were summed to obtain a general indicator of overall centralization of decision-making. An index reflecting the autonomy of the organization, defined as the number of decisions out of a subset of twenty-three which lay within its jurisdiction, was also calculated.

The relation of these indicators to contextual variables was then examined in both univariate and multivariate analyses (Pugh *et al.* 1969b). Forty variables describing the context of organizations were initially constructed and then combined into fourteen indicators. These included, among others: the age, size, and ownership status of organizations; the size and number of sites of their parent company, and the dependence of the organization under scrutiny on its parent (if there was any); the characteristics of the technology in use; and the type of outputs (e.g. service as opposed to manufacturing) and markets of the organization.

The results of the study indicated that decisions authority was more decentralized in relatively larger and older organizations that produce a wider range of non-standard producer goods. Conversely, it was found to be more concentrated at the top of the hierarchical pyramid in subsidiary branches of large organizations that operated a large number of sites, especially when dependence on the parent organization was great.[13] Technology was reflected by workflow integration. This variable was obtained through a PCA and captured, among other things, the rigidity of the workflow and the mean and maximum level of automation of the equipment in use (following the conceptualization proposed by Amber and Amber 1962). It was positively correlated with the concentration of decision authority (i.e. negatively correlated with delegation).[14] However, quite surprisingly in a multivariate analysis the explanatory power of most of these variables was found to be negligible, with only dependence on the parent organization and the number of sites of this latter exhibiting statistically significant coefficients.

Hickson *et al.* (1969) used the data collected by the Aston group to analyze in greater detail the role of technology. They considered both the workflow integration indicator mentioned above and an indicator of the continuity of production inspired by the work of Woodward (see n. 14).

They showed that in the thirty-one manufacturing establishments included in the sample analyzed by the Aston group, there was a lack of association between these indicators and the decentralization of decision authority. They interpreted these results as suggesting that technology had a negligible influence on this aspect of organizational design, especially if one considered organizations of large size.

2.3.2 More on the role of size and technology

Work carried out by the Aston group was then replicated and extended by several authors. In an influential article, Child (1973) further examined the effects on the decentralization of decision authority of the size of the organization. He also considered the use of advanced technology, with this latter variable being again proxied by workflow integration. In order to avoid bias possibly generated by the heterogeneity of the sample of organizations considered by Pugh and his colleagues, Child concentrated attention on eighty-two British business organizations stratified by size and selected from six industries.[15] None of these organizations was owned by local or central government bodies. In a multivariate regression he found that the degree of decentralization of decision-making increased with the size of the organization, and it was negatively affected by workflow integration, which allegedly reduced the complexity and variability of operations; so he concluded that both size and technology indeed affected the allocation of decision-making. Nonetheless, the former variable was found to enjoy a much closer relationship with decentralization than the latter one (on this issue, see also Child and Mansfield 1972).

Khandwalla (1974) analyzed the relation between operations technology and the degree of decentralization of strategic decisions in a sample of seventy-nine American manufacturing firms. The mass-output orientation of technology was captured by a composite index close in spirit to Woodward's. First, the firm's CEO was asked to rate, on a 7-point Likert scale, the extent to which each of five technologies were used in the manufacturing process of their firms – namely, custom, small-batch, large-batch, mass production, and continuous process technologies. These ratings were then weighted through weights ranging from 1 for custom technology to 5 for continuous process technology. As to the decentralization of decision authority, a perceptual measure was used. In fact, the president of the firm was asked to rate, on a 7-point Likert scale, the extent to which the CEO had delegated authority in each of nine key areas of strategic decision-making (e.g. raising of long-term capital, selection of investments, acquisitions, etc.). The delegation index was the average of the nine ratings. While the study provided evidence of a positive correlation equal to 0.49 between firm size measured by the log of annual sales and the decentralization index, this latter was found not to be correlated with the mass-output orientation of the firm's technology. Nonetheless, when the sample was split into two subsamples according to the profitability of firms, a significantly positive correlation between the two indexes emerged in the highly profitable firms' subsample.

The Aston group's argument that there is no "technological imperative" in organizational design was also questioned by other authors. For instance, Aldrich (1972) started from the assumption that the size of organizations is endogenous, being determined, among other factors, by the technology used by firms. He then re-examined the evidence provided by the Aston group through path analysis. He showed that operating variability, a dimension of technology, is positively correlated with workflow integration. Nonetheless, contrary to findings by Child (1973), this variable was positively correlated with decentralization of decision-making.[16]

Subsequent studies gave specific attention to the effect on the decentralization of decision authority of the widespread diffusion of computers in business organizations. In fact, as was argued by Blau *et al.* (1976), the effects on organizational design of the mechanization of production technology need not to coincide with those engendered by the automation of support functions through the use of computers. They considered a sample composed of 110 manufacturing plants with 200 or more employees and showed that in-house use of computers for the automation of support functions promoted decentralization of operational decisions (i.e. production and marketing decisions), in contrast to the centralizing influence of advanced production technology on these decisions.[17] These findings were replicated by Reimann (1980) in a study of twenty Ohio manufacturing plants.

Zeffane (1989) used survey data collected in 1983 on 149 Australian establishments to measure the effect of the extent of computer use in fourteen administrative functions on the decentralization of decisions. A distinction was made between operational, staffing, financial, and strategic decisions.[18] Informational and operational uses of computers (e.g. use in functions such as planning and market research as opposed to functions such as production, maintenance, and stock control) were captured by distinct variables. Quite interestingly, this study highlighted that operational, staffing, and financial decisions were more decentralized with greater operational use of computers, while the informational use of computers had a similar effect only on the decentralization of financial decisions. Conversely, strategic decisions were found to be unaffected by use of computers. These findings were relatively stronger among medium-sized and large establishments.

Dean *et al.* (1992) focused attention on the impact of adoption of computer-controlled automation in manufacturing (programmable automation, PA) on the extent of decentralization of decision authority. More precisely, they measured the extent of (i) computer usage in individual functions (e.g. computer aided design, CAD; computerized numerical control, CNC; etc.), (ii) computer-based integration between different functions (e.g. software downloading CAD data and creating CNC part programs), and (iii) sophistication of computer integration. Data were provided by the top-ranking manufacturing managers of 185 US metalworking plants. The computerization and sophistication of computer-based integration variables were significantly and positively correlated with the decentralization of decisions.

More recently, Collins *et al.* (1999) addressed the same issue, distinguishing between operating and strategic decisions, but resorted to longitudinal data.[19] Their empirical analysis was based on a stratified sample of large (i.e. number of employees equal to or greater than 250) US manufacturing establishments that were studied first in the early 1970s (time *T*1) and then in the early 1980s (time *T*2). Data referred to fifty-four establishments located in a highly industrialized mid-Atlantic state. The level of decentralization of decision authority was captured by the position in the corporate hierarchy of the person empowered to take action without consultation with others. "Strategic decentralization" referred to the average location of authority over the following decisions: set total operating budget, determine production quotas or goals, select suppliers, decide which type of equipment to buy. "Line operating decentralization" referred to the following decisions: determine methods of work, allocate work among production workers, set the pace of production work.

Quite unsurprisingly, strategic authority was found to be more centralized than operating authority, with strategic decisions resting on average with the highest executive at the site. Moreover, establishments with a higher number of hierarchical levels tended to decentralize strategic decisions and centralize operating ones to a larger extent than other establishments. As to the role of technology, PA was operationalized as the proportion of manufacturing capacity accounted for by machinery and equipment based on such technologies as CNC, robots, distributed numerical control, distributed process control, and automated material transfer devices. The study analyzed the effect of changes in the PA indicator between *T*1 and *T*2 on the level of centralization of strategic and operating decisions in *T*2 through a regression analysis. Several firm- and industry-specific factors were added to the set of explanatory variables. The former group included firm size, firm growth, the percentage of professionals in *T*1 and the growth of this indicator over the observation period. The latter included industry R&D intensity and growth. PA was found to positively influence the centralization of operating decisions, while it had a negligible (though negative) effect on the centralization of strategic decisions (that in fact were already highly centralized at the beginning of the observation period).

2.3.3   Country-specific effects

Several studies tried to replicate the Aston approach in other countries, in an attempt to highlight (or to negate) the role played by specific characteristics of the socioeconomic environments in which firms are embedded (which allegedly differ across countries: see, for instance, Inkson *et al.* 1970; McMillan *et al.* 1973; Hickson *et al.* 1974, 1979; Horvath *et al.* 1976; Kuc *et al.* 1980; see also Hickson and McMillan 1981). In general, differences across countries were found to be limited. Work on Japanese firms is especially interesting, as Japan is often mentioned as an example of a country with specific institutions, culture and management style.

In particular, in several studies Marsh and Mannari analyzed the organization of manufacturing plants employing 100 or more persons that were located in one medium city of the Okayama prefecture in Southwestern Japan (e.g. Marsh and Mannari 1981, 1988; Marsh 1992). The sample included fifty establishments that operated in fourteen industries, out of a population of eighty-four; half of them were branches of multi-unit companies. Survey-based data were first collected in the summer of 1976. A second survey wave in which forty-eight plants participated, was carried out in the summer of 1983. The authors used an indicator of decentralization very similar to that originally constructed by Pugh and his colleagues.[20] They analyzed how sample plants made the thirty-seven recurrent decisions that were considered by the Aston group. The dependent variable, the centralization score, was the sum of the scores across the thirty-seven decisions. In the 1981 study, specific attention was given to plants' size and technology: the degrees of both automaticity and production continuity were measured. The set of explanatory variables of decentralization also included the dependence of plants on their parent organization and their autonomy in decision-making, their dependence on customers and suppliers, the age of the parent company, and the number of dispersed sites it possessed. Contrary to the findings of Child (1973), decentralization turned out to be independent of size[21] and technology. In accordance with the results of the Aston group, it was mostly associated with autonomy from the parent organization.

In a later study based on the 1983 survey data, Marsh (1992) extended these results through the analysis of individual decisions. He showed that the greater the number of sites of the company to which plants belong, the greater the centralization of decision authority. In fact, this variable had a positive effect on the centralization of all thirty-seven decisions under scrutiny, and this effect was statistically significant at conventional confidence levels for twenty-four out of thirty-seven decisions. Conversely, the size of plants was found to favor decentralization, but this effect was statistically significant only for decisions relating to firms' personnel (e.g. methods of selection of personnel, promotion and dismissal, allocation of tasks among workers). Lastly, the automation of production processes failed to show any systematic influence on the allocation of decision power, in accordance with the view originally proposed by the Aston group that there is no technological imperative in the allocation of decision-making.

Marsh (1992) also considered environment-specific and decision-specific factors: he examined the influence exerted by task variability, defined as the extent to which an establishment changes products according to customer specification. This variable exhibited a negative statistically significant effect on the overall centralization score, and a negative effect, though generally not statistically significant in all individual decisions but one. The most centralized decisions had in common the creation of something new and other strategic issues like the choice of the market, price decisions, and major investments, while the most decentralized ones were those that involved either routine or localized issues, like production decisions.

In spite of the fact that the above-mentioned studies failed to consistently highlight relevant country-specific effects, the view that the determinants of the centralization of decision-making are largely culture-free is not unanimously shared in the empirical literature.

Lincoln *et al.* (1986) reported findings from parallel surveys conducted from 1981 to 1983, of fifty-five manufacturing plants in the US and fifty-one plants in Japan that operated in the same manufacturing industries and had comparable size. They departed from other studies in that they considered the decentralization of both formal and real authority; in other words, they resorted to the Aston group indicator of decentralization of decision-making but they measured which level within the organization was formally assigned the authority to make a given decision and at which level the decision under scrutiny was made in practice. Japanese plants were found to combine greater centralization of formal authority with greater *de facto* delegation of decisions than their US counterparts. More interestingly, the role of technological variables in molding the assignment of decision authority, both formal and real, differed between the US and Japanese samples. Using the indicators proposed by Woodward (1965), they found that in the US sample there was more delegation, with respect to both real and formal authority, in plants involved in custom/small batch and continuous production than in those involved in large batch/mass production. Nonetheless, this pattern was absent in the Japanese sample. Actually, the technological variables[22] turned out to have a far less significant effect on the organization of decision-making in Japan than in the US.

Wong and Birnbaum-More (1994) analyzed the organization of thirty-nine multinational banks from fourteen countries that operated in Hong-Kong between 1981 and 1984. The explanatory variables of the degree of centralization of decision authority included firm-specific factors (size, ownership status, and technology in use) and environmental factors associated with the cultural characteristics of the banks' home country. The centralization indicator was similar to that used by previous studies. Wong and Birnbaum-More resorted to confirmatory factor analysis and structural equation modeling with LISREL. The findings of their analysis highlighted that in accordance with most other studies (see again n. 21), size measured by the log of the number of employees, was positively associated with the extent of the decentralization of decisions. Quite surprisingly, dependence of the bank on its parent organization was found to have a similarly positive effect.[23] In addition, the power distance dimension of culture, mirroring the extent to which unequal distribution of power is accepted by members of a society, was positively related to the centralization of authority. Conversely, the uncertainty avoidance dimension, which captures the extent to which members of a society feel threatened by uncertainty, had no clear effect.

Similarly, Lin and Germain (2003) considered a sample composed of 205 Chinese state-owned enterprises (SOEs) that were observed in 1999. They measured the level of decentralization of four decisions relating to factory location planning, new product design and R&D budget, the adoption of EDI, and inventory planning. They again resorted to a confirmatory factor analysis using LISREL. The most interesting result is that the extent of foreign-induced industry competition, measured by the ratio of the sales of foreign funded enterprises that operated in a given industry to total industry sales, drove the decentralization of decision authority. Conversely, the remaining environment-specific and firm-specific variables – that is, technological turbulence proxied by perceived dynamism in products and processes, firm size measured by both sales and number of employees, and production technology routineness as reflected by orientation to mass output – failed to exhibit any explanatory power.

2.3.4   New directions in the empirical literature on the determinants of decentralization

More recently, there have been three interesting additions to the empirical literature that aims at highlighting the determinants of the allocation of decision authority.

Meagher and Wait (2007) used data from the Australian Workplace Industrial Relations survey 1995, covering 2001 workplaces with over 20 employees, to examine for those establishments that had implemented at least one significant non-routine change in the previous two years, who made the decision relating to the most important change. From these micro-data they obtained an index of establishments' decision-making decentralization, and they estimated an ordered probit model to assess the establishment- and environment-specific determinants of decentralization.

First of all, their estimates suggest that quite unsurprisingly, the relative size of the workplace to the size of the parent organization positively affects decentralization; however, the larger the parent organization, the more likely that decision authority be assigned to higher level managers. More interestingly, decentralization appears to be favored by the level of competition in the industry of the workplace. Moreover, exporting firms that allegedly face vigorous competition and need specialized knowledge on export markets, have more decentralized decision-making than other firms, with all else equal. Conversely, import competition does not have any statistically significant effect. Lastly, a change from predictable to unpredictable product demand substantially increases the probability that the decision under scrutiny be centralized.

Acemoglu *et al.* (2006) examined whether experience from other firms, while reducing the information advantage of middle managers, makes it less compelling for top managers to delegate decision authority down the corporate hierarchy. For this purpose, they used data provided by three sources: the COI database relating to a sample of around 4,000 French manufacturing firms observed in 1998; the 1998 wave of *Enquête Reponse* (ER), a survey of just under 3,000 French establishments covering all sectors of the economy; and the 1998 Workplace Employee Relations Survey (WERS) conducted in the UK with a similar structure to the ER survey.[24] They proxied decentralization of decision-making with three variables:

- a dummy variable provided by the COI, indicating whether a firm organizes its divisions into profit centers or is more centrally controlled; the assumption is made that delegation of decisions to division managers is greater in the former case than in the latter (for similar approach see Christie *et al.* 2003)
- a dummy variable provided by the ER, indicating whether the establishment's senior manager had "full" or "important" autonomy from the headquarters in making decisions about investments
- a dummy variable provided by the WERS, capturing the autonomy of establishments that are part of multi-unit firms in making staff recruitment decisions.

These dummies were regressed against explanatory variables that were aimed at reflecting the extent of the informational advantage of managers at division or establishment levels with respect to the corporate headquarters. This informational advantage is likely to be greater in more heterogeneous business environments in which benchmarking is more difficult, and for firms that are closer to the technological frontier and thus are dealing with technologies about which there is only limited public information.

In particular, Acemoglu and co-authors considered two explanatory variables:

- the *heterogeneity in annual average productivity growth* in the four-digit industry in which firms operated over the period 1994–7. This variable was measured by the difference in the rates of growth of productivity (i.e. value added per hour) between high- and low-productivity growth firms (i.e. the 90th and 10th percentiles of the distribution or the 95th and 5th percentiles). They also replaced productivity growth rates with productivity levels. In addition, they used an indicator that quantified (the inverse of) how many other firms were close neighbors to the firm under scrutiny in the product space. This indicator was inspired by Jaffe's (1986) approach to measuring technological proximity. This approach was followed closely, with sales in different industries replacing number of patents in different patent classes. The only difference was that closeness values relating to any firm *i* and *j* were weighted with firms' information technology (IT) investments, in accordance with the view that heterogeneity has a more decisive impact on delegation for IT-intensive firms

- the *proximity of firms to the technological frontier*. This variable was inversely measured by the ratio of the focal firm's productivity level to that at the 99th percentile of the distribution in the same four-digit industry.

The results of the estimates of probit models that also included several firm- and industry-specific controls,[25] suggested that both heterogeneity of the business environment and proximity to the frontier lead to greater delegation of decision authority. These results held true independently of the particular decentralization measure used in the model specification and independently of the country (i.e. either French or the UK) to which the estimates referred. However, they were far more robust in high-tech industries than in low-tech ones.[26]

Vázquez (2004) departed from most studies surveyed so far in that he tested the links between the allocation of decision rights on the shop floor and the attributes of labor transactions, while simultaneously controlling for several firm-specific characteristics. His empirical analysis was based on a sample composed of 329 firms that responded to a mail questionnaire out of the 3,004 with 3 million Euro sales or more in 2000 in the Spanish food and electronics industries. He distinguished strategic and operating decisions, following the categories proposed by Colombo and Delmastro (1999) and described in Chapter 1. He found that strategic decisions were more centralized than operating decisions, but only slightly so.

Among the characteristics of transactions that affected the relationships between workers and managers, and therefore allegedly influenced the extent of the decentralization of decision authority, the following five were considered:

- *frequency of transactions*, measured by the mean time that operators spend carrying out their main task
- *human specificity* – that is, the importance of localized industry-specific knowledge; this was proxied by the difference between the time that a newly hired worker with no experience in the industry spent to reach normal productivity and the corresponding time for a newly hired experienced worker
- *temporal specificity*, related to the extent of the technological interdependencies between different phases of the production process and proxied by orientation to a zero stock production and logistic system (i.e. a JIT system)[27]
- *workers' opportunism*, defined as the extent of workers' behavior aimed at consciously reducing the quantity and/or quality of output[28]

- *managers' opportunism*, defined as the propensity of managers to uni-laterally exceed previously agreed-upon limits in their relations with subordinates (see again n.28).

Vázquez also included in the set of explanatory variables an aggregate measure of the dynamism and uncertainty of firms' environment, reflecting characteristics such as the rate of introduction of new tech-nologies, new products and managerial innovations and the unpre-dictability of technological changes in the industry, and several firm-specific variables that were also considered in previous studies (e.g. size, age, and ownership status).

He estimated several ordered logit models, and the results of the esti-mates can be synthesized as follows. Decision-making is more centralized in subsidiaries than in independent firms; this holds true for both strategic and operating decisions. Firm size and age positively affect the decentral-ization of operating decisions, while they fail to show any significant effect on strategic decisions. Environmental uncertainty has no significant effect on the allocation of decision authority, be it strategic or operational.

As to variables that reflect the characteristics of transactions, they have greater influence on the allocation of operating decisions than on strategic ones. In particular, operating decisions are more decentralized in organizations that rely on a JIT logic and for which workers' learning-by-doing is crucial to obtaining high productivity levels. Conversely, they are more centralized in firms that have recurrent transactions. None of these characteristics has any influence on the allocation of strategic decision-making, with the partial exception of workers' learn-ing-by-doing which has a (weakly significant) unexpected positive effect on the centralization indicator.

Lastly, managers' and workers' opportunism failed to exhibit any explanatory power for the allocation of operating decisions, while man-agerial opportunism led to the centralization of strategic decisions, as was expected.

2.3.5   A synthesis

Altogether the studies surveyed above provide some interesting insights into the determinants of the decentralization of decision-making in business organizations. The evidence on this issue is summarized in Table 2.2a and 2.2b.

In particular, the results of these studies suggest that concerning the role of firm-specific variables, decisions tend to be more decentralized in larger, older, and independent organizations. For subsidiary branches, the larger the number of sites of the parent organization and the lower

Table 2.2a Quantitative empirical evidence on the determinants of the decentralization of decision authority: a synthesis

	Firm-specific variables										
						Multi-unit firm		Technology			
	Size	Levels	Age	Diversification	Skilled workforce	Dependence	Size of parent	Workflow integration/automation	Use of advanced manufacturing technologies	Use of computers	Closeness to technological frontier
Aston group Child and Mansfield (1972), Child (1973)	(+)		(+)			−	(−)	(−)			
Aldrich (1972)	+							(−)			
Khandwalla (1974)	+							+			
Blau et al. (1976)	+							//[a]			
Reimann (1980)	(+)					−		−[b]	−[b]	+[b]	
Zeffane (1989)	(+)							−[b]		+[b]	
Dean et al. (1992)	(+)					+		+		+[c]	
Collins et al. (1999)	+	−[d]/+[e]							−[d]	(+)	
Marsh and Mannari (1981, 1988)	//					−		//			
Marsh (1992)	+[f]	(+)				−		(−)			

Continued

Table 2.2a Continued

	Firm-specific variables										
	Multi-unit firm					Technology					
	Size	Levels	Age	Diversification	Skilled workforce	Dependence	Size of parent	Workflow integration/ automation	Use of advanced manufacturing technologies	Use of computers	Closeness to technological frontier
Lincoln et al. (1986)	+							U[g]			
Wong and Birnbaum–More (1994)			+[g]								
Lin and Germain (2003)	+					+		//			
Meagher and Wait (2007)	//						−	//			
Acemoglu et al. (2006)	+		−	+	+					+	+
Christie et al. (2003)				+							
Vazquez (2004)	+[d]		+[d]			−					+

Notes

+/−: Significant positive or negative effect. (+)/(−): weak positive or negative effect. //: no effect.
[a] Strategic decisions. Positive correlation in the subsample composed of highly profitable firms.
[b] Production and marketing decisions.
[c] Operational, staffing and financial decisions: operational use of computers. Financial decisions: informational use of computers.
[d] Operating decisions.
[e] Strategic decisions.
[f] Personnel decisions.
[g] U-shaped relation in US establishments. No relation in Japanese establishments. Age affects only formal authority.

Table 2.2b Quantitative empirical evidence on the determinants of the decentralization of decision authority: a synthesis

	Industry-specific					Country-specific	Decision-specific	
	Technological turbulence and uncertainty	R&D/IT intensity	Competition	Heterogeneity	Growth	Culture: power distance	Operating decisions	Importance of learning-by-doing
Reimann (1980)	(+)[a]							
Dean et al. (1992)	//							
Marsh (1992)	+						+	
Wong and Birnbaum-More (1994)						−		
Collins et al. (1999)							+	
Lin and Germain (2003)	//		+					
Meagher and Wait (2007)	−		+					
Acemoglu et al. (2006)		+	+	+				
Christie et al. (2003)	+				+			
Vázquez (2004)	//						+	+[a]

Note

[a] Operating decisions.

the autonomy of the subsidiary, the greater the centralization of decisions. Conversely, the effects of technology are ambiguous. They possibly depend on the specific characteristics of the technological innovations introduced by firms (i.e. automation of production as opposed to use of ICTs in support functions). They also seem to depend on other firm-specific characteristics (e.g. firm size). Nonetheless, scholars generally agree that, starting from the early 1980s, the use of ICTs is frequently associated with greater delegation of decision authority.

In addition, when the distributed specific knowledge possessed by subordinates is relatively more important, greater decentralization of decision authority follows. This situation applies to firms that are closer to the technological frontier or operate in a heterogenous business environment. There is also some evidence that greater decentralization is associated with greater urgency of decisions and stronger competitive pressures.

Concerning decision-specific factors, non-recurrent strategic decisions are more centralized than more routinized operating ones. In addition, the nature of the decision – be it related to the production, marketing, financial, or personnel spheres – also influences the degree of decentralization.

Lastly, these findings seem not to be substantially altered by the socioeconomic characteristics of different countries.

2.4   Evidence on the determinants of the allocation of decision authority based on the new empirical methodology[29]

In this section we report the results of the estimates of a series of econometric models of the determinants of the decentralization of decision authority that rely on the methodology and data on a sample of Italian manufacturing plants presented in Chapter 1 (see also the Appendix of this book).

The objective is to illustrate in detail how the quantitative indicators of decentralization that were illustrated in Chapter 1 can be used in econometric analyses based on large samples of organizations so as to provide empirical evidence that is both generalizable and robust, two characteristics that often are absent in the studies surveyed in Section 2.3.

2.4.1   The data*

The data used here concern who within the firm (that is, which hierarchical level) takes strategic decisions related to a plant's activity. We consider the following six strategic decisions: (i) introduction of new technologies, (ii) investments in new production lines, (iii) investments in stand-alone machinery, (iv) hiring and dismissal of plant personnel, (v) career paths, and (vi) design of individual and collective incentive schemes.[30]

We focus on the relationship between the plant manager (the agent) and her corporate superior (the principal), where the latter is either the firm's owner-manager or a salaried manager. In the latter case the principal is an intermediary of the owner(s), a situation typical of (even though not confined to) establishments that are owned by large multi-unit firms. The former case applies especially to small entrepreneurial firms. Further, notice that when firms are very small there may be no plant manager, at least formally. In such cases the agent is the person responsible for supervising production. In what follows, for the sake of brevity and simplicity, we shall always use the term "plant manager."

In order to test the determinants of the delegation of decision authority, we have distinguished three ranked modes of allocating a plant's strategic decisions:

- *Centralization (C).* Decisions under scrutiny are taken autonomously by the plant manager's corporate superior, with the plant manager being assigned an implementation role. In this case the plant manager can make proposals, but decision authority is a superior's matter. So this situation corresponds to the minimum degree of delegation of authority
- *Partial delegation of decision authority (DI).* The plant manager is in charge of the decision, but formal authorization by the corporate superior is needed. In this case, decision authority is partially delegated to the plant manager, even though her decisions may be overruled by the superior
- *Full delegation of decision authority (DII).* In this case, decisions are taken autonomously by the plant manager with no intervention by the superior. Note that the superior always keeps the right to overrule the plant manager, as she ultimately can fire her. Nonetheless, this situation corresponds to the maximum degree of decentralization of decision authority, as the plant manager has far greater autonomy than in case *DI*

Thus, for each sample establishment and for each of the six strategic decisions we know who (the plant manager or her corporate superior) is in charge and how the decision is taken. In other words, we know how authority is allocated between the two parties. In particular, in 42% of the 2,628 observations (i.e. 438 plants × 6 decisions) decision authority is centralized at the corporate superior's level; partial and full delegation account for 32% and 26% of total observations, respectively.

2.4.2   The econometric model*

2.4.2.1   *Specification of the econometric model**

We test the theoretical predictions illustrated in Section 2.2.2 by analyzing the impact of a set of explanatory variables which will be presented in the next section on the allocation of decision authority. The choice faced by the parent firm of plant j is the definition of the optimal degree of delegation of authority over decision i indicated by D_{ij}^*. This can be modeled as a discrete choice problem. As was said earlier, we let the firm allocate each of the six plant's strategic decisions into three different ranked modes: *Centralization (C)*, *Partial delegation of decision authority (DI)*, and *Full delegation of decision authority (DII)*, with $C < DI < DII$ in terms of degree of delegation of authority to the plant manager.

The choice of the decision mode reflects the maximization of the firm's profits. Let D_{ij}^* be the "optimal" degree of delegation – that is to say, the one that maximizes firm's profits, which is a random attribute of feasible choices. For each plant j ($j = 1,\dots,438$) and decision i ($i = 1,\dots,6$) we define D_{ij}^* as:

$$D_{ij}^* = V_{ij} + \varepsilon_{ij}$$

where ϵ_{ij} is a random disturbance and V_{ij} is a deterministic component, which depends on two sets of explanatory variables: one, denoted by X_j, includes plant-specific characteristics; the other, denoted by Z_i, includes decision-specific variables.

Clearly is D_{ij}^* unobserved. What we observe is D_{ij}, which assumes ranked values equal to C, DI, and DII, and whose relation with the optimal degree of delegation is:

$$D_{ij} = C \quad \text{if} \quad D_{ij}^* \leq \mu_0$$
$$D_{ij} = DI \quad \text{if} \quad \mu_0 < D_{ij}^* \leq \mu_1$$
$$D_{ij} = DII \quad \text{if} \quad D_{ij}^* > \mu_1$$

where μ_k ($k = 0,1$) are the thresholds that separate the different discrete categories of delegation of authority. With no loss of generality, we can set $\mu_0 = 0$ and $\mu_1 = \mu$.

Given the categorical ordered nature of the dependent variable we proceeded to estimate ordered probit models. Note that the sample is composed of 438 plants and for each plant there are six decisions so that the total number of observations is 2,628. However, these are not 2,628 independent observations. In fact, there are only 438 independent observations as observations relating to different strategic decisions in a given plant are likely to be correlated. This correlation is due to unobserved plant-specific effects that influence the overall allocation of plant decision-making, independently of the nature of individual decisions. For instance, in family-owned firms, that account for the large majority of the sample, owner-managers may be unwilling to delegate authority down to plant managers due to psychological motivations (i.e. personal preferences for autocratic decision-making). In addition, the allocation pattern of decision authority as observed at the survey date may depend on the specific history of each plant, due to irreversibilities and structural inertia in the organization (see Colombo and Delmastro 2002; see also Chapter 4). To deal with this problem we estimated ordered probit models with random effects.[31]

Before proceeding further with the definition of the explanatory variables, an additional remark is in order. In this chapter we focus on the optimal allocation of decision-making power and we relate the degree of decentralization of decision authority, the dependent variable of the econometric model, to a set of plant- and decision-specific characteristics. However, it is clear that the allocation of authority over strategic decisions is but one element in a set of decisions that firms make as regards the organization of plants. Such decisions include, for instance, the depth of the corporate hierarchy, the number and quality of employees, the use of incentive schemes to motivate employees, the type of technologies in use and, more generally, the overall organization of the parent firm. In other words, there likely is simultaneity between D_{ij}^* and other variables that in this work are considered as independent. Nonetheless, the great number of potentially endogenous variables and their non-linear nature makes it impossible to estimate a simultaneous equations structural model.

2.4.2.2 Explanatory variables*

In order to test the predictions of economic theory as to the determinants of the allocation of decision-making power, we considered plant-specific characteristics (X_j) and decision-specific variables (Z_i) that, in accordance with the conceptual framework presented in Section 2.2.2, reflect the following factors:

- factors that increase the need to decentralize
- factors that hinder decentralization because of coordination issues
- factors that influence the ability to decentralize.

Before presenting the explanatory variables, a preliminary comment is in order. While some variables are unambiguously associated with a particular set of factors, others capture various effects. In this latter case, as opposing forces may be at work, the sign of the coefficient of these variables cannot be predicted *ex ante*. In Table 2.3 we report the definition of the explanatory variables. A synthesis of their expected effects on the decentralization of decision authority is presented in Table 2.4. For a more detailed illustration and descriptive statistics, see the Appendix of this chapter (in particular, Table 2.A1).

Table 2.3 Explanatory variables of the econometric models

Variable	Description
Size	Logarithm of the number of employees
Level	Number of hierarchical levels of the organization
Just-in-time	1 for plants that have adopted JIT production methods; 0 otherwise
Multi-plant	1 for plants that belong to multi-unit parent companies; 0 otherwise
Multi-plant diversified	1 for plants that belong to multi-unit parent companies and meet the following two conditions: (a) the parent company has more than 25,000 employees and (b) no one of its product lines accounts for more than 70% of total sales; 0 otherwise
Multi-plant dominant business	1 for plants that belong to multi-unit parent companies and do not meet conditions (a) and/or (b); 0 otherwise
Subcontractor	1 for plants with more than 75% of total sales earned as a subcontractor; 0 otherwise
IMS	1 for plants that have invested in large-scale capital equipment, such as (inflexible) manufacturing line systems (IMS); 0 otherwise
Network	1 for plants that have adopted advanced network technologies (i.e. use of network technology to exchange technical data and general information with other departments, headquarters, and between different points on the factory floor); 0 otherwise
Monetary incentives	1 for plants that have adopted "non-traditional" individual incentive schemes (i.e. pay for skills and quality)

Continued

Table 2.3 Continued

Variable	Description
D-Capital	1 for decisions concerning purchase of capital equipment (i.e. technological innovations, large-scale capital equipment, stand-alone machinery); 0 otherwise
D-Labor	1 for decisions concerning the workforce (i.e. hiring and dismissal, career paths, incentive schemes); 0 otherwise
D-Technology	1 for decisions concerning the introduction of technological innovations; 0 otherwise
D-Capital equipment	1 for decisions concerning the purchase of large-scale capital equipment; 0 otherwise
D-Machinery	1 for decisions concerning the purchase of stand-alone machinery; 0 otherwise
D-Hiring and dismissal	1 for decisions concerning hiring and dismissal; 0 otherwise
D-Career path	1 for decisions concerning employees' career paths; 0 otherwise
D-Incentive schemes	1 for decisions concerning the design and/or implementation of incentive schemes; 0 otherwise

Table 2.4 Expected effects of the explanatory variables on the delegation of decision authority to the plant manager

Variables	Increased need for delegation	Increased need for coordination	Greater ability to delegate	Net effect
Complexity of plant's operations (Size, Level)	+			+
Urgency (Just-in-time)	+			+
Multi-plant diversified	+	−		?
Multi-plant dominant business	+	−	+	?
Subcontractor		−		−
IMS		−		−
Network	−		+	?
Network × Size	−			−
Network × Multi-plant	−	+	+	?
Just-in-time × Multi-plant	−			−
Just-in-time × Subcontractor	−			−
Monetary incentives			+	+
Labor decisions	+			+
Capital decisions		−		−

Notes
+ Predicted positive coefficient.
− Predicted negative coefficient.
? Ambiguous predictions.

2.4.3   Econometric results*

The aim of this section is to illustrate the results of the estimates of the ordered probit model with random effects specified above; they are synthesized in Table 2.5. Details of the estimates are provided in the Appendix. In fact, we run several estimates. *Model I* is a pooled model where the coefficients of the independent variables are restricted to be the same across the six types of decisions (see Table 2.A2). In order to provide further insights into the issues at hand, marginal effects have been calculated; they are presented in Table 2.A3. In *Models II* and *III* (see Table 2.A4) we introduced decision-specific variables. Lastly, in *Model IV* (see Table 2.A5) we allowed the coefficients of plant-specific variables to

Table 2.5   Detected effects of the explanatory variables on the delegation of decision authority to the plant manager

Variables	All decisions	Capital decisions	Labor decisions
Size	+++	+++	+++
Level	+++	+++	+++
Just-in-time	n.s.	n.s.	+
Multi-plant diversified	− −	− − −	− − −
Multi-plant dominant business	−	−	n.s.
IMS	− − −	−	− − −
Subcontractor	n.s.	n.s.	n.s.
Network	+++	++	+++
Network × Size	− − −	− − −	− − −
Network × Multi-plant	++	++	++
Just-in-time × Multi-plant	n.s.	n.s.	n.s.
Just-in-time × Subcontractor	−	− − −	n.s.
Monetary incentives	+++		
Labor decisions	+++		
Capital decisions	− − −		

Notes
For "All decisions" signs are detected effects of explanatory variables of Models I and II (see Table 2.A2).
For "Capital decisions" signs are detected effects of explanatory variables of Model V (see Table 2.A5).
For "Labor decisions" signs are results of linear tests on the sum of the coefficients of explanatory variables and their interactive effect (i.e. *Variable* + *Variable* × *D-Labor*) in Model V (see Table 2.A5).
n.s. effect not significant.
+/− Sign positive/negative and significant at 10%.
++/− − Sign positive/negative and significant at 5%.
+++/− − −Sign positive/negative and significant at 1%.

differ according to the type of decision, with a distinction being made between investment and personnel decisions.

Generally speaking, the evidence on the allocation of decision authority is rather robust and interesting. First, considering the complexity and size of plant organization, the number of hierarchic levels under the superior, measured by *Level*, significantly affects the allocation of authority. In particular, more complex organizational structures are characterized by greater decentralization of authority to the plant manager. Such a finding confirms the theoretical predictions relating to the alleged rapid increase of a superior's information costs when the organization becomes more complex. In other words, being close to operations seems a key factor for optimality of decision-making activity in complex organizations.

Similarly, a higher number of direct and indirect subordinates – that is, a larger value of *Size* – induces the superior to increasingly delegate authority to the plant manager: the coefficient of *Size* is positive and significant. However, our estimates suggest that concerning this aspect one has to distinguish between plants that have adopted advanced ICTs and plants that have not: the previous remark holds true only for the latter category (see below).

Let us now draw attention to the effects of a plant's ownership status. Multi-unit organizations turn out to be more likely to centralize decision-making activities outside the plant: the coefficients of *Multi-plant diversified* and *Multi-plant dominant business* are both negative and significant. This result confirms the importance of coordination issues: in a multi-unit firm locally optimal decisions are less likely to also be optimal for the firm as a whole, so that centralization of decision-making at the level of the plant manager's corporate superior is more likely. The fact that checking plant manager's actions is more difficult due to greater physical distance between her and her corporate superior reinforces this tendency. In addition, the (negative) coefficient of *Multi-plant diversified* is found to be significantly lower than that of *Multi-plant dominant business*; diversification of product lines, making benchmarking more difficult, implies less decentralization of decision-making at the plant level.

The impact of the adoption of advanced ICTs upon the allocation of decision authority is quite complex and deserves a detailed discussion. *Network* exhibits a positive, highly significant coefficient. This suggests that with all else equal, adoption of these technologies favors the delegation of authority. Such a positive impact is even more pronounced for plants owned by multi-unit organizations, as is apparent from the positive and significant coefficient of the interactive term *Network* × *Multi-plant*. This result indicates that coordination of a decentralized decision-making process is easier when advanced ICTs are in place. It also is consistent with the argument that ICTs enhance the monitoring capabilities of the corporate headquarters and that such an effect is especially important whenever monitoring the behavior of the plant manager is difficult – due, for instance, to the greater physical distance between the plant manager and her superior in multi-unit firms.[32]

In addition, as was noted above, in plants that have adopted sophisticated ICTs the allocation of decision authority turns out not to be dependent on plant size. In other words, in plants in which intra-firm communication capabilities are limited decision authority is more likely to be assigned to the plant manager the greater the number of plant employees. With better ICTs, the positive effect of plant size on delegation vanishes.[33] This may be a consequence of the fact that the extent of the information advantage of the plant manager with respect to the corporate superior no longer depends on the complexity of plant's operations. It follows that among larger plants (according to our estimates, plants with more than 100 employees), those that adopted advanced ICTs are characterized by less delegation of decision authority than those that did not. The opposite pattern applies to smaller plants; that is, when the number of employees is small (fewer than 100), decentralization of decision power at the plant manager level is more likely for plants that have introduced sophisticated ICTs. Figure 2.1 provides an illustration of this relation.

Plants involved in subcontracting do not display a different allocation of decision-making activities than other plants, with the coefficient of the variable *Subcontractor* being insignificant in the estimates. As to the

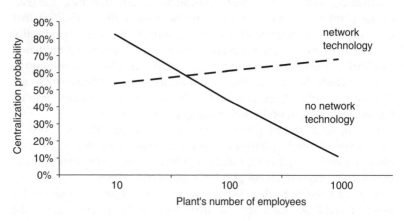

Figure 2.1 Size, use of advanced network technologies, and probability of centralization of decision authority

effect of urgency, the coefficient of *Just-in-time* is positive as predicted, though insignificant at conventional levels. In addition, the sum of the coefficients of *Just-in-time* and the interactive term *Just-in-time* × *Multi-plant* is significant. Adoption of JIT production techniques has a more positive impact on the probability of delegating authority to the plant manager for plants that belong to a multi-unit firm than for independent plants. For subcontractors, there again is no evidence that JIT requires greater coordination of decisions: the sum of the coefficients of *Just-in-time* and *Subcontractor* × *Just-in-time* is insignificant. Lastly, *IMS* displays a strong, statistically significant negative effect on the degree of delegation. For Tayloristic plants that invest in large-scale automated capital equipment, responsibility for strategic decisions is more likely to be centralized outside the plant.

As a final exercise we introduced into the estimates a variable which captures the adoption of monetary incentive schemes for personnel (see *Model II* in Table 2.A2). This dummy variable is one when plants have introduced non-traditional individual incentive schemes. In particular, we focus on monetary incentives which apply to individual workers and are sensitive to quality as well as quantity aspects of output (i.e. pay for quality and skills). The introduction of such incentive schemes may be considered as a proxy for the existence within a plant of measures of performance to which the compensation of the plant manager can be tied. With high-powered incentives in place, the objectives of the plant manager would be aligned with those of the firm: delegation of decision-making to the plant manager would follow. However, since the degree of decentralization of decision-making and reliance on incentive pay are chosen simultaneously, the estimates suffer from an endogeneity bias. Results confirm that decentralization of authority to the plant manager is more likely when monetary incentives are introduced.

Let us now focus attention on the evidence about the effects of decision-specific variables. We first tested whether capital investment decisions differ from decisions relating to the management of the labor force (see Table 2.A4). The coefficient of *D-Labor* is positive and significant in *Model III*. In accordance with the theoretical predictions, decisions concerning a plant's workforce are more likely to be delegated to the plant manager than those regarding capital investments. In *Model IV*, we considered each individual decision. The baseline is represented by the decision concerning the introduction of technological innovations (*D-Technology*). Overall, decision variables display a significant impact on plants' decision-making.[34] Moreover, the difference between decisions concerning capital equipment and those concerning the workforce that was highlighted by *Model III* is confirmed. In fact, dummy variables relating to the former decisions display a negative impact on the likelihood of decentralization of authority, while those relating to the latter generally have positive, statistically significant coefficients (*D-Incentive scheme* is the only exception, see below). Note also that the null hypothesis that the coefficients of all capital decisions be equal can be rejected at conventional confidence levels; the same holds true for the labor decisions. In particular, among capital decisions, the coefficient of *D-Capital equipment* is statistically different from that of *D-Technology*, the benchmark in the estimates, while the other differences are not statistically significant. Among labor decisions, the null hypothesis that the coefficients of *D-Hiring and dismissal* and *D-Incentive schemes* and those of *D-Career path* and *D-Incentive schemes* be equal can be rejected at conventional confidence levels; conversely, one cannot reject the equality of *D-Hiring and dismissal* and *D-Career path*. In sum, the individual decision dummies are better measures than the pooled dummies.

As to decisions concerning investments in capital equipment, the larger the amount of the investment the less likely the assignment of decision-making power to the plant manager. Concerning the decisions on labor, delegation of decision authority is more likely whenever decisions do not affect other units and have a direct impact on the plant manager's activity, as with decisions relating to the career of the plant's employees and to a lesser extent to hiring and dismissal of the plant's workers. Overall, these results provide support to the view that different types of decisions, having different importance to both the corporate superior and to the plant manager, are allocated following different patterns. Moreover, they suggest that exploitation of the plant manager's specific knowledge about the characteristics of plant's workforce plays a key role in shaping the plant's decision-making structure.

Lastly, we proceeded to estimate a model in which the coefficients of the explanatory variables were allowed to vary across the different types of decisions (i.e. either investment or personnel decisions). In order to do this, we run an econometric model (*Model V*) in which we included all interactive terms between the explanatory variables and *D-Labor*. Results for the sign and significance of the effects of the plant-specific explanatory variables on the allocation of personnel and investment decisions respectively, are synthesized in Table 2.5 (see Table 2.A5 for details of the estimates). Overall the results that have been illustrated above are confirmed, with some (but no major) differences in the determinants of the allocation of authority on capital and labor decisions. In particular, in plants that make use of a JIT production system, decisions on plant's workforce are more likely to be delegated to the plant manager; conversely the effect on delegation is insignificant for capital investment decisions.

2.4.4 A synthesis

In this section we have considered six strategic decisions relevant to a plant's activity and tested the theoretical predictions illustrated in Section 2.2.2 for a sample composed of 438 Italian manufacturing plants through the estimates of ordered probit models with random effects. The empirical results can be synthesized as follows.

First, the information advantage enjoyed by plant managers with respect to their corporate headquarters appears to be a key determinant of delegation. Accordingly, when a plant's organization is complex, consisting of a high number of hierarchical levels, the superior's information on the plant's internal activity is limited. This raises a stimulus toward delegation of authority to the plant manager, who is closer to and so has greater knowledge of the plant's activity. Such a finding is in line with those of the earlier studies surveyed in Section 2.3 (see Walton 2005 for a meta-analysis of this relation; see also Section 3.3 in Chapter 3). A similar reasoning applies to an increase in the number of the plant's employees if intra-firm communication efficiency is low: in fact, delegation of decision authority increases with size. Again, this result confirms those of most earlier studies (see also the meta-analysis of Donaldson 1986). Conversely, the effect of plant size vanishes for plants that have adopted advanced ICTs, possibly because these technologies increase both the information processing and communication capacities and the monitoring capabilities of the corporate headquarters.

Second, when strategic decisions involve substantial externalities there is no guarantee that decisions that are optimal for a given plant are also optimal for its parent company. Under such circumstances, the need to closely coordinate decisions across a firm's different units results in greater centralization, a phenomenon that was highlighted by the work of the Aston group. In accordance with this argument, in plants owned by multi-unit firms decision authority is far more centralized than in other plants. The fact that, absent efficient incentive schemes, it is quite difficult in such plants for the corporate superior to monitor plant managers' behavior due to great physical distance, reinforces the tendency toward centralization of decision-making. In contrast, when the pursuit of individual objectives is costly for the plant manager due to the use of sophisticated ICTs which enhance the monitoring capability of the corporate superior, the negative effect on delegation of a multi-unit ownership status disappears. In addition, such a negative effect is less pronounced in plants that belong to multi-unit non-diversified firms, which arguably can design incentive schemes based on some forms of yardstick competition among the different plants.[35]

Third, at least in small plants (i.e. those with fewer than 100 employees) which constitute the large majority of the sample examined here, the use of advanced ICTs seems to favor decentralization of decision-making.[36] This confirms the role played by ease of monitoring on the allocation of decision authority.

The evidence in support of the arguments raised by the information processing stream of the theoretical literature is weaker. In particular, we did not find compelling evidence that decentralization arises from leaks and delays in transmitting plans from the corporate headquarters to local managers, with the possible exception of large plants. From one side, as was said above, better ICTs favor delegation rather than centralization, except in large plants. From the other, the urgency of decisions turns out to have a positive, yet statistically insignificant, impact on delegation on decision authority, a result that is not new in the empirical literature (see, among others, Lin and Germain 2003; Vázquez 2004). Note, however, that this may be the result of the use of a rather crude proxy of decision urgency (adoption of JIT production techniques). It is therefore fair to recognize that, in this domain, additional empirical work is needed with explanatory variables that allow us to disentangle more clearly the predictions of the information processing and decentralization of incentives streams.

Lastly, in accordance with our theoretical predictions, authority over different types of plant's strategic decisions turns out to be allocated differently. Assignment of decision authority to the manager depends on: (a) the importance of the individual decision to the plant manager and to her corporate superior (i.e. the relative extent of the private benefits of the manager with respect to the monetary gains for the firm), (b) the extent of intra-firm externalities, and (c) the desire to take advantage of the manager's local knowledge and specific competence. Accordingly, when strategic decisions involve considerable financial resources, as is often the case in plants that have adopted capital-intensive production technologies, delegation of decision-making is quite unlikely. In addition, decisions concerning capital equipment are found to be more centralized than those relating to the workforce. Among the former, decisions regarding the purchase of large-scale capital equipment involving a larger amount of financial resources are more centralized than those relating to individual machinery. Among the latter, decisions on career paths of a plant's personnel and, to a lesser extent, on hiring and dismissal are less likely to affect other firm's units than decisions concerning the adoption of general payment schemes, while they have a more direct impact on plant managers' activity; therefore they are more frequently delegated to the plant manager. From this perspective, the findings reported in this section both confirm and extend the evidence provided by previous studies, according to which operating decisions are generally more decentralized than strategic ones (see, for instance, Marsh 1992; Collins *et al.* 1999; Vázquez 2004).

2.5 Concluding remarks

When and why should business organizations decentralize decision authority down the corporate hierarchy? In this chapter we illustrated a conceptual framework that helps us to highlight the determinants of the decentralization of decision-making. This framework rests on, and combines different streams of, the recent economic theoretical literature on organizational design, namely the information processing, decentralization of incentives, and transaction cost economics streams, and it leads to predictions suitable to empirical test. Then we reviewed the evidence that has been provided by previous quantitative empirical studies on the factors that induce or hinder decentralization of decision authority. Lastly, we tested (some of) the predictions of the conceptual model using the empirical methodology and data on Italian manufacturing plants that were described in Chapter 1.

Even though we think that much remains to be done in this field, this chapter documents some interesting "stylized facts" relating to the allocation of decision authority in business organizations that, broadly speaking, are consistent with the predictions of economic theory. In fact, it is important to bear in mind that there are both benefits and costs in decentralizing decision authority.

As to the benefits, good decisions are made by informed and competent decision-makers. The benefits of delegation thus materialize when subordinates are more informed and/or more competent than their bosses. This often occurs in large, complex organizations, leading to greater decentralization of decision-making, a situation which was documented by John Child's (1973) contribution. It is also more likely to occur in business environment in which learning-by-doing is important (Vázquez 2004) and firms are more heterogenous, with heterogeneity making it more difficult for firms' top management to imitate decisions made by other firms

(Acemoglu *et al.* 2006). A similar situation also arises when firms are closer to the technological frontier (see again Acemoglu *et al.* 2006).

In addition, in accordance with this principle, operating routinized decisions for which subordinates develop task-specific competence through learning-by-doing are shown by most studies to be far more decentralized than non-recurrent strategic decisions which, conversely, are generally kept at the top of the managerial pyramid.

The information processing stream claims that delegation occurs because of the leaks and delays in collecting information from and giving orders to subordinates. Actually, the empirical literature has so far been able to produce only limited evidence in support of this view. The econometric estimates presented in Section 2.4 indicate that use of advanced ICTs by large Italian metalworking plants which allegedly reduces the leaks and delays of transmitting information, indeed leads to greater centralization of decision authority than in otherwise similar plants with no ICTs. Nonetheless, the adoption of ICTs has an opposite effects in smaller plants, which actually constitute the large majority of the sample. Moreover, environmental uncertainty and turbulence enhance the importance of timely decision-making. However, previous empirical studies, including our own, failed to detect any significant effect of these factors on the allocation of decision authority, especially as regards strategic decisions.

Let us now turn attention to the costs of delegation. Again, the decentralization of incentives stream identifies two sources of costs: the externalities engendered by (strategic) decisions, an issue which is also considered by the information processing stream, and the principal's loss of control over them.

When decisions involve considerable externalities, there is no guarantee that locally optimal decisions are also optimal for the organization as a whole. Under these circumstances, coordination of decisions becomes crucial, leading to a greater likelihood of centralization of decision authority. Since the work of the Aston group in the 1960s, the empirical literature is almost unanimous in showing that decision authority is more centralized in subsidiaries of multi-unit organizations than in otherwise comparable independent firms. Moreover, the larger and the more diversified the parent organization and the greater the number of establishments it possesses, the stronger the inducement to centralize decision-making.

An informed and competent agent may make decisions that are very detrimental to the principal if she pursues objectives that are not aligned with those of the principal. Therefore, absent efficient monitoring, the principal will be forced to centralize decision authority. The evidence that decision authority is more centralized in subsidiaries of multi-unit firms than in independent firms may also be a consequence of the fact that monitoring agents' behavior is more difficult in the former organizations due to greater physical distance. In accordance with this argument we have shown that the effect of plants' ownership status on the allocation of decision authority vanishes when plants are equipped with advanced ICTs, which allegedly assure better monitoring and make coordination of dispersed decision-making easier.

The empirical studies illustrated in this chapter also indicate that there are different means to increase the effectiveness of monitoring, thus reducing principal's loss of control. They include:

- use of advanced ICTs that provide real-time information on an agent's behavior
- introduction of incentive-based compensation schemes, the purpose of which is to realign the objectives of agents with those of the principal
- yardstick competition based on the observation of the decisions taken by agents in charge of similar units of the same firms or by competitors, which discourage pursuit of private interests on the part of agents entitled with decision-making power.[37]

Conversely, limited empirical evidence has so far been provided in support of the argument that the opportunistic wish of top managers to conserve an advantageous bargaining position to the detriment of subordinates discourages delegation of decisions.

We think that the remarks made above are very helpful in bridging the gap between empirical findings and predictions based on economic theorizing relating to factors that influence the allocation of decision authority in business organizations. Nonetheless, we are also aware that this is just a first step forward. Two avenues for future research seem to us especially promising.

On the one hand, the allocation of authority over strategic and operating decisions is just one aspect of organizational design, which also includes several other aspects relating, for instance, to the depth of the corporate hierarchy (see Chapter 3), the introduction of high-powered incentive schemes to motivate employees (see Chapter 4), the number and quality of a plant's employees, and many others. Decisions as to these different aspects are likely to be made simultaneously by firms; therefore an endogeneity problem arises. This clearly demonstrates the need for a full structural theoretical model of organizational choice.

On the other hand, most previous empirical studies on this issue have adopted a cross-sectional approach. They analyze the allocation of decision authority at a given time in different organizations (and possibly over several decisions), and they try to relate it to environment-, firm-, and decision-specific variables that are measured at the same time. This type of econometric exercise suffers from severe methodological problems. In particular, lack of proper control for unobserved heterogeneity makes it difficult to interpret the results of the econometric estimates as evidence of a causal relation. For this purpose, one needs to follow the evolution over time of the allocation of decision authority in different organizations, trying to identify which factors trigger decentralization of decision-making. From this perspective we are convinced that the availability of longitudinal data sets with sufficient within-firm heterogeneity is crucial to extend our understanding of the determinants of firms' organizational choices (on this issue see Chapter 4).

Appendix

2.A.1 Definition and expected effects of the explanatory variables, and results of the econometric estimates

The complexity and size of plants' organization increase the need to delegate decision authority to managers; they are captured by two variables. *Level* is the number of hierarchical levels of the plant; *Size* is the logarithm of the number of plant employees.

A number of variables reflects the ownership status of plants and the organization of plants' parent companies. *Multi-plant* is a dummy variable that is one when a plant belongs to a multi-unit firm and is zero when the plant is owned by a single-unit firm. Furthermore, we distinguished multi-unit firms according to their mix of product lines: *Multi-plant diversified* is a dummy variable that is one when a plant's parent company is large and diversified (i.e. it has more than 25,000 employees and no one of its product lines accounts for more than 70% of total sales), while *Multi-plant dominant business* is a dummy variable that is one for the remaining multi-unit parent companies (i.e. smaller and/or non diversified multi-unit firms).[38] The expected signs of the two multi-plant variables are uncertain as opposed forces may be at work. From one side, in a multi-unit setting there is greater need for coordination, which may hinder delegation of authority to plant managers. From the other side, recourse to yardstick competition may increase the ability of the corporate headquarters to decentralize decision-making. This especially applies to dominant business multi-unit firms (i.e. when *Multi-plant dominant business* equals one). In addition, physical distance between the plant manager and her corporate superior is generally greater if the plant belongs to a multi-unit firm. This again may have opposing effects on delegation. On the one hand, greater physical distance reinforces the information advantage on local matters enjoyed by the plant manager and makes communication with the corporate superior more difficult, thus favoring decentralization of decision-making. On the other, it also makes it more difficult for the superior to directly check the decisions taken by the plant manager. Absent efficient incentive schemes and monitoring technology, this should lead to more centralization.

The fact that a plant is involved in subcontracting relations with customer(s) is likely to negatively affect delegation of authority to the plant manager due to a greater need for coordination. Since subcontractors are pressed to adjust their production operations according to the needs of their main customer(s), we expect them to have a more centralized allocation of decision-making power than other plants. We captured this effect by the dummy variable *Subcontractor* which equals one for plants with more than 75% of total sales earned as a subcontractor.

Conversely, urgency of decisions favors delegation. It is proxied by *Just-in-time*, a dummy variable which equals one whenever a sample plant makes use of JIT production methods. Indeed, firms that adopt JIT are pressed to deliver their products fast and to adjust production schedules over time in accordance with variations of demand; consequently, they heavily rely on the speed of taking and implementing production decisions. However, the expected sign of *Just-in-time* appears also to depend on the type of activity of a plant and the overall structure of its parent firm. If a plant belongs to a multi-unit firm and mostly produces goods that are used by other units of the same firm then the greater need for coordination engendered by the adoption of such new production techniques (Brynjolfsson and Hitt 2000) might determine less, and not more, delegation to the plant level. A similar reasoning applies to plants that are mainly involved in subcontracting. For this reason, we investigated possible interactions between *Just-in-time* and the ownership status (i.e. whether multi-unit or not) and main type of activity (whether subcontracting or not) of sample plants.

Adoption of advanced ICTs is captured by *Network*, a dummy variable that equals one if a plant has adopted a Local Area Network (LAN) and/or on-line connection with the corporate headquarters. More efficient ICTs may reduce both the information advantage of the plant manager on local matters and the leaks and delays of transmitting orders down the corporate hierarchy; accordingly, centralization of decision-making may follow. Nonetheless, we also stressed that the enhanced capabilities of the corporate headquarters to monitor the plant managers' decisions due to use of advanced ICTs positively influence firms' ability to decentralize decision-making. The net impact of *Network* on the allocation of decision authority is therefore uncertain.

In addition, the relative importance of these effects (i.e. decrease of the information advantage of the plant manager with respect to her corporate superior, greater efficiency of transmitting orders to the plant manager, and greater ability of monitoring her behavior) may be contingent on other variables (for a similar approach see, for instance, Zeffane 1989). Among them, the size and ownership status of plants figure prominently. For this purpose, we introduced into the econometric models the interactive terms *Network* × *Size* and *Network* × *Multi-plant*.

The former term aims to investigate the interaction between the complexity of a plant's operations and the decrease of the cost of using information due to the adoption of advanced ICTs; in particular, we expect the positive influence exerted by plant size on delegation of decision-making power to be considerably reduced if a plant is equipped with advanced ICTs. In fact, the plant manager no longer enjoys a substantial information advantage as regards local matters. Leaks and delay in information transmission are also reduced. The latter term concerns the interaction between decreases in the costs of communicating and of monitoring, due again to the use of advanced ICTs, and the physical distance between the plant manager and her corporate superior which, as said earlier, is generally greater in a multi-unit setting. Whatever the net effect (positive or negative) of *Network* on delegation of authority, such an effect is likely to be more pronounced the greater the distance between the agents and the principal, and hence the costs for the principal of being informed on local matters, communicating with and monitoring the behavior of agents. In addition, coordination of dispersed operations is easier with use of advanced ICTs; hence, the stimuli to centralize decision-making in a multi-unit firm because of coordination needs are reduced.

Lastly, let us draw attention to the nature of strategic decisions. First of all, one might argue that if decisions relating to a plant's activity involve on average a greater amount of financial resources, they also involve greater externalities as a plant competes with other organizational units (e.g. other functional departments, other manufacturing plants in multi-unit firms) for use of these resources. As more is at stake, less decentralization of decision-making follows due to the need for effective coordination of decisions. This condition depends, among other things, on the characteristics of a plant's production technology and organization of production activity. For instance, it generally holds true for Tayloristic plants that are involved in mass production of rather standardized goods and are characterized by large, highly indivisible investments in automated capital equipment, since strategic decisions relating to production factors (both capital and labor) are basically of a discrete nature (i.e. adding or closing a production line). So, we introduced into the econometric estimates the dummy variable *IMS*, that is set at one for plants that have introduced large-scale capital equipment such as IMS. This variable takes into account situations in which capital intensity is high, and hence decisions on a plant's activity involve on average a greater amount of financial resources.

In addition, in a given plant strategic decisions relating to different matters may be organized differently, with some being delegated to the plant manager and others being retained at the corporate superior level, according to the specific characteristics of the decision. As a general rule, decisions that have little (great) impact on the principal's economic returns and great (little) impact on the agent's private benefits should be decentralized (centralized). Furthermore, absent efficient incentive schemes, decisions that require greater coordination as the objectives pursued by a plant manager are likely to diverge from those of the firm as a whole should be retained with the plant manager's superior, while decisions for which the plant manager clearly enjoys an information advantage should be delegated. Such reasoning has a number of implications.

First, decisions concerning *capital investments* should be kept more centralized than those concerning the *workforce*, due to the greater amount of financial resources and the greater externalities involved in each individual decision. In addition, the information advantage of the plant manager with respect to her corporate superior is greater for decisions about whom to hire, promote, or fire, as such decisions rely on personal, largely tacit, knowledge of local conditions within the plant, as opposed to the more codified technical nature of capital investment decisions. Note also that control over such labor-related decisions is the very essence of a plant's manager personal power, and that her superior's choices in this matter may be very detrimental to her, as they may jeopardize personal relations with her own subordinates. This means that the private benefits the plant manager can extract from decisions concerning the workforce are on average larger than those relating to capital investment decisions.[39]

Second, with decisions concerning investments in capital equipment, the larger the amount of the investments the less likely to be decentralization. With decisions concerning a plant's labor force, decision authority is more likely to be kept centralized if decisions affect other units of the firm and decentralized if they have a larger impact on the plant manager's activity. Decisions on the adoption of general schemes of payment of the labor force belong to the former category, as generally congruence is needed within the same firm. Conversely, the latter category includes decisions on career paths within the plant as such decisions are key to motivating the plant manager's subordinates. Lastly, decisions as to hiring and dismissal of plant's personnel lie in a somewhat intermediate position, as both effects possibly are at work.

Table 2.A1   Descriptive statistics of the explanatory variables

	Mean	**Std dev.**	**Min.**	**Max.**
Size	4.4818	1.1854	1.6094	8.4118
Level	3.4726	0.8376	2.0000	6.0000
Just-in-time	0.4635	0.4988	0.0000	1.0000
Multi-plant	0.2283	0.4198	0.0000	1.0000
Multi-plant diversified	0.1050	0.3066	0.0000	1.0000
Multi-plant dominant business	0.1233	0.3288	0.0000	1.0000
Subcontractor	0.1370	0.3439	0.0000	1.0000
IMS	0.7169	0.4506	0.0000	1.0000
Network	0.5822	0.4933	0.0000	1.0000
Monetary incentives	0.3268	0.4694	0.0000	1.0000
D-Capital	0.5000	0.5001	0.0000	1.0000
D-Labor	0.5000	0.5001	0.0000	1.0000
D-Technology[a]	0.1667	0.3727	0.0000	1.0000
D-Capital equipment[a]	0.1667	0.3727	0.0000	1.0000
D-Machinery[a]	0.1667	0.3727	0.0000	1.0000
D-Hiring and dismissal[a]	0.1667s	0.3727	0.0000	1.0000
D-Career path[a]	0.1667	0.3727	0.0000	1.0000
D-Incentive schemes[a]	0.1667	0.3727	0.0000	1.0000

Note
[a] When one of the six dummies concerning capital and labor decisions is set to 1, then the others are equal to 0. Thus they are exhaustive and mutually exclusive (one has to be chosen as benchmark in the estimates). Obviously, they have the same mean, given by the ratio between the number of plants, 438, and the number of observations 2,628 (meaning for instance that one-sixth of the observations relate to decisions on the introduction of new process technologies) and standard deviation.

We measured the effect of decision-specific variables on the degree of decentralization by introducing the following six dummies: *D-Technology*, *D-Capital equipment*, *D-Machinery*, *D-Hiring&dismissal*, *D-Career path*, *D-Incentive schemes*. They are set to one when (once for each plant) the observation under consideration relates to the given decision – that is, the introduction of process innovations, the purchase of large-scale capital equipment, the purchase of stand-alone machinery, hiring and dismissal decisions, decisions relating to the career paths of employees, and the definition of incentive schemes, respectively. We initially aggregated different types of decisions into two homogenous groups: decisions concerning capital investments (i.e. *D-Capital*) and those concerning plant's workforce (i.e. *D-Labor*). With *D-Capital* being chosen as the baseline of

the estimates, we predict a positive coefficient for *D-Labor*. We also analyzed the impact of each individual decision. In that case, since the six
decision variables are exclusive and exhaustive, one (i.e. *D-Technology*)
was chosen as a baseline and does not appear in the estimates. As to the
remaining variables, in accordance with the arguments illustrated
above, we expect their coefficients in the estimates to be as follows:
D-Capital equipment < *D-Machinery* < 0; *D-Career path* > *D-Hiring and
dismissal* > *D-Incentive schemes* > 0.

Table 2.A1 shows descriptive statistics of the explanatory variables.
Details about the results of the econometric estimates are reported in
Tables 2.A2–2.A5.

Table 2.A2   Results of the estimates of a random effects ordered probit model

Variables	Model I	Model II
Constant	−3.0733 (0.6146) [c]	−2.4660 (0.6521) [c]
Size	0.4675 (0.1444) [c]	0.3392 (0.1496) [b]
Level	0.3535 (0.1105) [c]	0.2891 (0.1132) [b]
Just-in-time	0.2889 (0.1934)	0.1989 (0.1963)
Multi-plant diversified	−1.8575 (0.7714) [b]	−1.9576 (0.8385) [b]
Multi-plant dominant business	−1.1564 (0.6692) [a]	−1.1434 (0.7293)
Subcontractor	0.0658 (0.3089)	−0.3049 (0.3207)
Monetary incentives		0.3036 (0.1743) [a]
IMS	−0.6619 (0.1855) [c]	−0.5946 (0.1857) [c]
Network	2.1099 (0.7569) [c]	1.8499 (0.7726) [b]
Network × Size	−0.5499 (0.1790) [c]	−0.4481 (0.1876) [b]
Network × Multi-plant	1.6517 (0.6943) [b]	1.3867 (0.7470) [a]
Just-in-time × Multi-plant	0.4606 (0.4182)	0.7583 (0.4187) [a]
Just-in-time × Subcontractor	−0.9084 (0.4944) [a]	−0.5907 (0.5194)
μ	1.3940 (0.0299) [c]	1.3897 (0.0302) [c]
Log-likelihood	−1,925.640	−1,924.928
LR χ^2-test	34.186 (12) [c]	35.610 (13) [c]
Number of plants	428	428
Number of records	2,628	2,628

Notes
Usual *t*-tests. Standard errors and degrees of freedom in parentheses.
[a] Significant at 10%.
[b] Significant at 5%.
[c] Significant at 1%.

Table 2.A3 Marginal effects of the explanatory variables

Variables	Marginal effects[a]		
	P[D = C]	P[D = DI]	P[D = DII]
Size (Network = 0)	−0.1861	0.1088	0.0773
Size (Network = 1)	0.0255	−0.0478	0.0233
Level	−0.1362	0.0634	0.0729
Just-in-time	−0.1123	0.0550	0.0573
Multi-plant diversified (Network = 0)	0.4899	−0.3985	−0.0915
Multi-plant diversified (Network = 1)	0.0350	−0.0492	0.0142
Multi-plant dominant business (Network = 0)	0.3887	−0.3030	−0.0857
Multi-plant dominant business (Network = 1)	−0.1136	0.0923	0.0213
Subcontractor	−0.0261	0.0148	0.0114
IMS	0.2507	−0.1819	−0.0689
Network (Size = small)	−0.2885	0.2299	0.0587
Network (Size = average)	0.1328	−0.0887	−0.0441
Network (Size = large)	0.5697	−0.1711	−0.3986

Note

[a] In computing marginal effects, the estimates of *Model I* have been used. All dummy variables (with the exception of *Network*, see below) are set at zero and continuous (discrete) variables are evaluated at their mean (median) value (i.e. *Size* = 4.48, 195 employees, and *Level* = 3). The marginal effect of *Network* is computed for different values of *Size*: small (number of employees equals 10), average (employees = 195), and large (employees = 1,000). The marginal effects of *Size*, *Multi-plant diversified* and *Multi-plant dominant business* are computed with both *Network* = 0 and *Network* = 1. For dummy variables, reported values are the differences between the probabilities that result when the dummy variable under scrutiny takes its two different values.

Table 2.A4 Results of the estimates of random effects ordered probit models: fixed effects of decisions

Variables	Model III	Model IV
Constant	−3.2972 (0.6127)[c]	−3.2310 (0.6109)[c]
Size	0.4730 (0.1439)[c]	0.4847 (0.1435)[c]
Level	0.3622 (0.1088)[c]	0.3692 (0.1078)[c]
Just-in-time	0.2950 (0.1921)	0.2987 (0.1920)
Multi-plant diversified	−1.9088 (0.7691)[b]	21.9422 (0.7680)[b]
Multi-plant dominant business	−1.1729 (0.7691)[a]	21.1888 (0.6729)[a]
Subcontractor	0.0698 (0.3046)	0.0883 (0.3051)
IMS	20.6764 (0.1921)[c]	20.6913 (0.1834)[c]
Network	2.1319 (0.7507)[c]	2.1724 (0.7475)[c]
Network × Size	−0.5577 (0.1772)[c]	20.5687 (0.1760)[c]
Network × Multi-plant	1.7073 (0.6937)[b]	1.7437 (0.6942)[b]
Just-in-time × Multi-plant	0.4663 (0.4093)	0.4644 (0.4046)
Just-in-time × Subcontractor	−0.9143 (0.4864)[a]	20.9410 (0.4868)[a]
D-Labor	0.3509 (0.0367)[c]	–
D-Capital equipment	–	20.2903 (0.1673)[a]
D-Machinery	–	20.1191 (0.1462)
D-Hiring and dismissal	–	0.2526 (0.0998)[b]
D-Career path	–	0.4179 (0.1073)[c]
D-Incentive schemes	–	−0.0199 (0.1053)
μ	1.4204 (0.0313)[c]	1.4413 (0.0329)[c]
Log-likelihood	−1,907.065	−1,892.904
LR χ^2-test	71.336 (13)[c]	99.658 (17)[c]
Number of plants	428	428
Number of records	2,628	2,628

Notes
Usual *t*-tests. Standard errors and degrees of freedom in parentheses.
[a] Significant at 10%.
[b] Significant at 5%.
[c] Significant at 1%.

Table 2.A5 Results of the estimates of random effects ordered probit models: labor versus capital decisions

Variables	Model V
Constant	23.3233 (0.6301) [c]
D-Labor	0.2041 (0.3027)
Size	0.4660 (0.14678) [c]
D-Labor × Size	0.0437 (0.0689)
Level	0.3323 (0.1118) [c]
D-Labor × Level	0.0817 (0.0504)
Just-in-time	0.2109 (0.1996)
D-Labor × Just-in-time	0.1619 (0.0984) [a]
Multi-plant diversified	22.2182 (0.8504) [c]
D-Labor × Multi-plant diversified	0.5570 (0.4730)
Multi-plant dominant business	21.3531 (0.7619) [a]
D-Labor × Multi-plant dominant business	0.3163 (0.4324)
Subcontractor	0.2485 (0.3268)
D-Labor × Subcontractor	−0.2548 (0.1562)
IMS	20.3526 (0.1903) [a]
D-Labor × IMS	20.6659 (0.0915) [c]
Network	1.9498 (0.7592) [b]
D-Labor × Network	0.4907 (0.3864)
Network × Size	20.5366 (0.1789) [c]
D-Labor × (Network × Size)	−0.0750 (0.0875)
Network × Multi-plant	1.9973 (0.7857) [b]
D-Labor × (Network × Multi-plant)	−0.5433 (0.4284)
Just-in-time × Multi-plant	0.4763 (0.4156)
D-Labor × (Just-in-time × Multi-plant)	0.0342 (0.1850)
Just-in-time × Subcontractor	21.2722 (0.4889) [c]
D-Labor × (Just-in-time × Subcontractor)	0.5707 (0.2237) [b]
μ	1.4456 (0.0330) [c]
Log-likelihood	−1,889.795
LR χ^2-test	105.876 (25) [c]
Number of plants	428
Number of records	2,628

Notes
Usual *t*-tests. Standard errors and degrees of freedom in parentheses.
[a] Significant at 10%.
[b] Significant at 5%.
[c] Significant at 1%.

3
The Determinants of the Corporate Hierarchy*

3.1 Introduction

In Chapter 1 it was argued that the *depth* of the corporate hierarchy (or *vertical span*) measured by the number of hierarchical levels between the top and the bottom of the organization (i.e. between the top manager and line workers), was a key characteristic of firms' corporate hierarchy (see in particular Section 1.2.1.1 of Chapter 1).

The aim of this chapter is to analyze the determinants of such depth, at both firm and environment level. In other words, we are concerned with the following question:

- why do some organizations rely on an extensive sequence of principal–subordinate relations to manage their operations, while other organizations are much flatter?

Business history studies have fully documented that the birth of the modern corporation was linked with the rise of a hierarchy of salaried executives (Chandler, 1977; see Box 1.1 in Chapter 1). This evolution of business organizations was mainly due to (i) the increasing complexity of production, commercial, and financial operations to run and coordinate, and thus the increasing number of items of information to gather, store, and process, and decisions to take and implement (i.e. the increasing *size* of the modern corporation),[1] and (ii) the achievements of a *new technological paradigm* (i.e. the second industrial revolution) that raised the extent to which it was viable to internalize production and administrative activities into the corporate hierarchy (see Chandler 1962).

* Chapter 3 is reprinted from *International Journal of Industrial Organization*, Vol 20, No 1, Marco Delmastro, 'The Determinants of the Management Hierarchy: Evidence from Italian Plants', pages 119–137, Copyright (2002), with permission from Elsevier.

The relation between the depth of the corporate hierarchy and the extent of a firm's operations, as reflected by firm size, is nicely illustrated by the case of Siemens. Between 1890 and 1913, the number of Siemens' employees grew from 3,000 to 57,000, while the ratio between non-manual and manual workers went from 1:7.1 to 1:3.5. If we assume a constant span of control equal to 7, which is in line with empirical findings (see Chapter 1), this implies an increase in the number of hierarchical levels from four to nearly six (elaboration from Kocha, 1971).[2]

As to the empirical quantitative literature on organizational design, interest in the depth of the corporate hierarchy again dates back to the work of the Aston group (see Pugh *et al.* 1963, 1968, 1969b; Hickson *et al.* 1969). An important stylized fact highlighted by these studies and later confirmed by subsequent works that will be surveyed in Section 3.3 is that, in accordance with the qualitative evidence mentioned above, there is a positive *non-linear* (i.e. concave) relation between the *size* and the number of hierarchical levels of an organization. In addition, a positive correlation was found between the depth of the hierarchy and the *delegation of decision authority*.[3] Accordingly, large firms generally exhibit both a greater number of hierarchical levels and, as was extensively documented in Chapter 2, greater delegation than their smaller counterparts. Moreover, factors such as the *production* and *information and communication technologies* (ICTs) adopted by firms which in Chapter 2 were shown to influence the extent of delegation of decision authority, are also likely to have a bearing on the depth of the hierarchy.

Nonetheless, quantitative empirical studies that have focused attention on the determinants of organizational depth are less numerous than those concerned with delegation. Empirical findings are rather scattered and sometimes incoherent. To provide a through examination of this literature and to highlight its relation to theoretical work on the economics of organizational design is the main aim of this chapter.

The chapter proceeds as follows. We first present in Section 3.2 a conceptual framework aimed at highlighting the factors that influence the benefits and costs that business organizations obtain from increasing the depth of the corporate hierarchy; for this purpose, we rely on arguments proposed by different streams of the economic theoretical literature on organizational design, namely the information processing and decentralization of incentives streams. Special attention is devoted to the role played by (i) firm size and (ii) innovations in production technologies and ICTs. In Section 3.3, we survey the findings of previous quantitative empirical studies on this issue. Then, in Section 3.4, we illustrate the results of an econometric analysis of the determinants of organizational depth based on the data set on Italian manufacturing plants that was described in Chapter 1 and in the Appendix to this book. Some concluding remarks in Section 3.5 end the chapter.

3.2   A conceptual framework of the determinants of organizational depth

Since Williamson (1967), several theoretical papers have modeled the depth of the corporate hierarchy. The aim of this section is to present a simple eclectic conceptual model which combines insights offered by the information processing and decentralization of incentives streams of the economic literature that were briefly considered in the Introduction. The model will provide predictions on the factors that shape the depth of business organizations.

First, according to work in the information processing stream, if we define efficiency in terms of speed in processing information then "efficiency can be achieved by hierarchical networks" (Radner 1992); that is to say, the efficient organization takes the form of a hierarchy (see also Bolton and Dewatripont 1994). In particular, the larger the number of items of information to gather, process, and transmit, the larger the depth of the corporate hierarchy that minimizes total planning and implementation time (Radner 1993); hence, the positive relation between the depth and the *size* of the organization.

In this hierarchical framework, the productivity of workflow subordinates (line or direct workers) depends on the efficiency of administrative superiors who gather, store, and process information. In other words, administrative work enters the production function as well as other inputs (i.e. direct workers). Let N be the number of direct workers of an organization (e.g. firm, plant, shop). Assume a Cobb–Douglas production function, then the total output Q is given by

$$Q = \theta N^\alpha y_T^\beta \tag{1}$$

where T is the depth of the organization, y_T is the output of total administrative work, and θ is a parameter of the production technology that reflects the efficiency of line workers.

One of the main features of a hierarchical organization is its *serial structure*. This implies that the production technology of administrative work is recursive (Beckmann 1977). In any tier t, the administrative output (called "managerial effectiveness") depends on the efficiency of the manager of that level and of her superiors. That is, at every administrative layer t managers use their immediate superiors' administrative output y_{t-1} as an intermediate input, and combine it with their level of efficiency a_t to produce y_t for their immediate subordinates. Therefore,

$$y_t = F_t (y_{t-1}, a_t) \tag{2}$$

Suppose that (2) is simply given by $y_t = y_{t-1} a_t$; then, if one normalizes so as to make y_0 equal to 1, one obtains

$$y_T = a_1 a_2 \dots a_T \tag{3}$$

Equation (3) shows that the organization may suffer from administrative bottlenecks. In fact, if managers at level t are not effective ($a_t < 1$) then overall production declines. This phenomenon is called "loss of control."

There are two explanations of the extent of the loss of control. First, as highlighted by the information processing stream, a_t may reflect information processing and communication costs – that is, the costs of storing, processing, and understanding information, and of collecting information from and transmitting orders to subordinates (for a definition see Van Zandt 1998; see also Chapter 2 of this volume n.5 and n.6). *Advances in ICTs* reduce the information overload of managers and enhance their communication capabilities, leading to higher a_t ($t = 0, \dots ,T$). In turn, this allows managers to increase the number of immediate subordinates (i.e. their span of control), while avoiding information bottlenecks (Keren and Levhari 1979, 1983). So, "a reduction of communication costs leads to a flatter ... organization" (Bolton and Dewatripont 1994).[4]

However, the view that advances in ICTs result in a reduction of the number of layers of organizations is not unanimously shared in the theoretical literature. In fact, the relation between the depth of the management hierarchy and information processing and communication costs is still a puzzle in economic theory. Indeed, Lazear (1995) contrasts an organizational design in which agents specialize in different tasks (e.g. collecting information and making decisions) according to their comparative advantages with one in which agents engage in multiple tasks and take decisions autonomously. The former organizational design enjoys the gains from specialization, but incurs in greater communication costs. Lazear points out that since advances in ICTs lower communication costs among agents, they promote the specialization of agents in different tasks. Reliance on a more hierarchical organizational design follows. In other words "Technology-induced reductions in the cost of communication promote specialization and hierarchy" (1995, p. 125).

In a similar vein, Garicano and Rossi-Hansberg (2006) argue that in a knowledge hierarchy the reduction of information processing and communication costs associated with increasing use of ICTs favors reliance on a larger hierarchy; that is, the optimal number of hierarchical layers increases.

Second, a_t also reflects the effort of managers at level t. In this case, in accordance with the decentralization of incentives stream, the corporate hierarchy is depicted as a sequence of principal–agent relations. For each agent, effort is costly. As any superior only has a limited amount of time available to check the effort made by her immediate subordinates, the effectiveness of monitoring an individual's behavior and thus the probability of the individual being checked is a negative function of the span of control of his immediate superior (Calvo and Wellisz 1978). Hence, a_t again decreases if the span of control increases. Advances in the *monitoring technology* such as those associated with use of advanced ICTs, allow the superior to increase the number of immediate subordinates avoiding agents' shirking at the same time; hence, the optimal depth of the organization declines (Qian 1994). Note also that given the monitoring technology in use, this argument again implies that organizational depth increases with the size of the organization.

In addition to ICTs, *production technology* is likely to affect the optimal size of the management hierarchy. Williamson (1967) showed that if we assume the production function of (1) and (3), then, under certain conditions (i.e. a constant span of control), an increase in the parameter θ raises the optimal number of levels (see also Qian 1994). Nonetheless, the *type* of production technology in use also influences organizational depth. Lindbeck and Snower (1996) distinguished between production technologies of different vintages. They argued that the single-purpose automated technologies that are associated with the Tayloristic approach to production enjoy large returns to specialization of tasks; so they lead to the specialization of the line workers and the hierarchy. Adoption of multi-purpose PA technologies[5] while allowing labor to become more versatile favors the transition to a "holistic" type of organization based on multi-skilling and a sharp reduction of bureaucratization.[6] In accordance with this view, while mechanization of production associated with early-vintage automated production technologies led to an increase in organizational depth, subsequent innovations in production technologies associated with the PA paradigm had the opposite effect. The management literature points to the importance of complementarities in their use (see, for instance, Åstebro 2002); so they will have a strong allegedly negative impact on the number of hierarchical levels only when they work in clusters rather than in isolation.

Table 3.1 sums up the main theoretical predictions on the depth of the corporate hierarchy. The number of levels is positively related to firm size. As to production technologies, predictions are less clear; results depend on the vintage and extent of use of the production technology. In general, early-vintage mechanization is positively associated with the number of hierarchical levels, while adoption of PA technologies is expected to lead to a flatter hierarchy. In the decentralization of incentives approach, the asymmetry of information and the related opportunistic behavior of workers shape the form of the organization. In this context, the depth of the management hierarchy is a negative function of the efficiency of the monitoring technology. Indeed, a better monitoring technology allows the firm to increase the number of immediate subordinates under each manager, thus to decrease the number of levels. In the information processing approach, the focus is on the total planning time. The depth of the organization depends on information overload and communication costs. Better information processing and communication capabilities may again lead to greater span of control and a reduction of the depth of the hierarchy. Nonetheless, the effects of an increase in the efficiency of the communication technology are ambiguous, as it may favor specialization of tasks and a more extended hierarchy.

Table 3.1 Determinants of organizational depth: theoretical predictions

Determinants	Expected effect on the number of hierarchical levels
Size (log of the number of employees)	+
Efficiency of production technology	+/− (the effect depends on type, vintage, and extent of use of production technologies)
Efficiency of monitoring technology	− (increasing efficiency in monitoring allows a greater horizontal span of control, hence a "flatter" organization)
Efficiency of ICT	− (increasing efficiency in ICTs reduces overloads, allows a greater horizontal span of control, hence a flatter organization)
	+(increasing efficiency in ICTs promotes specialization of employees, hence a deeper organization)

3.3   Empirical evidence on the determinants of organizational depth

The aim of this section is to survey the quantitative empirical literature on the determinants of the depth of the corporate hierarchy. The origin of this literature again dates back to the work carried out by the Aston group (Pugh *et al.* 1968, 1969b; Hickson *et al.* 1969). As was indicated in Chapters 1 and 2, the Aston group considered depth as among the key measurable aspects of the organization. These authors assumed that all these aspects were designed by firms so as to conform to the requirements of the context in which they operate. In accordance with this view, one would expect depth to be correlated with other dimensions of the organization such as the (horizontal) span of control and the centralization of decision authority.[7]

In fact, several authors have highlighted the existence of a negative correlation between the number of levels of the corporate hierarchy and the degree of *centralization of decision authority*. In their study of fifty-two organizations located in the Birmingham area in the early 1960s, Pugh *et al.* (1968) found a −0.28 correlation between the depth of organizations and their overall centralization indicator.[8] Child (1972) and Marsh and Mannari (1981) replicated the same calculation in a national sample of eighty-two British business organizations and in a Japanese sample of fifty manufacturing plants (the Okayama sample); the values of the correlation again were negative and equal to −0.41 and −0.24, respectively. More recently, Collins *et al.* (1999) while analyzing fifty-four manufacturing plants in a highly industrialized mid-Atlantic state, discriminated between strategic and operating decisions. The correlation between the number of levels of plants and the centralization of the strategic decisions was negative (−0.24). Conversely, they found a positive, though weak (0.18) correlation with the centralization of operating decisions: that is, in plants with flatter hierarchies operating decisions were more decentralized.

Empirical findings relating to the correlation between the depth of the organization and the *(horizontal) span of control* were more ambiguous. Pugh *et al.* (1968) found a positive correlation equal to 0.24 with the CEO's span of control, measured by the number of managers that directly reported to the CEO, but almost no correlation (−0.06) with the span of control at shop floor level, measured by the subordinate ratio (i.e. the ratio of the number of line workers to the number of first-line supervisors; this latter was defined as the lowest job that did not include prescribed direct work). Conversely, in Child's (1972) national sample the latter correlation was negative (−0.28), while there was no correlation (−0.06) between depth and the CEO's span of control. Lastly, in Rajan and Wulf's (2006) study of the organization of more than 300 US public (generally large and mature) companies that were observed over the period 1986–99, the correlation between depth and CEO's span of control was found to be significantly negative (−0.27).[9]

3.3.1 Size

The most agreed-upon stylized fact on the determinants of the number of hierarchical levels relates to the role of the size of organizations, generally measured by the number of employees. In particular, the number of hierarchical levels of the organization is found to increase with size, but at a decreasing rate. Hence, the relation between the number of hierarchical levels and the number of employees of firms (or establishments) is suitably described by a concave (e.g. logarithmic) function. In Table 3.2 we illustrate the results found by previous empirical studies concerning the univariate correlation between these two variables. With the partial exception of the Okayama sample of Japanese manufacturing plants examined by Marsh and Mannari (1981), the values are systematically positive and rather large, ranging

Table 3.2 Correlation between the number of hierarchical levels and the log of the total number of employees of organizations

Study	Sample	Correlation
Pugh *et al.* (1968,1969b); Hickson *et al.* (1969)	Aston total sample ($N = 46$)	0.67
	Aston subsample of manufacturing plants ($N = 31$)	0.77
Child (1972)	National UK sample ($N = 82$)	0.65
	National UK subsample of manufacturing plants ($N = 40$)	0.63
Blau and Schoenherr (1971)	US sample of employment security agencies ($N = 53$)	0.73
Blau *et al.* (1976)	New Jersey sample of manufacturing plants ($N = 110$)	0.49
Reimann (1980)	Ohio sample of manufacturing plants ($N = 20$)	0.54
Marsh and Mannari (1981)	Okayama sample of manufacturing plants ($N = 50$)	0.15
Collins *et al.* (1999)	Mid-Atlantic sample of manufacturing plants ($N = 54$)	0.39

between 0.39 (in Collins *et al.* 1999) and 0.77 (in the Aston subsample of manufacturing establishments).

The logarithmic relation between organizations' depth and size is generally confirmed when other regressors are considered. The most recent and most extensive documentation of this relation is offered by Rajan and Wulf's (2006) study of US firms.[10] Nonetheless, there are a few exceptions. For instance, Reimann (1980) found that the coefficient of the log of the number of employees, though positive, was not significant in multivariate regressions that also included technological variables (see below). Similar results were obtained by Marsh and Mannari (1981) in the Okayama study.[11]

3.3.2   Technological variables

Since Woodward (1965) claimed that there was a "technological imperative," with technology being the key driving force that shaped the form of organizations, the relation between technological variables and the number of hierarchical levels of organizations has been a hot issue in the empirical literature on organizational design. Woodward (1965, pp. 51–60) considered eighty firms located in south-east Essex that were observed in 1954–5; most of them were of small and medium size (i.e. with fewer than 1,000 employees). She relied on an indicator capturing the degree of mechanization of production, from single batch through small batches, large batches, mass production, up to continuous flow process production, and found a positive correlation between this indicator and the depth of the organizations under scrutiny. Nonetheless, subsequent studies failed to confirm this evidence. For instance, Hickson *et al.* (1969) replicated Woodward's analysis on the Aston group sample and found that the correlation of organizations' depth with an index of workflow integration was only weakly positive. In addition, the statistically significant positive univariate correlation (0.51) with an index of production continuity similar in spirit to Woodward's mechanization index largely vanished after controlling for the effect of size.

Similarly inconclusive results were found in samples composed of Japanese plants. For instance, in Marsh and Mannari's (1981) study, after controlling for internal dependence on the parent organization (if any), external dependence on customers and suppliers, autonomy, age, and number of sites of the parent company, none of the technological indicators that were introduced in multivariate regressions (i.e. Woodward's scale of mechanization, an automaticity index based on Amber and Amber's 1962 scale, and Khandwalla's 1974 technology score, see Chapter 2) exhibited any statistically significant association with the number of hierarchical levels (see also Lincoln *et al.* 1986 for similar results).

Actually, as was argued in Chapter 2 concerning the delegation of decision authority, the effect of technology on the number of levels is likely to depend on the type of technology under consideration. From this perspective, an important distinction was originally made by Blau *et al.* (1976) between mechanization technology, the purpose of which is to automate production processes, and use of computers in functions other than production. In line with the Aston group's tradition, in their study of 110 New Jersey medium- and large-sized manufacturing plants (i.e. with 200 or more employees) they found a weak positive correlation (equal to 0.1) between depth and mechanization; this latter variable was measured by both a version of the Woodward production continuity score and the percentage of total production equipment that operated at or above an Amber III level of automation (i.e. self-feeding machines which repeat cycles automatically). Moreover, establishments in the intermediate "large batch, assembly, and mass production" category turned out to have (slightly) smaller depth (average number of hierarchical levels equal to 5.08) than those included in both the "unit and small batch" and the "continuous production processes" categories (5.14 and 5.35, respectively); this possibly suggested the existence of a curvilinear U-shaped relation between mechanization and depth. Conversely, the degree of computer automation of plants measured by the number of functions for which a computer on site was used[12] turned out to be positively correlated with the number of levels (0.27). This positive association persisted after controlling for plant size.[13] Similar results were obtained by Reimann (1980), who found a positive univariate correlation between the number of hierarchical levels and the presence of a computer on site (0.61), the number of computerized functions (0.31), and the degree of mechanization of production (0.18). Note, however, that in multivariate regressions only the former variable had a positive statistically significant coefficient.

Nonetheless, the view that the computerization of operations leads to an increase in the number of hierarchical levels is not confirmed by more recent studies. In particular, Collins *et al.* (1999) found that in multivariate regressions, the extent of adoption of PA equipment (i.e. computer numerical control, robots, distributed process control, and automated material handling devices) had a negative statistically significant effect on organizational depth. Pinsonneault and Kraemer (1997) analyzed the effects of the general accessibility of computer applications, and of the penetration of control-oriented, coordination-oriented, and efficiency-oriented computer applications on the presence of middle managers among the managerial ranks of 155 US cities. One may assume that the lower the incidence of middle managers the flatter the organization.[14] The authors split the sample according to whether authority over organizational and computing decisions in the city under scrutiny was centralized or decentralized. They found that use of computers was positively associated with the flatness of the organization but only in extensively centralized cities (that is, cities where both organizational and computing decisions were centralized). Conversely, in extensively decentralized cities the penetration of computer applications led to a moderate increase of the percentage of middle managers.

To sum up, the effect of technological factors on organizational depth depends on the type and vintage of the technology under consideration. While old-vintage mechanization turns out to be associated with a deeper organizational design, the adoption of PA equipment seems to have a negative effect on depth. For ICTs, empirical studies concentrate upon the effect of information technology (that impacts on the cost of using information about the environment – i.e. collecting, processing, and understanding information), while there is no evidence on the role played by communication innovations (i.e. network technology, that influences the cost of monitoring and transmitting data and orders within the managerial hierarchy) on the depth of organizations. In any case, findings are not robust, since they seem to depend on the measure of the use of computers.

3.3.3   Other firm-specific and industry-specific effects

Quite surprisingly, very few studies have considered the effects on organizational depth of other variables beyond size and technology.

For firm-specific variables, establishments that were part of larger organizations were generally found to have flatter hierarchies than independent plants (see, for instance, Marsh and Mannari 1981, Lincoln *et al.* 1986). Nevertheless, this may simply be due to a measurement error arising from the fact that in the former plants a portion of the corporate hierarchy is not considered (i.e. the portion above the plant manager level). Conversely, findings as to the role of age were inconclusive. For instance, Marsh and Mannari (1981) highlighted a positive statistically significant effect of this variable on the number of levels, while in Lincoln *et al.*'s (1986) study age had no effect. Lastly, Collins *et al.* (1999) found that the number of hierarchical levels was positively associated with the incidence of professionals in firms' total workforce.

For industry-specific factors, the evidence is even scarcer and confined to Collins *et al.*'s (1999) analysis, according to which organizational depth is smaller in R&D-intensive industries and greater in rapidly growing ones.

3.4   Evidence on the determinants of organizational depth based on the new empirical methodology[15]

In this section we report the results of an econometric analysis of the determinants of organizational depth based on the data set of Italian manufacturing plants described in Chapter 1 (see also the Appendix to this book). The aim is to provide a more direct test of the theoretical predictions illustrated in Section 3.2 of this chapter, with special emphasis being placed on the role of plant size and of technological factors (i.e. both production and network technologies).

3.4.1   Specification of the econometric model*

The organizational unit of analysis of the econometric model described below is the plant. The optimal number of levels of plant *j* that operates in industry *i* is given by:

$$T_j^* = \arg \max(\pi_j) = F(N_j, x_j, y_j, z_i) \tag{4}$$

where π_j is the profit function, N_j is plant *j*'s (log of the) number of employees, x_j is a vector of variables reflecting the production technologies and ICTs in use in the plant, y_j is a vector of other plant-specific characteristics (e.g. ownership status), and z_i is a vector of environment-specific characteristics (e.g. R&D intensity, concentration).

The conceptual framework illustrated in Section 3.2 identified several factors that influenced organizational depth. For instance, T_j^* should be a positive function of the (log of the) number of plant employees. Moreover, production technologies and ICTs are likely to affect the choice of optimal depth. We test these and other determinants of organizational depth through the estimates of a discrete choice model.

T_j^* is unobserved. The observable number of levels T_j differs from the optimal value due to adjustment costs and other unobserved factors. For instance Schaefer (1998) has noted that influence costs may lead to delays in adjusting the organizational structure towards its efficient configuration (on this issue, see Chapter 4).

In any case, the relation between the optimal depth of the organization and its actual value is assumed to be as follows:

$$T_j = 2 \ if \ T_j^* \leq \mu_0$$
$$T_j = 3 \ if \ \mu_0 < T_j^* \leq \mu_1$$
$$T_j = 4 \ if \ \mu_1 < T_j^* \leq \mu_2$$
$$T_j = 5 \ if \ \mu_2 < T_j^* \leq \mu_3$$
$$T_j = 6 \ if \ T_j^* > \mu_3$$

where μ_k are the thresholds that separate the different discrete categories of the number of levels of a plant's hierarchy, $T_j = 2$ represents the simplest two-layer organizational structure, and $T_j = 6$ is the maximum observed level of organizational complexity, corresponding to a situation in which a plant has six or more levels.[16] Observations are thus censored to the right-hand side of the distribution of T_j^*. Given the censored and categorical ordered nature of the dependent variable, an ordered logit model with censoring will be estimated (see Maddala 1983).

3.4.2   Explanatory variables*

In Table 3.3 we present the explanatory variables of the econometric model and their description (see the Appendix to this chapter for a more detailed description of explanatory variables and their descriptive statistics). These variables can be grouped into three categories.

The first category includes the following *plant-specific variables*:

- plant size measured by the log of the number of employees
- variables capturing the production technologies and ICTs used by plants.

In production technologies, a distinction is made between conventional automated technologies (IMS) close in spirit to those measured by Woodward's production continuity scale and the Aston group's workflow rigidity score, and PA technologies. These latter include the following advanced manufacturing technologies (AMTs): NC or CNC stand-alone machine tools, programmable robots, machining centers, and flexible manufacturing systems and cells (FMS). For ICTs, we consider use of both within-firm and interfirm (i.e. with suppliers and customers) advanced network technologies. These technologies inversely

Table 3.3   The explanatory variables of the econometric models

Variable	Description
Size	Log of the number of employees
IMS	1 for plants that have adopted IMS; 0 otherwise
DAMT 1	1 if a plant has adopted 1 AMT (PA production technologies, i.e. numerically or computerized numerically controlled stand-alone machine tools, programmable robots, machining centers, and FMS); 0 otherwise
DAMT 2	1 if a plant has adopted 2 AMTs; 0 otherwise
DAMT 3	1 if a plant has adopted 3 AMTs; 0 otherwise
DAMT 4	1 if a plant has adopted 4 AMTs; 0 otherwise
Intra-firm network	1 for plants that have adopted advanced network technologies for intra-firm communication (i.e. use of network technology to exchange technical data and general information with other departments, headquarters, and between different points on the factory floor); 0 otherwise
Interfirm network	1 for plants that have adopted advanced network technologies for interfirm communication (i.e. use of network technology to exchange technical data and general information with customers and suppliers); 0 otherwise
State-owned group	1 for plants that are state-owned; 0 otherwise
Private Italian group	1 for plants that belong to private Italian multi-unit parent companies; 0 otherwise
European MNE	1 for plants that belong to European (non-Italian) multi-unit parent companies; 0 otherwise
American MNE	1 for plants that belong to American multi-unit parent companies; 0 otherwise
R&D	Number of R&D employees to total employees in the industry in which plants operate (three-digit NACE–CLIO)
Herfindahl	Herfindahl concentration index in the industry in which plants operate (three-digit NACE–CLIO)
Just in time	1 for plants that have adopted JIT production methods; 0 otherwise

reflect the costs incurred by managers to communicate information to and monitor the behavior of subordinates (and firms' partners).

The second category includes *plant-specific controls*. They consist in a series of dummy variables indicating the ownership status of plants. In particular, we consider whether a plant is state-owned or privately owned, and in this latter case whether it is part of an Italian business group or multi-unit firm, a foreign multinational enterprise (MNE) (with a further distinction being made between European and American multinationals), or it belongs to a single-plant firm.

The third category includes *environment-specific controls*. These reflect the technological intensity (*R&D*) and market concentration (*Herfindahl*) of the industries of plants, and the uncertainty of the business environment in which they operate, proxied by the adoption by plants of just-in-time production techniques *(Just in time)*.

3.4.3 Econometric results*

The results of the econometric estimates are synthesized in Table 3.4 (for a detailed report of the estimates see Tables 3.A2 and 3.A3 in the Appendix).

Generally speaking, the results are quite robust. The positive, highly significant, coefficient of (the log of) plant size comes as no surprise. *Size*

Table 3.4 Detected effects of the explanatory variables on organizational depth

Variables	All establishments	Establishments belonging to single-unit firms	Establishments belonging to multi-unit firms
Size	+++	+++	+++
IMS	+++	n.s.	+++
DAMT 1	n.s.	n.s.	n.s.
DAMT 2	n.s.	n.s.	n.s.
DAMT 3	n.s.	n.s.	n.s.
DAMT 4	−	n.s.	− −
Intra-firm network	+++	++	+
Interfirm network	−	n.s.	n.s.
State-owned group	+	n.a.	+
Private Italian group	n.s.	n.a.	n.s.
European MNE	−	n.a.	− −
American MNE	n.s.	n.a.	n.s.
R&D	n.s.	n.s.	n.s.
Herfindahl	n.s.	n.s.	n.s.
Just in time	n.s.	n.s.	+

Notes
+++: positive effect significant at 1%; ++: positive effect significant at 5%; +: positive effect significant at 10%.
− −: negative effect significant at 5%; −: negative effect significant at 10%.
n.s.: effect not significant.
n.a.: not applicable.

is the individual variable which exhibits the greatest explanatory power in all models, showing that the number of hierarchical levels is a positive and concave function of the number of plant employees; so the number of levels increases with plant size, but at decreasing marginal rates.[17] As was shown earlier (see Section 3.3), span of control and organizational depth are closely entwined. The (positive) concave relation between the depth of the organization and plant size implies that the (average) span of control is increasing with the number of employees (see Chapter 1 for a more detailed discussion of this finding).

A second interesting result relates to technological variables. With all else equal (in particular, plant size), production technology plays a key role in influencing the choice of organizational form. There is a positive significant relation between the depth of the organization and the use of IMS. Such finding seems to confirm the view originally advanced by organizational scholars (e.g. Woodward 1965) that early-vintage single-purpose automated technologies are associated with a more rigid separation of tasks and ranks, and hence a larger number of hierarchical layers. In other words, IMS are tightly related to the Tayloristic approach to production which is based upon the specialization of blue-collar workers and a sharp separation of tasks in production. IMS are, therefore, typical of organizations in which the number of hierarchical layers is rather high.

In contrast, previous studies have argued that the use of PA technologies tends to increase the probability of adoption of a flatter hierarchy. Nonetheless, the results of our estimates show that the effect of adopting these technologies is negligible up to three AMTs, with the coefficients of *DAMT*1, *DAMT*2, and *DAMT*3 being insignificant at conventional levels, while those of *DAMT*4 denoting the adoption of all four AMTs under consideration, is positive, significant and of large magnitude. Indeed, only when a plant adopts a cluster of complementary PA technologies is the depth of the organization affected. More than the use of an AMT in isolation, it is the combination of different AMTs that leads to an organization characterized by a flat corporate hierarchy.[18]

Concerning the adoption of advanced ICTs, the results are rather articulated. First, the depth of the organization increases with the use of intra-firm network technology. Note, however, that from our cross-sectional estimates one cannot derive any robust conclusion on the causal link between organizational depth and technology. Hence, this result may also be interpreted the other way round: plants characterized by a deep organizational structure are more likely to introduce network technologies so as to improve the efficiency of intra-firm communication.

It is further interesting to note that while plants using advanced intra-firm communication technologies are more likely to have a multi-layered structure, improvements in interfirm communication (with customers, suppliers, and/or subcontractors) decrease this probability. The coefficient of *Interfirm network* is negative and significant (at 10%). In particular, this result might be the outcome of a process of *outsourcing*: the link of suppliers and subcontractors with a plant's communication network might capture a process of delegation of production activities outside the plant. In turn, this process is likely to be associated with the flattening of a plant's hierarchy.

Let us now consider the effects of plant ownership status. State-owned plants tend to be relatively more bureaucratic than private independent plants, the reference category of the estimates, with the coefficient of *State-owned group* being positive and significant (at 10%). The opposite applies to plants that are part of European MNEs. Actually, it turns out that there is a great difference between plants according to the home country of their parent organization. In particular, Wald-tests of the difference between the coefficients of the ownership status variables show that plants owned by a European MNE are significantly less bureaucratic than other plants (independent national plants, state-owned plants, plants owned by national multi-unit firms or business groups, and those owned by American MNEs). This result might point to the role played by the distance between the plant and its headquarters. Indeed, plants that belong to European corporations can be directly controlled by their headquarters being rather close, thus reducing the need for some intermediate levels. Conversely, North American MNEs whose headquarters are very far from Italian production units may prefer to delegate activities completely to the plant level. Note also that Italian private business groups are on average smaller than foreign MNEs: 65% of them have less than 10,000 employees against 33% and 25% of European and North American MNEs, respectively. So, plant and firm boundaries of Italian groups are more likely to overlap.[19]

Finally, there is no evidence of any relation between the organizational depth of plants and the characteristics of their business environment. As to industry characteristics, the coefficients of *R&D* and *Herfindahl* are insignificant. Similarly, uncertainty in the business environment, proxied by adoptions of JIT production techniques, fail to exhibit any explanatory power of organizational depth. Remember that in Chapter 2 we showed that adoption of these techniques pushes firms to decentralize decision-making authority down the corporate hierarchy. So, while the urgency of decisions associated with environmental uncertainty affects the allocation of authority, it seems not to affect the number of levels of the corporate hierarchy.

We also ran LR tests on the joint significance of the estimated coefficients for various groups of explanatory variables (see Table 3.A2). The tests confirm that (i) plant size, (ii) the production technologies in use, and (iii) the adoption of advanced ICTs are crucial in explaining differences among sample plants in the depth of their organization. In addition, they show that the ownership status of plants matters. Conversely, environment-specific factors play a negligible role.

Within a further analysis we split the data into two subsamples, composed of plants that belonged to single-unit firms and multi-unit corporations, respectively. Regression models similar to those illustrated above were estimated. The results of these estimates are presented in Tables 3.4 and 3.A2 (Models *II* and *III*).

Generally speaking, the results highlight differences between the determinants of the boundaries of the firm's organization and those of the plant's hierarchy. In single-plant firms, the boundaries of the plant coincide with those of the firm. Administrative, financial, and marketing activities, in addition to production operations, are incorporated into the plant's organization. The impact of production technology vanishes, whereas the overall role played by network technologies remains key. As to plants owned by multi-unit firms or business groups, the boundaries of a plant's organization relate only to the production unit. In this case, production technology is key in shaping the corporate hierarchy. In addition, results on multi-unit establishments (see also Models *IIIa* and *IIIb* of Table 3.A2) confirm that state-owned plants are very bureaucratic compared to all the other categories of plants, and plants owned by private European corporations have adopted flatter organizations with respect to those owned by Italian and North American companies.

3.4.4 A synthesis

The aim of this section was to provide new insights into the determinants of the depth of organizations through the estimates of econometric models. For this purpose, we examined the decision relating to the number of hierarchical levels for the sample of Italian manufacturing plants described in Chapter 1. Particular attention was devoted to variables usually considered in both the theoretical economic literature on organizational design and earlier quantitative studies of the determinants of organizational depth. Among these variables plant size and the production technologies and ICTs in use figured prominently. In addition, we introduced into the specification of the econometric models (i) several variables reflecting the ownership status of plants which is traditionally considered in the theory of the firm, but is rarely examined in empirical studies of organizational depth (for exceptions, see Marsh and Mannari 1981; Lincoln *et al.* 1986), and (ii) environment-specific effects, upon which theoretical work has just started to concentrate and for which empirical evidence is almost non-existent. We obtained a number of interesting results that can be summarized as follows.

First, quite unsurprisingly, the stylized fact highlighted by earlier empirical studies (see again Table 3.2) that the number of levels of an organization increases with the log of the number of employees is confirmed by the results of our estimates.

Second, in accordance with Woodward's (1965) claim for the existence of a technological imperative, technological variables have indeed been found to play a central role in shaping plant organization.

Quite interestingly, for production technologies our results are in line with the evidence provided by previous studies that their impact crucially depends on the type and vintage of the technologies in use (see, for instance, Blau *et al.* 1976; Reimann 1980; Collins *et al.* 1999). In this perspective a crucial distinction is that between early-vintage mechanization technologies and the PA technologies that began to diffuse in the 1970s. The former technologies were linked to the Tayloristic approach to production, so that they needed a high specialization of line operators and turned out to be associated with a more hierarchic organization of plants. The latter technologies were intertwined with the holistic approach to production based on multi-skilling and job rotation.[20] In addition, there exists large empirical evidence that demonstrates that different PA technologies are positive complements in the adoption process (see, for instance, Stoneman and Kwon 1994; Colombo and Mosconi 1995; Stoneman and Toivanen 1997; Åstebro *et al.* 2006) – that is, these technologies tend to operate in clusters rather than in isolation. In accordance with these arguments, plants in our sample that exhibit the greatest extent of use of PA technologies have a flatter organization than other plants, with all else equal. Conversely, a moderate extent of use of these technologies seems to have no effect on organizational depth.

A similar reasoning applies to ICTs. In fact, our results support the view that the effects of ICTs on organizational depth again depend on the specific use that establishments make of these technologies.

Accordingly, we highlighted two opposite effects of network technologies on the number of hierarchical layers of sample plants, depending on the specific locus of improvements in communication efficiency. On the one hand, in contrast with the predictions of part of the information processing stream of literature but coherently with Lazear (1995) and Garicano Rossi-Hansberg (2006), advances in *intra-firm* network technologies increase the likelihood of plants adopting an organization characterized by a deep management hierarchy. On the other, the opposite applies to *interfirm* network technologies. Note, however, that our cross-sectional estimates do not allow us to highlight the direction of causality relations. Therefore the positive association of organizational depth with the use by sample plants of advanced intra-firm communication technologies might well be explained by the need of bureaucratic plants with a larger number of hierarchical levels to reduce communication costs. Similarly, the negative association of organizational depth with the use of interfirm network technologies might indicate that flatter plants have greater recourse to outsourcing, so they need better communication technologies with suppliers and subcontractors.

Finally, we provided evidence that the ownership status of establishments matters, an issue on which earlier empirical literature is almost silent. State-owned plants generally adopt more bureaucratic forms of organization (Shleifer 1998). Moreover, there are sizable differences according to whether a plant is owned by a private Italian group, an American firm, or a European (non-Italian) MNE, with the latter plants being less hierarchic than other plants. These findings may indicate that the distance between production units and their corporate headquarters, while affecting the cost of communication and monitoring, is positively associated with the organizational depth of production units. They also suggest that the number of hierarchical levels of establishments may be positively influenced by the overall size of their parent firms, which is considerably smaller for Italian private groups than for their foreign counterparts.

Conversely, environment-specific factors relating to the uncertainty and urgency of decisions in the business environment in which firms operate, and the technological intensity and market concentration of their industries, fail to display any explanatory power.

3.5 Concluding remarks

The aim of this chapter was to highlight the determinants of organizational depth, the main dimension of corporate hierarchy. Why are some business organizations rather flat, while other have a large number of hierarchical levels? In order to address this question, we first illustrated a simple eclectic conceptual model that combines the predictions of different streams of the theoretical economic literature on organizational design (notably, the information processing and the decentralization of incentives streams). Then we surveyed the empirical results of earlier quantitative studies on this issue. Lastly, we illustrated a new econometric test of the determinants of organizational depth based on the data set described in Chapter 1.

From the previous sections it is clear that the most important factor that determines the number of hierarchical levels of an organization is its *size*. The empirical evidence presented in this chapter almost unanimously points to the existence of a logarithmic relation between the number of employees of firms (and establishments) and the number of hierarchical layers; in other words, the number of layers increases with size, but at a decreasing rate.

Another important factor is the technology in use, in accordance with Woodward's (1965) early claim that there is a technological imperative shaping organizational design. Nonetheless, both the predictions of economic theory and the available empirical evidence are rather ambiguous as to the direction of this influence. In general, they suggest that the relation between technology and organizational depth depends on the type and vintage of the technologies under consideration, and the extent of their use. For the type of technology, one should first distinguish production technologies and ICTs. The former technologies determine an increase of productivity, while the latter affect information processing, communication and monitoring costs.

For production technologies, it is important to distinguish early-vintage mechanization technologies from PA technologies whose diffusion started in the 1970s and gained speed in the 1980s and 1990s. It is often argued that early mechanization of production processes is associated with the Tayloristic approach to production based upon specialization of line operators and an extensive hierarchy; however the empirical results in support of this argument are far from robust (see, for instance, the inconclusive evidence produced by the studies of the Aston group and their replications in different contexts, e.g. Hickson *et al.* 1969; Marsh and Mannari 1981; Lincoln *et al.* 1986). Conversely, the available empirical evidence (see Collins *et al.* 1999 and the findings presented in Section 3.4) indicates that adoption of

PA technologies leads to a reduction in organizational depth, at least when such technologies are used in clusters rather than in isolation.

For ICTs, while early studies conducted in the 1970s (e.g. Blau *et al.* 1976; Reimann 1980) suggested a positive association of use of computers with the number of levels of a firm's hierarchy, later studies indicated that, in accordance with the predictions of economic theory, the effects of ICTs on organizational depth depended on their nature (i.e. information versus communication technology), the type of use (e.g. intra- versus interfirm communication technologies, see again the findings illustrated in Section 3.4), and the characteristics of the adopting organizations (e.g. centralized versus decentralized, see Pinsonneault and Kraemer 1997).

A weakness common to most of these studies is a recourse to cross-sectional estimates. This makes it very difficult to disentangle causality relations. For instance, greater use of ICTs by highly hierarchical organizations may simply be a consequence of the need of these organizations to reduce communication costs. Similarly, the negative association between the use of interfirm network technologies and organizational depth that was highlighted in Section 3.4 may be explained by a greater recourse to outsourcing on the part of flatter organizations, and the associated greater needs for efficient communication with suppliers. In order to go a step further in this domain there is a need for longitudinal econometric analyses; while taking endogeneity issues properly into account, they could highlight the marginal effects in terms of the addition or elimination of one or more hierarchical layers induced by the adoption of advanced production, communication, and monitoring technologies. These dynamic issues are left for Chapter 4.

Quite surprisingly, both the theoretical and empirical literature have so far devoted insufficient attention to other aspects that, beyond size and technology, may influence organizational depth. In Section 3.4 we clearly documented that the number of levels of Italian manufacturing plants depended on their ownership status (e.g. single-unit versus multi-unit firms, private firms versus state-owned ones) and the home country of the controlling firm; this evidence echoes that produced by early studies that compared US and Japanese establishments (e.g. Lincoln *et al.* 1986). However, the sources of these differences remain largely unexplored. Moreover, there may exist other factors at both firm level (e.g. firm age) and environment level (e.g. knowledge intensity, demand uncertainty, competitive pressures) that affect organizational depth. So far, this is again a largely unexplored terrain.

Appendix

3.A.1 Definition and expected effects of the explanatory variables, and results of the econometric estimates

Size is measured by the number of employees. In order to account for declining marginal effects, plant size is introduced into the econometric model in a logarithmic form. In other words, in accordance with previous findings, we assumed the relation between plant size and organizational depth to be concave.

Several explanatory variables refer to technologies in use in sample plants that pertain to the production sphere. We considered advanced PA manufacturing technologies (AMTs) and inflexible manufacturing systems (see Dunne 1994). *DAMT* is a dummy variable which is equal to one if a plant is among the adopters of one or more of the following AMTs: numerically (or computerized numerically) controlled stand-alone machine tools, programmable robots, machining centers, and flexible manufacturing systems and cells. Further, we defined four additional dummy variables *DAMT1*, *DAMT2*, *DAMT3*, and *DAMT4*; they equal one if a plant has adopted one, two, three, and four AMTs, respectively. They allow us to treat the intensity of use of AMTs as a categorical variable. Finally, *IMS* is a dummy variable that is one when plants have adopted inflexible manufacturing line systems.[21]

Turning to ICTs, we have considered two variables that allegedly capture advances in communication and monitoring efficiency. *Intrafirm network* is a dummy variable that equals one for plants that adopted local area network (LAN) and/or on-line connection with headquarters; *Interfirm network* is set to one for plants that introduced electronic data interchange (EDI) with customers, suppliers and/or subcontractors.[22] Whereas the former variable accounts for advances in intra-firm communication technology, the latter relates to improvements in interfirm communication system (i.e. shared databases between different firms, see Johnston and Vitale 1988; Mukhopadhyay *et al.* 1995). Not only do advanced ICTs increase the efficiency of both intra- and interfirm communication, they also enable managers to access information about production more easily (see Hubbard 2000). This increases their ability to collect and process information on a plant's operations and decrease the principal's costs of investigation. Adoption of advanced ICTs therefore both reduce communication costs and improve monitoring efficiency.

Let us now turn to plants' ownership status. We defined the two dummy variables *State-owned* and *Private group* that denote whether a plant belonged to a state-owned group or to a private multi-unit company respectively, with private single-plant companies being the reference category of the estimates. Moreover, we distinguished group nationality by introducing three additional dummy variables *Private Italian group*, *European MNE* and *American MNE*, indicating the Italian, European, or North American nationality of the private business group to which a plant eventually belonged.

Finally, environment-specific effects were captured by three variables: *R&D* is the proportion of R&D to total industry employment (three-digit NACE–CLIO classification), and *Herfindahl* is the three-digit Herfindahl concentration index. These variables are introduced in order to control for the scientific base and market competition of industries in which plants operate. *Just in time* is a dummy variable that equals one for plants that adopt JIT production techniques.[23] This latter variable is intended to proxy for the urgency of decisions and need for flexibility in the business environment in which plants operate.

Descriptive statistics on the explanatory variables of organizational depth are reported in Table 3.A1. In Table 3.A2, and 3.A3 we present the results of the estimates of the econometric models.

Table 3.A1 Descriptive statistics of the explanatory variables

Variable	Mean	Std dev.	Min.	Max.
Size	4.4818	1.1865	1.6094	8.4118
IMS	0.3219	0.4677	0	1
DAMT 1	0.2215	0.4157	0	1
DAMT 2	0.3311	0.4711	0	1
DAMT 3	0.1530	0.3604	0	1
DAMT 4	0.0959	0.2948	0	1
Intra-firm network	0.5822	0.4938	0	1
Interfirm network	0.1849	0.3887	0	1
State-owned group	0.0320	0.1761	0	1
Private Italian group	0.0525	0.2233	0	1
European MNE	0.0890	0.2851	0	1
American MNE	0.0548	0.2278	0	1
R&D	0.0206	0.0375	0	0.2204
Herfindahl	0.0177	0.0348	0.0001	0.2425
Just in time	0.4635	0.4992	0	1

Table 3.A2 Determinants of organizational depth: ordered logit models with censoring

Variable	All establishments	Single-unit firms	Multi-unit firms	
	I	II	IIIa	IIIb
a_0 Constant	-1.0573[b] (0.4573)	-.9856[a] (.5131)	-1.4992 (1.7632)	.1540 (2.1259)
a_1 Size	.8647[c] (.1241)	.8368[c] (.1433)	.8520[c] (.3191)	.8266[c] (.3173)
a_2 IMS	.6256[c] (.2264)	.3924 (.2802)	1.2734[c] (.4712)	1.3351[c] (.4855)
a_3 DAMT 1	-.1565 (.3070)	.0405 (.3401)	-1.2812 (.8750)	-1.4893 (.9145)
a_4 DAMT 2	-.1584 (.2900)	-.0744 (.3245)	-.6849 (.8491)	-.6810 (.8386)
a_5 DAMT 3	-.1008 (.3774)	.2243 (.4334)	-1.3451 (1.0277)	-1.2882 (1.0464)
a_6 DAMT 4	-.7966[a] (.4684)	-.1839 (.6938)	-2.4364[b] (.9617)	-2.4003[b] (.9394)
a_7 Intra-firm network	.5998[b] (.2433)	.5002[a] (.2584)	1.8219[a] (1.0710)	1.9652[a] (1.1571)
a_8 Interfirm network	-.5142[a] (.2965)	-.5427 (.3647)	-.3734 (.5497)	-.5642 (.5901)
a_9 State-owned group	1.0423[a] (.6086)	–	1.2848[a] (.7452)	–
a_{10} Private Italian group	.5844 (.5185)	–	–	-.6658 (.8135)
a_{11} European MNE	-.6910[b] (.3819)	–	–	-2.0649[b] (.8208)
a_{12} American MNE	.0393 (.4271)	–	–	-1.1603 (.9548)

a_{13} R&D	−1.2626 (3.3148)	−1.3292 (4.8530)	.0234 (3.7562)	−.0831 (4.1771)
a_{14} Herfindahl	.1885 (2.8528)	.5502 (3.4326)	4.2389 (6.0194)	1.8447 (6.3615)
a_{15} Just-in-time	.3088 (.2229)	.1819 (.2483)	1.0678[a] (.5808)	1.0957[a] (.6087)
μ_1	3.7198[c] (.2273)	3.6448[c] (.2624)	4.4873[c] (.5388)	4.5419[c] (.5357)
μ_2	5.8358[c] (.2325)	5.7102[c] (.2958)	6.7537[c] (.4647)	6.9921[c] (.4637)
μ_3	7.8368[c] (.4259)	8.0150[c] (.6983)	8.6141[c] (.6115)	8.913[c] (.5742)
Log-likelihood	−440.5843	−368.9929	−105.9846	−102.5765
LR test	151.47[c] (15)	75.87[c] (11)	48.25[c] (12)	55.07[c] (14)
No. of censored obs.	10	3	7	
No. of obs.	438	338	100	

Notes

Standard errors and degree of freedom in parentheses.

[a] significant at 10%.

[b] significant at 5%.

[c] significant at 1%.

Table 3.A3 Determinants of organizational depth: results of tests on groups of explanatory variables

Determinants	LR tests (on the coefficients of Model I Table 3.A2)	Results	Comments
Size	$a_1 = 0$	48.55^c (1)	Positive concave relation
Production technologies	$a_2 = a_3 = a_4 = a_5 = a_6 = 0$	9.99^a (5)	Significant effect; the sign depends on the type (i.e. vintage) and extent of use of production technology
Network technologies	$a_7 = a_8 = 0$	8.12^b (2)	Significant effect; the sign depends on the type of network technologies (i.e. intra-firm versus interfirm network technology)
Ownership status	$a_9 = a_{10} = a_{11} = a_{12} = 0$	8.95^a (4)	Significant effect, with state-owned plants being more bureaucratic than private plants; existence of national differences
Environment characteristics	$a_{13} = a_{14} = a_{15} = 0$	2.18 (3)	Negligible effect

Notes
Standard errors and degree of freedom in parentheses.
[a] significant at 10%.
[b] significant at 5%.
[c] significant at 1%.

4
Evidence on the Determinants of Organizational Dynamics

4.1 Introduction

In Chapter 1 we depicted organizational design as a coherent bundle of different dimensions: structural organizational variables (SOVs, i.e. organizational depth measured by the total number of hierarchical levels, span of control, and allocation of decision authority) and work and human resource management practices (i.e. IWPs and HRMPs). In Chapters 2 and 3 we provided evidence as regards the static determinants of the structural dimensions of organizational design. In particular, Chapter 2 was devoted to the allocation of decision-making, while in Chapter 3 we discussed the determinants of corporate hierarchy.

In this chapter, we turn to organizational dynamics. In accordance with our comprehensive definition of organizational design, under the heading "organizational dynamics" we consider changes in one (or more) of these dimensions. We are interested here in highlighting factors that favor or hinder these changes.

In principle, the static analysis developed in previous chapters also provides predictions relating to changes in organizational design. For instance, it has been shown that the depth of the organization increases with (the log of) its size. So when firms grow in size, they are expected to add additional layers to their hierarchy. The opposite should occur when they cut the workforce. Nevertheless, we will show in this chapter that other factors need to be taken into account to gain a satisfactory understanding of organizational dynamics.

In fact, both the economic press and studies in business history suggest that powerful conservative forces are at work preventing firms from implementing the organizational changes that would supposedly improve their economic performance, a phenomenon usually referred to in the literature as "structural inertia" (e.g. Schaefer 1998). In addition, the quantitative empirical work that will be surveyed in Section 4.3 has highlighted that the diffusion of organizational innovations has been extremely slow when compared to the diffusion of technological innovations, thus again suggesting the existence of structural inertia (for evidence see also Section 1.3 of Chapter 1). But why are firms so reluctant to modify their organizational structure? In other words, what are the sources of structural inertia?

The present chapter aims to analyze the determinants of organizational dynamics and the origins of structural inertia. The chapter proceeds as follows. We first present in Section 4.2 a conceptual framework aimed at highlighting the factors that influence the benefits a firm obtains, and the costs it incurs, in changing its organizational design. Special attention is devoted to the role played by (i) complementarities among technological and organizational innovations (Milgrom and Roberts 1990b), (ii) sunk costs (Dixit and Pindyck 1994), and (iii) influence activity (Milgrom 1988, Milgrom and Roberts 1990a). In Section 4.3, we survey the findings of quantitative empirical studies on the determinants of adoption of new organizational practices (both IWPs and HRMPs). Then, in Section 4.4, we concentrate on empirical findings on the determinants of changes in the structural dimensions of organizational design. In particular, we first present international evidence on the factors that determine changes in the depth of the corporate hierarchy, and then use the data on Italian manufacturing plants described in Chapter 1 to get further insights into the determinants of these changes through the estimates of appropriate econometric models. Some concluding remarks in Section 4.5 end the chapter.

4.2   A conceptual framework of the determinants of organizational dynamics

4.2.1   A general framework of organizational dynamics

We adopt here a very simple conceptual framework. We assume that a firm changes its organizational design only when the *discounted additional operating revenues* it generates through such change are greater than the costs it incurs (for a similar approach, see Ichniowski and Shaw 1995). These changes may pertain to the structural characteristics of organizational design or to the adoption of new organizational practices. For the sake of simplicity, we will use the term "organizational innovation" to refer to all these changes. In what follows, we will distinguish the determinants of the adoption of organizational innovations depending on whether the factors under scrutiny are expected to influence the additional operating revenues generated by, or the adjustment costs associated with, the change.

4.2.1.1 Factors affecting the additional operating revenues from organizational innovations

The additional operating revenues generated by organizational innovation are given by the difference between the operating revenues a firm is able to reap after the modification of the organizational design has been implemented and those that would have been obtained with the "old" design. Let us first consider the factors affecting the former category of operating revenues.

Several studies have argued that changes in different organizational dimensions constitute a bundle of *complementary* organizational innovations: hence "using one more intensely increases the marginal benefits of using others more intensely" (Hölmstrom and Milgrom 1994, p. 973; see also Milgrom and Roberts 1995 and the literature surveyed in Chapter 5, Sections 5.3 and 5.4). So the additional revenues from an individual organizational innovation are greater if other complementary organizational variables are already in place, or are contextually changed by the firm under scrutiny. For instance, it is well known that SMT are more effective if workers are allowed to rotate across jobs – in other words, there are *complementarities* among different IWPs. They also are more effective if workers are trained in, and have incentives to exercise, decision power and the exploitation of their individual skills; in other words, complementarity extends to HRMPs relating to selection procedures, training, and compensation schemes. The same argument applies to the structural dimensions of organizational design such as delayering and decentralization of decision authority down the firm's corporate hierarchy.

A similar contention is often made as regards the use by firms of ICTs and PA equipment (Milgrom and Roberts 1990b; Lindbeck and Snower 1996). In fact, these technologies are instrumental to the implementation by firms of a product/market strategy that hinges on the variety and rate of change of the product mix. Hence, they make it more profitable to adopt organizational innovations like IWPs that are intended to obtain greater flexibility and quicker response from the production system. This argument obviously implies that, all else equal, in more ICT- and PA-intensive firms the additional operating revenues from the adoption of these organizational innovations are greater, and thus their adoption is more likely than in other firms.

Concerning the operating revenues generated by use of an "old" organizational design, they will be lower for firms that are subject to stronger competitive pressures. From this perspective, we expect that firms that operate in businesses open to competition and face entry of new, more efficient competitors will have greater stimuli to change their organization, with all else equal.

4.2.1.2   The adjustment costs associated with organizational innovations

Several studies have argued that there are powerful forces within firms that oppose changes in organizational design. In what follows we will analyze the sources of these adjustment costs.

First, sizable investments of a tangible (i.e. equipment) and an intangible (i.e. training costs of the workforce) nature, are tied up with a specific organizational design. For instance, in a Tayloristic organization the specialization of tasks among workers is the result of investments in carefully designed production processes. Technical equipment is often specialized to the individual tasks that need to be performed. Moreover, workers, supervisors, and managers are all trained to perform clearly defined jobs. The associated *sunk costs* may prevent firms from switching to a more effective organizational design, unless the very existence of the firm is threatened (Dixit and Pindyck 1994). For the same reason, switching costs will be lower if a radical shift in a firm's strategy and organization occurs (e.g. the opening of a new production site, a radical change of the product mix).

Second, as is claimed by the evolutionary theories of technical change, human behavior is highly routinized (see Nelson and Winter 1982; Cohen *et al.* 1996). Firms (and the individuals within them) develop established patterns of operations that are reproduced almost automatically over time, making them increasingly efficient. To the extent that a change in organizational design involves a disruptive, competence-destroying organizational evolution, firms' workers and managers need first to unlearn the old practices and adjust their collective behavior to the new ones. The performance obtained through use of a new design increases more or less rapidly over time through learning-by-doing. Nonetheless, in the short term this performance may well be inferior to the one obtained with the old organizational design. In turn, the pace of learning (and unlearning) depends on factors such as the age and the education of the workforce, with younger and more educated individuals being more apt to rapidly learn how to effectively adapt to a new organizational design. Because of the very essence of routinization, however, more experienced workers and managers are likely to be entrenched in the old design and to incur higher adjustment costs. Learning also requires personal effort on the part of these individuals; so the creation of an institutional environment apt to promote the personnel firm-specific investments that support this learning process will play a key role in favoring a rapid switch to a new organizational design.

Third, an additional source of structural inertia is highlighted by incentive theory. A change in organizational design modifies the distribution of quasi-rents among employees. Therefore, they will devote time and energies to trying to influence the person in charge of the decisions so as to turn the change to their own advantage. This influence activity (Milgrom 1988; Milgrom and Roberts 1990a) is detrimental to production activities. A firm may decide not to change the organization (or, at least, to postpone change until the expected revenues reach a certain threshold level) in order to avoid these influence costs.

These remarks are rather general and apply more or less to every change in organizational design (i.e. the adoption of new organizational practices and/or a change in a structural dimension of organizational design). However, one has to acknowledge that in practice changes in various aspects of the organization may follow related but distinct patterns, just as the static determinants of these factors may be different (see Chapters 2 and 3). Consequently, in the next subsection we concentrate on one (structural) aspect, that will be extensively treated in the empirical part of the chapter (see Section 4.4) – that is, the determinants of changes in organizational depth (for a static analysis, see Chapter 3).

4.2.2 Testable predictions on the determinants of changes in the organizational depth

In Chapter 3 we have analyzed the determinants of organizational depth. In particular in Section 3.2 we argued that the number of hierarchical levels increases with the *size* of the organization. With almost no exception, the quantitative empirical studies surveyed in Section 3.3 provided compelling evidence in support of this view.

On the one hand, as is argued by the information processing stream, larger organizations need to process a larger amount of information than their smaller counterparts. In order to avoid information overload and minimize information processing time, firms resort to increasingly complex managerial hierarchies (Keren and Lehvari 1979, 1983; Radner 1993; Bolton and Dewatripont 1994). On the other hand, when the organization expands with a fixed number of layers, the span of control (i.e. the number of subordinates under each superior) increases and thus the effectiveness of monitoring decreases (Calvo and Wellisz 1978). Greater shirking follows; alternatively, higher efficiency wages must be paid to employees. In order to restore proper incentives in the workforce without increasing wages, the number of hierarchical levels must be increased (Qian 1994). These arguments imply that changes in size will be associated with changes in the organizational depth in the same direction.

The drawback of the proliferation of hierarchical layers is an increase of the likelihood of organizational failures, a trade-off originally highlighted by Williamson (1967). In a hierarchy, decisions taken by top managers must be implemented by workers at the bottom of the pyramid. The larger the number of layers, and thus the larger the distance between the top manager and line workers, the more likely that actions collectively undertaken by the latter will be suboptimal due to leaks and delay in transmitting information between the top and the bottom of the organization (Beckmann 1977). This poses an upper limit to the increase in organizational depth when size increases.

These arguments also imply that changes in the costs of processing information, communicating with and monitoring the behavior of agents such as those originated from adoption of advanced ICTs, should trigger changes in organizational depth. Nonetheless, as was extensively discussed in Chapter 3, there is no general consensus as to the direction of these changes.

The change in the number of hierarchical levels of an organization will also be influenced by the use of advanced production equipment and new organizational practices. Generally speaking, adoption of these technological and organizational innovations increases the productivity of line workers.[1] If the span of control at the bottom of the hierarchy is larger than that at the top, a condition which is usually met in real-world business organizations (see for instance Smeets and Warzynski 2006), Qian (1994) shows that higher productivity results in an increase of the optimal number of tiers.

Nonetheless, we believe that there is more than this as regards the relation between innovation and change in organizational depth. In a seminal paper, Milgrom and Roberts (1990b) contend that adoption of PA technologies, use of new organizational practices and organizational changes leading to a flatter organizational design are characterized by strong complementarities and non-convexities: the marginal return to the adoption of any of them increases with the adoption of the others and with the extent of their use (see also Lindbeck and Snower 1996).[2]

Use of a bundle of PA technologies such as flexible manufacturing systems and cells, machining centers, programmable robots, CAD, CAM and CAD–CAM equipment, substantially reduces the cost of designing and manufacturing an increased variety of product versions and of introducing new products over time, thus making it easier for firms to implement a market strategy based on a broad product line, short product life cycles and quick response to environmental changes. In order to shorten decision time and assure greater responsiveness, firms have to reduce the delays caused by the communication of information up and down the corporate hierarchy. This, in turn, requires delegation of decision authority down the organizational pyramid, assignment of greater responsibility to line workers, increased reliance on a multi-skilled workforce so as to assure greater flexibility, and recourse to suitable incentive-based payment schemes. As a consequence, intermediate managerial positions and staff functions are eliminated, with this leading to a flatter organization with a smaller number of layers.

We should thus expect the adoption of PA technologies, new HRMPs and IWPs, to be a major driver of changes in organizational depth. We should also expect the likelihood of these changes to positively covariate with the extent of the use of PA technologies.[3]

As was highlighted in Section 4.1, it is important to recognize that there are powerful forces within firms that oppose any change in organizational depth. Two of these deserve special attention.

First of all, structural inertia may be the (efficient) outcome of a firm's attempt to avoid *sunk costs*. Any change in organizational depth involves irrecoverable investments due to the need to reallocate decision authority within the structure (and across different units that belong to the same firm), reassign tasks to employees, redefine communication flows, and modify administrative procedures. As the business environment is by definition uncertain, such investments may engender substantial sunk costs should future conditions differ from those expected at the time when the decision to change the organizational depth was made. Under such circumstances, real option theory (Dixit and Pindyck 1994) claims that there is an additional opportunity cost in implementing this change due to the lost option value of waiting for new information. So, it may be optimal for a firm to stay with the current number of hierarchical layers, even though it is not the optimal one given present business conditions. The larger the sunk costs involved in organizational change, the larger the incentive to postpone it – that is, the larger the structural inertia. We contend that the amount of sunk costs entailed by a change of the number of hierarchical layers depends on the firm's type of organization. More specifically, in plants that adhere to a Tayloristic organization of production, there is a rigid division of labor among workers, tasks are specialized, organizational procedures are standardized and codified in a formal way, and authority relations and communication flows tend to be defined once for all at the start of production. Subsequent modifications of the organization are thus likely to involve substantial costs, so we can expect inertial forces to be quite strong in such firms.

Second, the literature on *influence activities* (Milgrom 1988, Milgrom and Roberts 1990a; see also Schaefer 1998) claims that structural inertia may be engendered by the willingness of firms' management to limit the costs associated with such activities. As was said earlier, a change in a dimension of the organizational design of a firm is likely to modify the distribution of quasi-rents among employees; this is especially true for the structural dimensions of business organizations such as the allocation of decision authority and organizational depth. As a consequence, if employees anticipate that such a change will occur, they will devote time and energies to trying to turn it to their own advantage, an activity obviously detrimental to the firm. The incentives to indulge in such activity, and thus the associated loss for the firm in terms of reduction of the productive effort of employees, depend on the marginal benefits and costs to individual employees (Perri 1994). These in turn are contingent on a number of factors. First, the expected benefits arising from influence activities depend on the nature of decision-making within the organization: the more discretionary decision-making power, the higher the influence costs, everything else being held constant (Milgrom 1988). If there is no room for influencing decisions because the decision-maker has no discretionary power, the benefits of influence activities will entirely vanish. Second, closeness to the agent endowed with decision authority determines the personal costs incurred by individual employees in trying to affect the outcome of her decisions. In accordance with such an argument, how responsibility for decisions relating to a firm's organizational chart is allocated within firms should figure prominently in explaining structural inertia.

As a final remark on the determinants of structural inertia, the literature on organizational ecology claims that large, very complex organizations are subject to structural inertia to a larger extent than their smaller counterparts (Hannan and Freeman 1984). There are actually reasons to believe that the opposite may be true, at least in the last thirty years. Increasing emphasis was placed by large firms on time to market and quick response, so as to cope with the increasing uncertainty and turbulence of the business environment. In accordance with the lean production paradigm (see, Box I.4 in the Introduction), firms with a large number of hierarchical layers reorganized operations, eliminating middle management positions so as to assure faster decision-making.[4]

Table 4.1 summarizes the theoretical predictions on the determinants of changes in organizational depth. A rigorous econometric test of these prediction will be illustrated in Section 4.4.3.

Table 4.1 Theoretical predictions on the determinants of organizational dynamics

Variables	Effect on organizational change	Theory
Changes in size	+	Information processing, Incentive theory
New practices (IWPs and HRMPs)	+	Complementarities
Technological innovations (PA)	+	Milgrom and Roberts (1990b): positive relation with contraction of the corporate hierarchy
		Qian (1994): positive relation with expansion of the corporate hierarchy
Sunk costs	−	Real option theory
Influence activity	−	Incentive theory
Size	−	Organizational ecology

4.3 Empirical evidence on the determinants of the adoption of organizational practices[5]

In this section we will illustrate the results of quantitative empirical studies that examined the factors that favored or hindered the adoption of organizational practices (i.e. IWPs and HRMPs). We will first survey studies that considered specific industries, starting with the seminal work of Ichniowski and his colleagues on steel plants; we will then turn attention to cross-industry studies.

4.3.1 Work in the steel industry

In a series of papers Ichniowski and his colleagues adopted an insider econometric approach to the study of the diffusion of IWPs and associated

HRMPs (Ichniowski and Shaw 1995; Ichniowski *et al.* 1996; see Ichniowski and Shaw 2003 for a summary of this and related work). They focused attention on a narrowly defined production process in the steel industry – a specific kind of steel finishing line. Of the approximately sixty lines that were in existence in the US in the early 1990s, they personally visited forty-five owned by twenty-one different companies. They were interested in assessing the diffusion of a large number of organizational practices including the use of teams, either on the line or for the purpose of quality improvements, rotation of operators across tasks, profit-sharing, non-traditional incentive pay plans aimed at compensating workers for skill improvements, off-the-job training, sophisticated recruiting practices, and labor–management communication. They managed to collect longitudinal data on the adoption of these practices in thirty-six lines. They also interviewed the personnel, managers, and union representatives of these lines. Here we report the evidence provided by these studies on the adoption of these practices (see Table 4.2), while we postpone to Chapter 5 the analysis of the effects of their adoption on productivity (see section 5.3.1.1).

First of all, there is considerable heterogeneity across practices in the speed of diffusion, with some practices being much more common than others (see Chapter 1). For instance, SMT were adopted by a large number of steel finishing lines, but only a few adopted job rotation. Similarly, for complementary HRMPs, while profit-sharing was almost ubiquitous, non-traditional incentive schemes aimed at compensating workers for skill development and other qualitative aspects of their job were rather rare.

Second, as predicted, organizational practices tended to be adopted in clusters. This is documented by the high values of the correlation index between some of the practices under scrutiny (e.g. SMT, job rotation, non-traditional incentive schemes, and off-the-job training). This evidence was interpreted by the authors as a signal of the existence of *complementarities* between different practices.

In order to study the determinants of adoption, Ichniowski and his colleagues resorted to two different methodologies. On the one hand, they grouped the different practices using several statistical procedures that created a unidimensional adoption index. Variations of this index across lines and over time allowed them to analyze the factors that drive adoption through the estimates of panel data models. On the other hand, they looked at breakpoints in the values of this index and used these breakpoints to define four different clusters of "Systems of practices." At one extreme (System 4), one finds lines that had a very traditional work organization and did not adopt any new practices. At the other extreme

Table 4.2 Determinants of the diffusion of organizational practices: evidence from steel finishing lines

Independent variable	Ichniowski and Shaw (1995) Panel data, mid 1980s–early 1990s		
	Multinomial logit model of adoption of systems of practices, High-performance WP system	Pooled OLS estimates, Linear index of practices adoption	Fixed effects model, Linear index of practices adoption Old lines only
Size[a]		−	
Age of employees	−	−[b]	
Age of employees^2	+	+	
Tenure of managers	−	−	
Tenure of managers^2	+	+	
Tenure of union president	−	−	
Tenure of union president^2	+	+	
Industry experience of line manager	−	−	+
National market	−	−	
No. of new competitors	+	+	−
Threat of shut down	+/−[c]	+/−[c]	+/−[c]
Use of layoff		+	
New or reopened lines		+	

Notes
[a] Dummy variable = 1 if line is part of an integrated mill.
[b] Coefficient becomes insignificant when adding a dummy that captures whether the plant is new/reopened or old.
[c] Effect generally is positive. The effect of a plant's partial shut down is negative if the workforce is quite young.

(System 1) were lines with all the practices under examination; in 1992 these innovative lines accounted for only 11% of the sample. Systems 2 and 3 lay in between, being somewhat closer to Systems 1 and 4, respectively. The authors resorted to multinomial logit models to study the assignment of firms to the four clusters of Systems of practices.

The key result of the econometric analysis is that in spite of the fact that new organizational practices led to non-negligible productivity increases, as will be documented in Chapter 5, substantial adjustment costs hindered their rapid diffusion. In accordance with the arguments illustrated in Section 4.2.1, these costs arose mainly from the relation-specific investments that had been made by firms' personnel in learning how to effectively operate plants with an old-fashioned organizational design, and by the difficulties involved in unlearning. In fact, the value of the knowledge relating to the old organizational design vanished with the adoption of innovative organizational practices. Moreover, their adoption required personal effort to learn new skills on the part of workers and managers that were accustomed to a traditional work environment. If they doubted the personal returns to these relation-specific investments, they resisted change. In addition, even if adequate incentives were in place, the costs of learning and unlearning were greater with an older and less educated workforce. Several findings support this view.

- New plants that were built after 1983 and plants that reopened after a temporary closure exhibited greater values of the index that measures the adoption of new practices. The authors interpreted this result as indicating that the likelihood of adoption of an innovative organizational design decreased with the tenure of plant personnel.

- The value of the adoption index decreased with both the age of production workers and the tenure of plant managers. The industry experience of plant managers also had a negative, statistically significant effect on the adoption index.

- Conversely, the reluctance of workers and managers to make relation-specific investments in the skills required by the new organizational practices was considerably weakened if a plant risked being shut down or layoffs were likely. Under such circumstances, adoption of innovative practices was clearly favored.

- Competition from new entrants proved to stimulate adoption.

- Lastly, there was very strong persistence in the organizational practices used by sample plants: when the lagged dependent variable was introduced into the specification of the model, its coefficient was close to unity and the coefficients of most of (but not all) the other explanatory variables became insignificant.

In later work, Boning *et al.* (2001) applied the same methodology to the study of thirty-four rolling lines in minimills. They focused attention on two innovative organizational practices: quality circles (QC, an IWP) and group-based incentive pay (a HRMP). Again, there were significant differences in the diffusion speed of these two practices.

While by the end of the study period incentive schemes had been adopted by 91% of the sample lines, the adoption rate of QC was 42%. More interestingly, the production processes analyzed in the minimills study were much less homogenous than those in the finishing lines study. This allowed them to highlight the role of technology-specific factors in determining the speed of adoption. In particular, more complex production lines where the potential for productivity increases from team-based problem-solving practices was greater, exhibited a far greater likelihood of adopting this practice than other lines.

These findings provide interesting insights into the determinants of the adoption of IWPs and HRMPs. The key issue is whether they are generalizable or not. We turn to this issue in the next subsections.

4.3.2 Work related to other industries

Studies relating to the auto assembly and apparel industry basically confirmed the key insights provided by the work examined in the previous subsection.

4.3.2.1 Automobile assembly industry

Pil and MacDuffie (1996) considered thirty-nine automobile assembly plants located in different countries and observed in 1989 and 1993–4. They developed a composite index measuring the extent of adoption of IWPs. More precisely, the index included the percentages of employees working in teams and of those involved in problem-solving groups, the extent of rotation of production workers across different tasks, the intensity of suggestions from employees, the rate of acceptance of those suggestions, and the extent of involvement of production workers in quality control tasks. The level of the IWP index at the end of the observation period was regressed against the value of the same index in 1989 and a set of explanatory variables which aimed to capture the benefits and costs of adoption of these practices. The results of the econometric analysis can be summarized as follows.

First, there was great persistency in the use of IWPs, with the coefficient of the lagged dependent variable being positive and highly significant in all specifications. Second, the value of the IWP index was found to increase with the value in 1989 of an index measuring the extent of adoption of allegedly complementary HRMPs. These included selection and hiring procedures based on individuals' manifested willingness to learn new skills and work with others, training of production workers, pay for quality and skills compensation schemes, and reduction of status differentials between managers and workers. The extent of the use of PA technologies proxied by the ratio of programmable robots to workers, however, turned out to have no effect on adoption of IWPs. According to the authors, this result may be explained by the presence in the sample of several plants for which investments in PA technologies were primarily intended as a means to reduce labor costs, and so they were a substitute for rather than a complement of IWPs. Third, the extent of IWP adoption was greater in plants that in the period under consideration were more involved in the introduction of new models, with this reducing the barriers to adoption that arose from sunk costs. Fourth, and quite surprisingly, the tenure of production workers was found to have no effect on adoption, and that of the five top managers of the plant had a beneficial effect. This evidence is in contrast with the argument that routinization hinders the adoption of new practices. The authors suggest that in the early 1990s the high competitive pressures in the automobile industry generated a shock that motivated workers and managers to be open to changes of work practices, independently of their tenures. This argument also helps explain why the layoffs and adoption of early retirement schemes that occurred in a plant between 1989 and 1993–4 did not affect the extent of adoption of IWPs. In fact, in the period under observation the threat of losing their job was quite ubiquitous among workers in this industry. Alternatively, this result may highlight the dual nature of these restructuring measures. On the one hand, they help overcome reluctance to change from plant personnel. On the other, they create an unfavorable environment to the commitment by workers and managers in the firm-specific personnel investments that are necessary for efficient assimilation of new practices.

4.3.2.2   Apparel industry

Dunlop and Weil (1996) examined the adoption of modular production systems between 1988 and 1992 in forty-two business units that operated in different apparel production lines. Modular production entails grouping tasks and assigning them to teams of workers. Hence, it involves team work and (some) rotation of workers across tasks. It is also usually associated with compensation schemes based on the module's output rather than the individual's output.

Dunlop and Weil's empirical analysis revealed that competitive pressures from big retailers to provide products on a rapid replenishment basis and to reduce throughput time were the key driving force behind the diffusion of modular production. Larger business units that allegedly suffered most from the lack of flexibility of bundle production (i.e. mass- production) were found to be more rapid adopters than their smaller counterparts. Lastly, there was no evidence that investments in ICTs positively affected the adoption of modular production.

4.3.3 Cross-industry evidence

A limited number of studies used data produced by national surveys to estimate econometric models of the determinants of the adoption of a set of new organizational practices (Osterman 1994; Gittleman *et al.* 1998; Bauer 2003; Eriksson 2003; Greenan and Mairesse 2004).[6] Other econometric studies focus attention on specific practices (e.g. Barron and Gjerde 1996 on TQM; Eriksson and Ortega 2004 on job rotation). The results of these studies are synthesized in Tables 4.3a and 4.3b. In spite of the heterogeneity of the data used, the empirical evidence is surprisingly coherent and provides rather clear indications as to the key factors that drive the diffusion process.

At the beginning of Section 4.2.1, we argued that the first movers in the adoption of organizational innovations will be the firms that, in so doing, expect to increase their operating revenues the most. Conversely, firms that would incur the greatest adjustment costs in abandoning a traditional organizational design will be among the laggards. This view is clearly confirmed by the econometric studies described in Tables 4.3a and 4.3b.

First of all, in almost all studies large, multi-plant firms exhibited a greater likelihood of adoption. Large firms are those that allegedly suffer the most from lack of flexibility, slow response, and inadequate involvement of the workforce. As IWPs are designed precisely to deal with these weaknesses, the stimuli to their adoption will be greater for larger firms than for their smaller counterparts. In addition, with all else equal, adoption costs are likely to increase less than proportionately with firm size; a positive scale effect similar to that highlighted in the technology diffusion literature follows (see, among others, the pioneer studies of Mansfield 1968; David 1975; Romeo 1975).

Second, the additional operating revenues generated by IWPs are likely to depend on the technological characteristics of the production process and the strategy adopted by firms. Osterman (1994) found that diffusion proceeded more rapidly among US firms that used skill-intensive production technologies and adopted a competitive strategy based on factors other than costs. Gittleman *et al.* (1998), while analyzing a nationally representative sample of British establishments observed in 1993, showed that adoption was more likely when firms had already in place other complementary HRMPs relating to recruiting

Table 4.3a Determinants of the diffusion of organizational practices: cross-industry evidence

Independent variable	Osterman (1994) cross-sectional estimates			Barron and Gjerde (1996) cross-sectional estimates		Gittleman et al. (1998) cross-sectional estimates
	Logit, any practice out of four practices used by 50% or more of core employees[a]	Principal component of % of core employees involved in use of four practices[a]	Ordered probit of no. of practices used by 50% or more of core employees[a]	Probit, TQM	Logit, adoption of one or more practices	Ordered logit, no. of practices
Size (no. of employees)	−	−	−	+	+	+
Foreign owned						
Part of multi-establishment organization	+	+	+			
Skills-intensive production process	+	+	+			
Strategy based on factors other than cost	+	+	+			
Exposure to international markets	+	+	+			
Profitability						
Competition	n.s.	−	n.s.			

	SMT	Job rotation	QC	TQM
Introduction of new technology in previous years			+	+
Investment in IT				
Age of establishment	—		n.s.	n.s.
Age of employees				
% of employees with higher education			+	+
Individual compensation schemes			+	+
Collective compensation schemes		+	+	+
Turnover of employees			—	+
Manufacturing		+	+	+

Notes

[a] Four practices: (1) SMT (2) job rotation; (3) QC (4) TQM.

+ positive effect.

− negative effect.

n.s. effect not significant.

Table 4.3b Determinants of the diffusion of organizational practices: cross-industry evidence

Independent variable	Eriksson (2003) Cross-sectional estimates			Bauer (2003) Cross-sectional estimates OLS,
	Logit for each of three practices, hourly-paid workers[b]	Logit for each of three practices, salaried workers[b]	Ordered logit, no. of practices	Index of org. change in 1993–5 (PCA three dummies indicating: reduction of the no. of levels, delegation of decisions, teams)
Size (no. of employees)	+[c]	+	+	+
Foreign owned	+	+	+	
Part of multi-establishment organization				(+)
Skills-intensive production process				
Strategy based on factors other than cost				
Exposure to international markets				(+)
Profitability				
Competition				−

Introduction of new technology in previous years		
Investment in IT		+
Age of establishment		−
Age of employees		−
% of employees with higher education	+[c]	
Individual compensation schemes		
Collective compensation schemes		
Turnover of employees		
Manufacturing		

Notes

[b] Three practices: (1) SMT; (2) Job rotation; (3) TQM.

[c] Except for teams.

+ positive effect.

(+) nearly positive effect.

− negative effect.

procedures, training of the workforce and compensation schemes, and advanced technologies. Caroli and Van Reenen (2001) showed that British plants that introduced computer-based equipment were more likely than other plants to be involved in organizational changes that allegedly implied the introduction of innovative organizational practices.[7] Similarly, for German establishments, Bauer (2003) considered a composite index of organizational change reflecting adoption of teams, delegation of decision authority, and delayering during the period 1993–5. He found that investments in ICTs in 1992 had a highly significant positive effect on this factor. Greenan and Mairesse (2004) analyzed the pattern of joint adoption over time of ICTs and organizational innovations. They resorted to COI data to build, through a multiple correspondence analysis, two aggregate indicators measuring the use of ICTs and the adoption of several innovative organizational practices in 1994 and 1997, respectively. After dichotomizing these indicators, they found that French manufacturing firms were either intensive users of both new organizational practices and ICTs or used both innovations to a fairly limited extent. Moreover, the likelihood of a transition to a high use of organizational innovations (ICTs) was greater if a firm was already an intense user of ICTs.

Conversely, diffusion of IWPs was found to be slower among old firms that employed older, relatively unskilled employees. In fact, old unskilled workers are those that exhibit the greatest adjustment costs to new routines and practices. This evidence is in line with the arguments proposed by the skill-biased organizational change literature (see, for instance, Caroli *et al.* 2001; Caroli and Van Reenen 2001; Piva *et al.* 2005, 2006), according to which investments in human capital are complementary to the introduction of organizational innovations. It also confirms that the adjustment costs arising from the firm-specific investments that are required from a firm's workforce was order for IWPs to be used efficiently represent a crucial barrier to adoption. The effect of the tenure of the workforce, however, is more ambiguous. On the one hand, the necessary relation-specific investments are more likely to be made by workers if employment relations are stable. A high turnover rate of the workforce was found by Barron and Gjerde (1996) to deter the adoption of TQM among US firms. On the other hand, Eriksson and Ortega (2004) highlighted an opposite effect on the adoption of job rotation by Danish firms. A high average tenure of the workforce (i.e. lower turnover) may be indicative of highly routinized behavior, thus involving greater adjustment costs.

4.4 Empirical evidence on the determinants of changes in structural organizational variables[8]

4.4.1 Empirical evidence on the determinants of the adoption of organizational forms

In Chapter 1 we documented the existence of an extensive business history and management literature on organizational forms. We also claimed that the findings coming from this work were based mainly on case studies and anecdotal evidence. There are, however, a few quantitative papers that present econometric results on the determinants of the adoption of the M-form by large companies (for a definition of the M-form, see Box I.3 in the Introduction).

Thompson (1983) found that the diffusion of the M-form followed a symmetric sigmoid process and that early adopters were relatively more diversified and of greater size. Palmer *et al.* (1987, 1993) confirmed the importance of (product and geographic) diversification, and hence complexity of firm operations, but not of size which is only indirectly related, through complexity, to the adoption of a divisional structure. In addition, these studies pointed to the role played by both ownership status and imitation of firms that operated in the same line of business.

The imitation hypothesis, however, is still much debated. Whereas Mahajan *et al.* (1988) found no evidence of any imitation process for the adoption of the M-form within 127 very large US companies, Venkatraman *et al.* (1994), using the same data set, showed that the results reflected the role played by external influence (i.e. information outside the same line of business) instead of internal information (i.e. the number of firms that operated in the same line of business and had adopted the M-form). Finally Kogut and Parkinson (1998) found that imitation emerged as a (significant) explanatory variable of the diffusion process only if one extended the time of observation sufficiently – that is, if one analyzed history from the start.

4.4.2 Empirical evidence on the determinants of the "flattening" of the corporate hierarchy

In Chapter 1 we saw that since the 1980s firms, especially of large size, were becoming flatter, reducing the number of middle management positions and eliminating intermediate levels in their corporate hierarchy (see, in particular, Box I.4 in the Introduction and Section 1.3 in Chapter 1). They also increasingly decentralized decision authority down the corporate hierarchy. But why were firms doing so? In other words, what were the determinants of the flattening of hierarchies and the decentralization of decision power? And how general is this phenomenon across different types of firms (e.g. small as opposed to large firms), industries and countries?

So far, very few large-scale quantitative studies have addressed these issues. Most have focused on *delayering* – that is, the elimination of some managerial levels – and have tried to relate it to firm-specific (or establishment-specific) and industry-specific factors. The aim of this section is to survey these studies and to synthesize the empirical evidence they have provided (see Table 4.4).

First of all, as was shown in Chapter 3, most studies agree on the existence of a logarithmic relation between the *depth* and the *size* of organizations, measured by the number of employees. This stylized fact has a simple dynamic extension. When firms grow larger, they tend to add layers to their corporate hierarchy; when they downsize, reducing the workforce, they also reduce the number of hierarchical levels. For instance, Collins *et al.* (1999) showed that the change in the number of levels experienced by the manufacturing plants in their sample between the early 1970s and the early 1980s was positively associated with the percentage change in the number of their employees. Similarly, in Rajan and Wulf's (2006) panel data estimates, firm size turned out to be positively associated with organizational depth after controlling for a firm-specific fixed effect; this result indicates an increase (decrease) over time of the number of hierarchical levels when size grows (declines).

One may wonder whether or not this relation between employment growth and change of organizational depth is symmetric. Wang (2006) addressed this issue. He examined a large sample composed of both public firms and privately held firms with at least $10 million in revenues located in the US and observed over the period 1993–2003. He considered whether in a given year a firm had increased or decreased the number of hierarchical levels. He then split the available firm-year observations in two subsamples, according to whether in the previous year a firm had increased or decreased the number of employees. He found that in the growing firms subsample, the proportional growth in the number of employees in a given year was a significant predictor of the likelihood of an increase in the number of hierarchical levels in the subsequent year; similarly, the proportional decrease in the number of employees among declining firms was positively related to the likelihood of a decrease in the number of levels. However, the latter effect turned out to be much stronger than the former, indicating that downsizing of a firm's workforce had a more

Explanatory variable	Collins et al. (1999)	Ruigrok et al. (1999)	Whittington et al. (1999)	Caroli and Van Reenen (2001)	Brews and Tucci (2004)	Rajan and Wulf (2006)	Acemoglu et al. (2006)	Wang (2006)
No. of hierarchical levels	+							+
Size	−			+				−
Decline of size	+					+		+
Decline of size ×public company								−
Public company								+
Effective governance						n.s.		
Firm age							(+)	n.s.
R&D intensity		n.s.	n.s.			−		
Capital intensity								
Intensity of use of high-tech equipment	+[a]	n.s.	n.s.	+[b]				
International sales intensity		+	+	n.s.	+[c]			
Competitive pressures							+	
Local wage differential between highly educated and less educated workers				+				
Proportion of educated workers in region–industry				+				
Proximity to technological frontier							+[d]	
Heterogeneity of business environment							+[d]	

Notes

n.s. effect not significant.

+ positive effect.

(+) nearly positive effect.

− negative effect.

[a] Percentage of PA equipment out of total production capacity.

[b] Percentage of workers using computers and PA equipment.

[c] Depth of use of and operating performance associated with Internet communication technologies.

[d] Stronger evidence for IT-intensive firms.

fundamental impact on delayering than an increase of the workforce had on the addition of hierarchical levels.

Second, both Collins *et al.* (1999) and Wang (2006) found that a reduction in the number of hierarchical layers was more likely the greater the *depth* of the organization. In other words, all else equal, delayering seems to be more likely if firms have a more bureaucratic, less flat organization. Similarly, in their study of French establishments (see below) Caroli and Van Reenen (2001) found that the likelihood of delayering increased with establishment size (measured by the log of employment).[9]

Third, several studies considered the effects of *technological variables* on changes in the depth of organizations. Ruigrok *et al.* (1999) and Whittington *et al.* (1999) analyzed organizational changes that occurred between 1992 and 1996 in a large sample of European firms with more than 500 employees. In their estimates, the knowledge intensity of firms, measured by the ratio of R&D expenses to firm sales, had a positive, though statistically insignificant influence on the likelihood of delayering. Conversely, Rajan and Wulf (2006) showed that as firms became less capital-intensive over time, they also tended to become flatter. This finding is in line with the argument that a greater intensity in the knowledge-based intangible assets of firms' activities has led to a decrease over time in organizational depth.

Other studies that focused on PA technologies and ICTs found more compelling results. In particular, they generally supported the view that it was the increase in the extent of the use of computers in both production and administrative functions that allowed organizations to become flatter.[10] For instance, Collins *et al.* (1999) considered the percentage of plants' production capacity accounted for by PA equipment (i.e. CNC, robots, distributed process control, and automated material handling devices) and found that high-tech plants were also those where organizational depth had declined most. Caroli and Van Reenen (2001) showed that in their sample of French establishments the proportion of workers using high-tech equipment (i.e. robots, computers, and numerically controlled machines) was positively associated with the likelihood of delayering. More recently, Brews and Tucci (2004) analyzed the effect on delayering of the adoption of Internet-based advanced communication technologies. They examined an international sample composed of 469 firms, some managers of which participated in thirty executive training programs offered by five leading business schools. As a consequence of the sampling criteria, most of these firms were large, well-established, multinational enterprises.

The reduction in the number of hierarchical levels of sample firms was captured through a qualitative categorical index. This index was regressed against a composite Internet depth index measuring both reach and richness in Internet use by firms, and a variable that reflected operating performance ratings assigned by firm managers to the use of the Internet. Both Internet-related explanatory variables were positively and significantly associated with hierarchy reduction, even though the amount of explained variance of the dependent variable was fairly low (7%).

Fourth, specific attention has been given by the empirical literature to the effect of *competition*. The argument here is that greater competitive pressures connected with the globalization of markets and the entry of new players have increasingly forced firms to eliminate (allegedly unnecessary) intermediate managerial levels. Unfortunately, the evidence on this issue is far from robust. For instance, in Ruigrok *et al.*'s (1999) study, firms' openness to international (and allegedly more competitive) markets, proxied by the ratio of sales abroad to total sales, was unrelated to delayering. Conversely, an index capturing the perception by firm managers of greater competitive pressures had a strong positive association with delayering. Measures of market competition were included in the set of controls by both Caroli and Van Reenen (2001) and Acemoglu *et al.* (2006):[11] the results were ambiguous. In the former study these measures failed to exhibit any explanatory power of the likelihood of delayering. In the latter one, the Lerner index (i.e. a proxy for price–cost margins calculated as the ratio of gross operating profits to sales) was found to be negatively and significantly associated with delayering.

If delayering is explained by adoption by firms' top managers of a behavior more in line with the creation of shareholder value because of competitive pressures, improvements in corporate governance should have a similar effect. However, Rajan and Wulf (2006) found no evidence of a positive relation between adoption by firms of more effective governance and a reduction in organizational depth.[12]

The role of *ownership status* was more thoroughly analyzed by Wang (2006). He distinguished public firms from privately held ones and argued that the former were more sensitive to institutional pressures, making them more likely to conform to normative practices and indulge in herding behavior. In accordance with this view, public firms were far more likely than private ones to change the number of hierarchical levels in either direction. Moreover, after controlling for the lagged number of levels, the effect of firm size on changes in the depth of the organization was found to be contingent on ownership status. More precisely, larger firms were more likely to decrease their number of levels if they were privately held, while no such effect was detected for public firms. Similarly, the positive effect of a size increase on the likelihood of an increase in organizational depth mentioned earlier was again confined to private firms.

Two recent studies on the determinants of delayering deserve special mention. In accordance with the skill-biased organizational change theory, Caroli and Van Reenen (2001) examined the influence exerted on the reduction in organizational depth by the decrease in the relative cost of skilled workers. Data were provided by the 1992 wave of the ER survey conducted in French in 1992 and by the ESE establishments-level survey of employment structure. In the ER survey senior managers of a nationally representative sample composed of about 2,500 establishments in all sectors of the economy were asked whether in the previous three years one or more hierarchical levels in their establishments had been removed (or were in the process of being removed); affirmative answers proxied delayering. About half of the ER establishments were matched to ESE establishments. Estimates of the determinants of delayering were run on this reduced sample of establishments. The delayering dummy variable was regressed against the difference in mean log hourly wage in the region where an establishment was located between highly educated and less educated individuals,[13] after taking into account several controls (e.g. establishment size, extent of use of computers by the establishment's workforce, level of competition faced by the establishment). This explanatory variable exhibited a negative statistically significant coefficient in the estimates. Similarly, when this variable was replaced by the proportion of educated workers in the region–industry cell of sample establishments, this latter variable exhibited a positive statistically significant coefficient. The authors concluded that the abundant availability of cheap skilled labor in the local market was an important inducement of delayering.

Acemoglu *et al.* (2006) relied on data provided by the 1998 wave of the ER survey. The question on delayering captured whether in sample establishments there had been any reduction in the number of hierarchical levels between 1996 and 1998. The ER sample was matched with the FUTE data set which contains the entire population of French firms with more than twenty employees. The matching procedure provided a data set of about 2,200 establishments. However, the estimates were run on data relating to a subsample of establishments that were part of larger groups. The key argument in this study is that delayering is closely associated with the decentralization of decision-making processes (on this issue see Chapter 2). It is thus induced by the need of firms' top managers to rely on the proprietary individual knowledge dispersed in the firm, and their inability to learn from the experience of other firms regarding the implementation of new technologies. In accordance with this argument, the authors focused attention on two explanatory variables:

- the *proximity of firms to the technological frontier*. This is inversely measured by the gap between the log labor productivity of a firm and the frontier log labor productivity in the primary four-digit industry of the firm (see Section 2.3 in Chapter 2 for further details on these measures)
- the *heterogeneity of the business environment* in which firms operate. Heterogeneity is captured by three variables: (i) the dispersion of firms' productivity growth within a four-digit industry; (ii) a similar indicator based on productivity levels, and (iii) an index capturing how many close neighbors a firm has in the product market space (i.e. an inverse proxy of heterogeneity)[14]

The authors also considered firm age through a series of dummies. The idea here was that younger firms cannot capitalize on learning-by-doing for the implementation of new technologies, and are thus more likely to delegate decision authority and reduce the number of hierarchical layers.

The results of the estimates indicated that the likelihood of delayering was significantly greater the more heterogenous the business environment of firms and the closer they were to the technological frontier. The evidence was considerably stronger for the subsample of IT-intensive firms. Conversely, age turned out to have a modest influence on delayering; only the dummy indicating firms less than five years old exhibited a positive statistically significant coefficient. Moreover, contrary to theoretical predictions, this result was more robust for low-tech than high-tech firms, with all age dummies being insignificant in the estimates relating to the high-tech subsample.[15]

4.4.3   Evidence on the determinants of organizational dynamics based on the new empirical methodology[16]

In this section we provide quantitative evidence on the determinants of organizational dynamics. By using our empirical methodology (see Chapter 1 and the Appendix to this book) we are able to test econometrically the determinants of changes in organizational depth on a sample of Italian manufacturing plants observed for a very long period of time (more than twenty years, the period 1975–96). More precisely, we specify and test a duration model of the likelihood of an individual plant changing the number of hierarchical levels after a spell *t*, provided that no change has occurred up to *t*.

4.4.3.1   *Specification of the econometric models**

The empirical results rely on the estimates of two duration data econometric models. Such models aim to analyze the factors that drive changes in the number of layers of the corporate hierarchy of sample plants, and the direction of such changes (that is, expansions are distinguished from contractions of the corporate hierarchy).

Modeling organizational change

The first econometric model aims to model the spell needed for a change in the number of hierarchical levels to occur; that is, the model is specified in terms of duration τ, the dependent variable, of a plant not changing its organizational depth. The basic tool for modeling duration data is the hazard function $h(\cdot)$, which may be viewed as the instantaneous probability of turning to a different corporate hierarchy at τ, provided that no change has occurred by τ:

$$h(\tau, \chi_i, \theta) = \lim_{\Delta \downarrow 0} \frac{P\left[T < \tau + \Delta \mid T \geq \tau, \chi_i, \theta\right]}{\Delta} \tag{1}$$

with T being a random variable indicating the spell needed for organizational change to occur for the *i*th observation. The hazard function depends on the duration τ, a set of explanatory variables x, and the unknown parameter vector θ, which is supposed to be the same for all observations.

In order to specify the model, one should consider the following two limitations of the data set. First, for sample plants that changed the number of hierarchical levels twice or more between 1975 and

1996 the available data relate to the period that starts in the year following the organizational change before the last one and ends in 1996. Second, for the remaining plants, we do not have any information prior to 1975. Therefore, the observation of such plants is left-censored.

The usual way of dealing with left-censoring problems (see Andersen *et al.* 1993) would be to estimate the unobserved date of the last organizational change that occurred before the observation period.[17] However, this was not possible as we had no information on sample plants before 1975 and the hazard rate was unlikely to be constant over time, due to both the presence of time-dependent covariates and possible duration dependence. What we did know is that such date is between t_j^E, plant j's year of foundation, and 1975. In addition, should a plant not have changed the number of hierarchical levels from the year of establishment up to 1975, it would be natural to compute the time spell from t_j^E.

Relying on such considerations, we proceeded to determine the duration origin. For plants that did not change the number of hierarchical layers during the entire observation period the origin was initially assumed to coincide with the maximum (say t_0) between the plant's year of foundation t_j^E and 1975. Observations of plants that changed organizational structure only once were divided into two intervals: the first period of observation goes from t_0 to the date of the first organizational change (t_1), while the time span of the second interval is delimited by t_1 and 1996. Lastly, observations of plants that changed twice or more times, and thus are left-uncensored, were divided into two intervals: the first period starts with the year that follows the organizational change before the last one and ends with the date of the last change (t_2); the time spell of the second interval is delimited by t_2 and 1996. The three cases are illustrated in greater detail in the Appendix to this chapter. Then, we recalculated the time spell after replacing t_0 with t_j^E and repeated the estimates. This means that in this latter case plants that were in operation before 1975 (and did not change the number of levels more than once in the 1975–96 period) were assumed to have maintained the number of levels constant from the date of establishment up to 1975.[18] Note that with the first method we underestimate the duration of no change in organizational depth, whereas with the second one we overestimate it. What is important to emphasize here is that the econometric results proved to be robust with respect to the choice of the (unobserved) duration origins.

Under the above assumptions, the log-likelihood function $L(\boldsymbol{\theta})$ can be written in terms of the hazard rate, as follows (Cox and Oakes 1984; Kiefer 1988, p. 671):

$$L(\boldsymbol{\theta}) = \sum_i d_i \ln\{h[\tau_i, \boldsymbol{\chi}_i(\tau_i), \boldsymbol{\theta}]\} - \sum_i \int_0^{\tau_i} h[u, \boldsymbol{\chi}_i(u), \boldsymbol{\theta}] du \qquad (2)$$

with d_i being a dummy variable that indicates right-uncensored observations. Such observations coincide with plants that changed organizational depth between 1975 and 1996 when they are observed in the first interval out of the two into which the observation period has been divided. The set of right-censored duration observations comprises: (a) plants that stayed with the same organizational depth in the whole period under scrutiny; (b) plants that changed organizational depth and are observed in the second interval of observation – that is, after the year in which the last change in organizational depth occurred.

In order to estimate (2) a functional form allowing for duration dependence must be chosen for the hazard function. Following work on technology adoption (see Karshenas and Stoneman 1993; Colombo and Mosconi 1995), we assumed $h(\cdot)$ to be Weibull:[19]

$$h[\tau, \boldsymbol{\chi}_{i\tau}, \boldsymbol{\theta} \neq (p, \boldsymbol{\beta})] = hp(h\tau)^{p-1}, \qquad h = e^{\boldsymbol{\chi}'_{i\tau}\boldsymbol{\beta}} \qquad (3)$$

where p is the parameter that rules duration dependence. When p equals one, there is no duration dependence; when it is greater than one there is positive duration dependence, while a negative duration dependence arises when p is smaller than unity. The effects of the covariates included in vector $\boldsymbol{x}$ are accounted for by the parameter vector $\boldsymbol{\beta}$. Note that (3) is an accelerated lifetime model, with the effect of the explanatory variables being to rescale duration (see Kiefer 1988, p. 669).

Modeling contraction and expansion
of the managerial hierarchy

In order to distinguish contractions and expansions of the corporate hierarchy we resorted to the literature on competing risks (see Kalbfleisch and Prentice 1980, Lancaster 1990); increases and decreases in the number of hierarchical levels were considered as multiple destinations. Let $h^k(\cdot)$, $k = E,C$, denote a cause-specific hazard function, with superscript E indicating expansion of the number of layers and superscript C contraction. The dummy variables D^k, $k = E,C$, equal one if failure is of type k. If one assumes that the hazard rates of expanding ($h^E(\cdot)$) and shrinking ($h^C(\cdot)$) the corporate hierarchy do not depend on the nature and time of previous changes in organizational depth, it results that:

$$h^k(\tau,\chi_i,\boldsymbol{\theta^k}) = \lim_{\Delta \downarrow 0} \frac{P\left[T<\tau + \Delta, D^k = 1 | T \geq \tau, \chi_i, \boldsymbol{\theta^k}\right]}{\Delta}, \qquad k = E,C. \qquad (4)$$

$h^k(.)$ can be interpreted as the instantaneous rate for failure of type k, $k = E,C$, occurring after a spell τ given x and in the presence of the other failure type. It results that: $h(\cdot) = h^E(\cdot)+h^C(\cdot)$. Under the above assumption the likelihood function factors into a separate component for each failure type. Therefore, we obtain the two following log-likelihood functions $L^k(\boldsymbol{\theta^k})$:

$$L^k(\boldsymbol{\theta^k}) = \sum_i d_i^k\{h^k[\tau_i^k,\mathbf{x}_i(\tau_i^k),\boldsymbol{\theta^k}]\} - \sum_i \int_0^{\tau_i^k} h^k[u,\mathbf{x}_i(u),\boldsymbol{\theta^k}]du, \quad k = E,C, \qquad (5)$$

with d_i^k being two dummy variables that indicate right-uncensored observations – that is, observations for which an increase ($k = E$) or a decrease ($k = C$) of the number of layers occurred at duration τ_i^k. Such observations coincide with plants that augmented ($d_i^E = 1$) or reduced ($d_i^C = 1$) the depth of the corporate hierarchy between 1975 and 1996 when they are observed in the first interval out of the two into which the observation period is divided. The set of right-censored duration observations, for which $d_i^k = 0$, $k = E,C$, comprises: (i) plants that did not increase ($k = E$) or decrease ($k = C$) the number of tiers in the whole period under scrutiny; (ii) plants that did expand ($k = E$) or shrink ($k = C$) the hierarchy when they are observed in the second interval of observation – that is, after the year in which the increase ($k = E$) or the decrease ($k = C$) occurred.

Again we assumed $h^k(\cdot)$ to be Weibull:

$$h^k[\tau,\chi_{i\tau},\boldsymbol{\theta^k}\equiv(p^k,\boldsymbol{\beta^k})] = h^k p^k (h^k \tau)^{p^k-1}, \qquad h^k = e^{\mathbf{x'}_{i\tau}\boldsymbol{\beta^k}} \qquad (6)$$

4.4.3.2 Explanatory variables*

In order to test the predictions of economic theory as to the determinants of change in organizational depth, we considered variables that, in accordance with the conceptual framework presented in Section 4.2, reflect the following factors:

- factors that increase the need to change
- factors that oppose organizational change
- factors that control for other plant-, firm-, and industry-specific effects.

In particular, for factors that increase the need to change the number of hierarchical levels we considered the effects of complementarities with organizational (both IWPs and HRMPs) and technological (PA) innovations. The second group, aimed at reflecting forces that oppose organizational change, is composed of measures of sunk costs (of organizational change) and of influence activities within sample plants. Finally, we introduce plant- (i.e. number of levels, size), firm- (ownership status, age), and industry- (growth, competition, technological intensity) specific control variables.

In Table 4.5 we report the definition of the explanatory variables (for a more detailed illustration and a discussion of their expected effects, see the Appendix to this chapter).

Table 4.5   Explanatory variables of change in organizational depth

Variables[a]	Description
$DAMT1,2,3,4_t$	1 for plants that by year $t-1$ have adopted 1,2,3,4 AMTs[b] respectively; 0 otherwise
$Team_t$	1 for plants that by year t-1 have adopted formal team practices; 0 otherwise
$Rotation_t$	1 for plants that by year t-1 have adopted job rotation; 0 otherwise
$Incentive_t$	1 for plants that by year t-1 have adopted non traditional individual line incentives (pay for quality and skills); 0 otherwise
$Line_t$	1 for plants involved in line production of a limited number of standardized designs; 0 for plants characterized by job-shop operations
$Owner_t$	1 for plants owned by a single-plant firm in which the decision on the plant's organizational structure is taken by the firm's owner–manager; 0 otherwise
$Powerowner_t$	Proportion of plant's strategic decisions taken by the firm's owner-manager
$External_t$	1 for plants owned by a multi-plant company in which the decision on the plant's organizational chart is taken by corporate officers outside the plant; 0 otherwise

Variables[a]	Description
$Level_t$	No. of hierarchical levels of plant's organization
Size	Logarithm of the number of plant's employees in 1989
ΔSize	Percentage growth rate of the number of plant employees between 1989 and 1996
Age_t	Plant age
I-Growth	Industry growth rate (three-digit NACE–CLIO classification), in 1981–91
R&D	Proportion of R&D employees to total sector employment (two-digit NACE–CLIO classification) in 1994
Herfindahl	Herfindahl concentration index (three-digit NACE–CLIO classification) in 1991

Notes

[a] The subscript t indicates time-varying variables.

[b] AMTs: machining centers, programmable robots, NC or CNC stand-alone machine tools, and FMS. See description in the Appendix of the book.

4.4.3.3   Econometric results*

Table 4.6 synthesizes the results of the econometric analysis (the results of the estimates are fully reported in the Appendix to this chapter, Tables 4.A1–4.A4). In particular, we estimated two Weibull duration models. In both, the dependent variable was the time spell needed for a change (either an increase or a decrease) in the number of layers of a plant's hierarchy to occur. In Model I (Table 4.A1) we dealt with left-censoring problems by defining the starting value of the dependent variable as the maximum between the year of plant's foundation and 1975, while in Model II we calculated the time spell after replacing its starting value with the year of the plant's foundation (or 1947 for plants founded before the Second World War). Results do not change from one model to the other, except for duration dependence which is positive in the first model and null in the second. In the following we concentrate on the results of Model I, that are synthesized in Table 4.6.

The results of the econometric estimates are robust and are generally in line with the predictions of the conceptual model illustrated in Section 4.2. In order to assess the joint contribution of the explanatory variables to the fit of the models, we proceeded to run χ^2 tests (reported at the bottom of Table 4.A1) for the joint hypothesis that all coefficients apart from the constant are equal to zero (see Kiefer 1988, p. 674). The tests are equal to 174.27 for Model I and 278.43 for Model II, showing that overall independent variables are highly significant. We also computed the generalized residuals e_i of

Table 4.6 Determinants of change in organizational depth: results of the econometric models

Variables	Change of the organizational depth	Expansion of the organizational depth	Contraction of the organizational depth
DAMT1	+++	+++	n.s.
DAMT2	+++	+++	+++ (DAMT2 > DAMT1)
DAMT3	+++ (DAMT3 > DAMT2, DAMT1)	+++	+++ (DAMT3 > DAMT1)
DAMT4	+++ (DAMT4 > DAMT3, DAMT2, DAMT1)	++	+++ (DAMT4 > DAMT3, DAMT2, DAMT1)
Team	+++	++	+++
Rotation	++	++	+
Incentive	n.s.	n.s.	n.s.
Line	− −	−	n.s.
Owner	− − −	−	n.s.
Powerowner	++	+	n.s.
External	n.s.	n.s.	n.s.
Level	+++	− − −	+++
Size	n.s.	n.s.	n.s.
ΔSize		++	n.s.
Age	n.s.	n.s.	n.s.
I-Growth	++	n.s.	n.s.
R&D	n.s.	n.s.	n.s.
Herfindahl	−	n.s.	−

Notes
n.s. effect not significant.
+/− Sign positive/negative and significant at 10%.
++/− − Sign positive/negative and significant at 5%.
+++/− − − Sign positive/negative and significant at 1%.

both models. If the model is correctly specified the e_i are a right-censored sample of a unite exponential variate. Their survivor function can be estimated at each uncensored value by the Kaplan–Meyer method. The minus log of the residual survivor function at point e_i should lie approximately on a 45 degree line (see Lancaster 1990, p. 308). Plots of the value of such a function against the e_i relating to Models I and II highlight a concave function. With an exponential model, such concavity would be indicative of neglected heterogeneity (see again Lancaster 1990, pp. 309–10); however, such a result does not generalize to other models. While in Model I parameter p turned out to be significantly greater than unity, in Model II the null hypothesis that $p = 0$ could not be rejected (see Table 4.A1), with the Weibull function becoming exponential. Therefore we re-ran the models by allowing for heterogeneity (see Greene 2003). Results of the estimates have been omitted for the sake of synthesis. They show that parameter θ is significant, thus confirming the presence of heterogeneity. However, the values of the estimated coefficients are very close to those presented in Table 4.A1.[20]

Before addressing the role played by factors that increase the need for or oppose organizational change, let us consider other plant-, firm-, and industry-specific explanatory variables.

First, *Size* fails to register any additional significant impact upon the likelihood of a plant changing its organizational depth once we consider the characteristics of the plant's organization (notably, the number of levels of the corporate hierarchy). *Age* displays a positive coefficient, even if it fails to register any significant explanatory power. As all sampled plants are at least three years old, such a result suggests that should young organizations suffer from organizational instability such an effect would rapidly vanish over time.

Turning to industry-specific variables, they overall display a significant impact on change in organizational depth, with the coefficient of *I-Growth*, *R&D*, and *Herfindahl* being jointly significant at conventional levels (see the LR-tests at the bottom of Table 4.A1). In particular, in industries that are expanding, changes in organizational depth are more likely to occur than in declining industries, with the coefficient of *I-Growth* being positive and significant. In addition, the negative (weakly significant) sign of *Herfindahl* highlights that, as was expected, industry concentration may favor structural inertia. The estimates fail, however, to support the view that a higher scientific base induces more change, as the coefficient of *R&D*, though positive, is insignificant.

As to the complexity of a plant's organization, this turns out to be positively related to changes in organizational depth, with the coefficient of *Level* being positive and significant at the 1% level. This result contrasts with predictions of organizational ecology theory, confirming instead the evidence mentioned in Section 4.4.2.

Next, let us focus attention on the adoption of PA technologies and new organizational practices. Technology variables overall display considerable explanatory power, as is witnessed by the value of the LR-test of joint significance. The coefficients of the dummy variables

DAMT1, DAMT2, DAMT3, and *DAMT4* are all positive and statistically significant at 1%. Even more interestingly, these results show that the higher the intensity of use of AMTs, the larger the impact on the likelihood of changes in the number of hierarchical levels. This evidence is further confirmed by the Wald-tests (see Table 4.A2), which demonstrate that the increasing magnitude of the effect of adoption of multiple PA technologies on the likelihood of a change in organizational depth is statistically significant in almost all cases: the larger the number of PA technologies in use, the higher the probability of changing the organizational depth. Such result points to the complementarity between the adoption of PA technologies and consequent changes in organizational design. Lastly, the results on new organizational practices (both IWPs and HRMPs) confirm the predictions that the corporate hierarchy often changes with the introduction of other organizational innovations. The coefficients of *Incentive, Team,* and *Rotation* are positive, with the last two being significant at conventional levels.[21]

The result of the variable *Line*, which has a negative and significant (at 5%) coefficient, suggests that sunk costs are key in explaining structural inertia. Given that (i) plants whose layout of production is in line incur in high sunk costs when changing their organizational design and (ii) the decision on organizational change implies uncertain returns, then in accordance with real option theory (Dixit and Pindyck 1994) it may be rational for a plant's management to postpone any change until new information is collected. This in turn leads to the detected inertial process.

Let us now turn to variables reflecting the allocation of decision-making. They overall display a significant impact on the likelihood of changing the organizational chart (see again the LR-tests at the bottom of Table 4.A1). Contrary to expectations, the variable *External*, which indicates plants in which decisions relating to plant's organizational design are taken by corporate officers outside the plant, has a negative though statistically insignificant coefficient in the estimates; this possibly suggest that, all else being equal, the proximity of a plant's employees to the decision-maker does not influence organizational change when the decision-maker is a salaried manager. Instead, the variables *Owner* and *Powerowner* are significant at conventional levels. As was expected, plants owned by a single-plant firm where the owner–manager is in charge of decisions relating to the plant's organizational chart are most likely to be characterized by structural inertia: the coefficient of *Owner* is negative and significant at the 1% level. In addition, the negative effect of *Owner* on the likelihood of change decreases with the extent to which authority over strategic decisions is centralized in the owner–manager's hands, as is apparent from the positive, statistically significant (at 5%) coefficient of *Powerowner*. In other words, the more centralized is decision-making in owner-managed plants, the more likely is organizational change. Such evidence clearly provides support for the role played by influence activities in inhibiting organizational change. Agents are very likely to try to influence the decisions of the principal so as to defend or augment their personal quasi-rents, especially when (i) the principal is endowed with discretionary decision power, a condition which distinguishes situations where the owner–manager is in charge of decisions relating to a plant's hierarchy from those where responsibility for such decisions is delegated to a salaried manager, and (ii) influence activities are likely to be successful; this in turn is signaled by the fact that the owner–manager partially allocates authority over strategic decisions to lower levels, even though she keeps authority over decisions as to the depth of the corporate hierarchy. If the negative coefficient of *Owner* were to be explained by psychological motivations connected with the aversion of owner–managers towards organizational changes which often imply a delegation of decision-making authority to salaried managers, then *Powerowner* should display a negative coefficient, as very autocratic owners would likely be most resistant to organizational change. Such an argument is not supported by our findings.

A further inquiry on the direction of organizational dynamics

We also analyzed the direction of changes in organizational depth and its determinants (see again Table 4.6 and Models III and IV in Table 4.A3).

(a) The determinants of the expansion of organizational depth For the determinants of the expansion of the depth of the corporate hierarchy, the adoption of PA technologies still plays a key role, with the coefficients of *DAMT1*, *DAMT2*, *DAMT3*, and *DAMT4* being positive and significant at conventional levels. The same holds true for new organizational practices: the coefficients of *Rotation* and *Team* are positive and significant at 5%, while that of *Incentive* is insignificant. Such findings are congruent

with the theoretical model by Qian (1994), according to which productivity increases due to the introduction of process and organizational
innovations will result in an increase of the number of hierarchical layers.
Note, however, that the previously detected increasing magnitude of the
impact of the adoption of multiple PA technologies upon organizational
change does not show up when one focuses on the expansion of the corporate hierarchy: the results of Wald-tests (see Table 4.A4) show that the
differences between the coefficients of the AMT variables are insignificant. Nor is there any additional effect connected with the introduction
of several new organizational practices, as was the case in Model I.

Turning to the remaining organizational variables, their effects on
the likelihood of a plant increasing the number of levels are similar to
those highlighted in the previous section. In particular, sunk costs
inhibit the expansion of the corporate hierarchy, with the coefficient
of *Line* being negative and significant at 5%. Decision variables display
a similarly significant role, supporting predictions based on influence
costs. Plants where the owner–manager keeps authority over decisions
relating to the organizational chart but decentralizes other more technical decisions are less inclined towards introducing new hierarchical
layers than plants in which responsibility for the former decisions is
allocated to the plant manager. Instead, there seems to be no difference according to whether the plant manager or an external salaried
manager is in charge of such decisions. Finally, as one might expect,
organizations characterized by a large number of levels are less prone
to further enlarge their structure: the coefficient of *Level* is negative
and significant at 1%.

Industry- and other plant-specific variables generally are insignificant
at conventional levels; the only exception is $\Delta Size$ which has a positive
coefficient, significant at 5%. Such a result indicates that, quite unsurprisingly, growing plants (in terms of employment) often tend to
increase the depth of the corporate hierarchy, thus confirming dynamically the positive relation between number of employees and number of
hierarchical layers highlighted in Chapter 3.

(b) The determinants of the contraction of the organizational depth Let us
now consider the determinants of the shrinking of the corporate hierarchy (i.e. delayering). The introduction of PA technologies significantly
impacts upon such organizational change. Even more interestingly,
unlike the expansion of organizational depth, technological complementarities turn out to play a key role in the reduction of the depth of
the corporate hierarchy. In this case, the results of Wald-tests (reported
in Table 4.A4), show that the magnitude of the impact of AMTs on a

hierarchy's downscaling increases with the number of AMTs in use. If one adds results relating to new organizational practices which have the expected positive coefficient and are jointly significant at 1%, then we may say that the adoption by firms of a flatter organizational design[22] has been driven to a substantial extent by the adoption of a bundle of technological and organizational innovations. Such findings confirm both the predictions of theoretical work concerned with complementarities between technological and organizational changes (see Milgrom and Roberts 1990b) and earlier empirical evidence on this issue (Colombo and Mosconi 1995). Moreover, evidence provided by the variable *ΔSize*, whose coefficient is insignificant, highlights the fact that delayering is not determined a by company downsizing.

Turning to the other organizational variables, results generally are less strong. *Level* has a positive, highly significant coefficient: quite unsurprisingly, it is fatter organizations characterized by a complex hierarchy that are relatively more likely to reduce the number of layers. *Line* has a negative but insignificant coefficient. Decision variables are jointly insignificant. In particular, the coefficients of *Owner* and *Pownerowner* maintain their expected (negative and positive, respectively) signs; however, the null hypotheses cannot be rejected. Overall, such findings seem to suggest that the likelihood of shrinking the corporate hierarchy is less sensitive to the allocation of the decision authority of plants than the likelihood of expanding it.

Lastly, let us consider control variables. None of the plant-specific control variables introduced into the models (*Size* and *Age* in addition to *ΔSize*) displays any significant explanatory power. Contrary to expansion of the corporate hierarchy, industry-specific variables do exhibit a significant impact upon the shrinking of plant organization: they are shown to be jointly significant at conventional levels by an LR-test. In particular, plants that operate in less competitive markets tend to be less inclined to delayer.

4.4.3.4 A synthesis

In this section we considered changes in organizational depth and tested the predictions of economic theory for a sample composed of 438 Italian manufacturing plants (see Chapter 1 and the Appendix of this book) through the estimates of several duration models. The empirical results can be synthesized as follows (see Table 4.7).

First, organizational dynamics is characterized by an inertial process. In this regard, we showed that the existence of *sunk costs* and the extent

Table 4.7   Evidence on organizational dynamics

Variables	Detected effect on organizational change	Comments
Variation in size	+/n.s.	Positive relation with the expansion but not the contraction of the corporate hierarchy
Industry- specific variables: R&D intensity, growth rate, concentration	+/−	Positive relation with industry growth, negative with concentration, no effect of technological environment
Size	n.s.	No detected relation
Technological innovations (PA)	+	Strong effects of PA production technologies; key role of complementarities, especially for delayering
New organizational practices (HRMPs and IWPs)	+	Co-evolution of different dimensions of organizational design
Sunk costs	−	Tangible and intangible sunk costs hinder organizational change
Influence activity	−	Influence activity of workers strongly opposes organizational change

Notes
+ positive effect.
− negative effect.
n.s. effect not significant.

of *influence activities* within a plant were important determinants of structural inertia, opposing organizational change.

On the one hand, plants that adhere to a Tayloristic organization of production turn out to change the number of hierarchical levels (especially to increase it) more rarely than those characterized by job-shop operations; the reason may be that in the former plants such changes involve substantially greater sunk costs, due to the rigid specialization of the tasks performed by workers, the formal codification of procedures, and the formal definition of authority relations and communication flows. Of course, there may be other sources of sunk costs in organizations – associated, for instance, with the specificity of physical assets or the irrecoverable nature of investments in human capital. The findings illustrated in this section suggest that it may be worthwhile investigating their effects on the persistence of the organizational design of firms.

On the other hand, our findings show that the allocation of decision authority has a considerable impact on the likelihood of changes in organizational depth. Independent family-owned plants where it is up to the owner–manager to modify the plant's organizational chart are more resistant to changes in the depth of the organization than the remaining plants – that is, both independent plants where such responsibility is allocated to the plant manager and plants that belong to multi-unit firms. In the former plants the owner–manager is generally quite close to the plant's employees, unlike the salaried middle-manager of a multi-unit organization who works outside the production unit under consideration; in addition, the owner–manager has a rather discretionary decision power in the sense that her decisions are not limited by the existence of formal procedures, a situation typical of a salaried manager. Among independent plants where the owner–manager is directly in charge of modifying the number of hierarchical levels, the most resilient ones turn out to be those where strategic decisions relating to other aspects – such as the introduction of new technologies or the purchase of new capital equipment – are delegated by the owner–manager down the corporate hierarchy. In plants with a very autocratic owner–manager who centralizes decision-making in her own hands, modifications of the organizational chart are relatively more frequent. Such results are easily interpreted in the light of the theoretical contributions on influence costs. Following Schaefer (1998), in owner-managed plants the centralization of decision-making may be interpreted as signaling the difficulty for a plant's employees to affect the outcome of the decisions of the owner–manager. Under such circumstances, incentives for them to indulge in influence activities are weak. On the contrary, incentives will be stronger if the owner–manager has the reputation of taking into account the opinion of others, a situation which is more likely if decision authority is assigned at least partially to subordinates. It is worth emphasizing that our findings cannot simply be explained by psychological motivations which trace back structural inertia to the aversion of the owner–manager of a family business to delegate power to subordinates. Such reasoning especially applies to the evidence that autocratic owner–managers are relatively more likely than democratic ones to introduce new hierarchical layers, a move which usually implies delegating (some) decision authority to subordinates.

Second, adoption of AMTs associated with the PA paradigm and new organizational practices such as job rotation, team work, and non-traditional incentive-based payment schemes (i.e. pay for quality and skills), figure prominently in explaining the likelihood of changes in organizational depth. This holds true for both expansions and contractions of the corporate hierarchy. In addition, when one focuses attention on the likelihood of delayering, there are cumulative effects due to the adoption of PA technologies, with the likelihood of reducing the depth of the hierarchy rapidly increasing with the extent of the use of these technologies. Altogether, such results provide clear support to the argument that the use of PA technologies, recourse to innovative organizational practices, and changes in the structural dimensions of organizational design are characterized by strong complementarities: they are highly profitable only if they are all carried out together (for a confirmation of such reasoning see Chapter 5, in particular Section 5.5).

Third, in contrast to the predictions of ecological organization theory, the econometric estimates confirm the anecdotal evidence provided by the managerial literature that in the 1980s and 1990s bureaucratic organizations characterized by a large number of hierarchical levels were more prone to changes in organizational depth, generally implying the adoption of a flatter organization, than plants having a simpler hierarchy. Such effect is on top of the effect determined by corporate downsizing; nor it can be explained by industry-specific effects connected with the restructuring of mature, capital-intensive, and highly concentrated industries, dominated by bureaucratic organizations.

Lastly, for industry-specific effects, growth and competition have been found to stimulate changes in organizational depth, as firms struggle to adapt to changing business conditions.

4.5   Concluding remarks

This chapter aimed to analyze the factors that favor or hinder changes in organizational design. More precisely, we considered a broad notion of organizational dynamics including both adoption of new organizational practices and changes of the structural dimensions of organizations (notably the number of hierarchical levels). First, we presented the findings of the empirical literature on this issue; then we illustrated the results of the estimates of duration models of the likelihood of an organization changing its depth based on the data set on Italian manufacturing plants described in Chapter 1.

For organizational practices, we encountered several methodological problems. First of all, there is no general consensus about the notion of practices (see also Chapter 1). Some studies exclusively focus on practices that modify how work is performed (i.e. IWPs), other studies include in their definition HRMPs relating to incentive-based compensation schemes, training, and recruitment. Other authors further extend the scope of the analysis to changes in organizational design involving the flattening of the managerial hierarchy (i.e. delayering) and the assignment of decision authority to subordinates. Second, there is heterogeneity across studies that examine the diffusion of organizational practices as to the industries and firm size classes that are the target of the analysis, and the indicators used to measure diffusion. As was emphasized in Chapter 1, this makes international comparisons of diffusion levels, and of the determinants of diffusion speed, rather difficult. Lastly, long longitudinal data sets on the adoption of new practices are very rare, and they are often confined to specific industries (e.g. the data collected by Ichniowski and his colleagues on the steel industry).

In spite of the above shortcomings, this body of literature has highlighted some interesting regularities relating to the determinants of the adoption of new organizational practices. These stylized facts are consistent with the view that there are substantial differences across firms as to both the additional operating revenues that are reaped by use of these practices and the extent of their adoption costs. In turn, these differences explain differences in the speed of adoption. The key findings can be summarized as follows.

- In almost all studies the likelihood of adoption of new organizational practices increases with *firm size*. In fact, large firms are those that are likely to suffer most from lack of flexibility, slow response, and inadequate involvement of the workforce. These practices are indeed designed to deal with these weaknesses.

- Adoption of IWPs and HRMPs is also more likely for firms that have *complex production processes* and exhibit a *rapid rate of introduction of new products*. In fact, for these firms it is very important to be able to take advantage of the specific skills and tacit knowledge possessed by line workers.

- IWPs and HRMPs tend to be *adopted in bundles*. In other words, firms either adopt several of them or do not adopt them at all. Moreover, the use of these organizational practices is often associated with changes in organizational design leading to a flatter, more decentralized organization. Even though it is almost impossible to be sure that this pattern of adoption is not determined by unobserved heterogeneity alone, it is generally interpreted as a signal of the existence of complementarities between these organizational innovations.

- Several authors contend that these complementarities extend to the adoption of PA technologies and advanced ICTs. Nonetheless, it is fair to recognize that the evidence on this issue is far from conclusive (on this issue see also Chapter 5, Section 5.5).

- There is great *persistence in* the use of organizational practices. In all econometric models that attempted to explain the extent of adoption of IWPs and HRMPs, the coefficient of the lagged dependent variable is positive and statistically significant, with its value being close to unity. This evidence is interpreted as documenting the high adjustment costs involved in the adoption of these practices. For one thing, sizable investments are generally tied up with a specific bundle of organizational practices. The associated sunk costs prevent radical organizational changes which would diminish the value of these investments. The fact that the benefits of new practices are reaped only when several complementary practices are used in combination also helps explain the persistence of firms' organizational choices. Moreover, because of the routinized behavior of individuals (Nelson and Winter 1982; Cohen *et al.* 1996), in order for the new organizational practices to be operated efficiently firms' managers and production workers need first to unlearn the old practices and then to become skilled in the new ones. This learning requires commitment of personal firm-specific investments. The risk therefore arises of managers and workers being entrenched in an old organizational model and reluctant to embrace a new one, even though the latter is far more efficient.

- Adjustment costs are consistently shown to be higher in firms that have an *older, less educated workforce*. In fact, for these individuals learning new practices is more difficult and the rewards from the associated personal firm-specific investments more uncertain. This evidence echoes the argument set out by the skill-biased organizational change literature (see, for instance, Caroli *et al.* 2001) that new organizational practices are complementary to a skilled workforce.

- The risk of entrenchment with a bundle of old organizational practices is reduced when *competitive pressures* and the associated threat of being fired help overcome the reluctance to organizational changes of firms' personnel.

As was said earlier, use of these organizational practices is often associated with broader changes in organizational design. In this chapter we devoted specific attention to *changes in organizational depth*, a crucial structural characteristics of organizational design, and particularly to the flattening of the corporate hierarchy (i.e. delayering). We clearly documented that, broadly speaking, the factors that explain the likelihood of the occurrence of this change are similar to those mentioned above. Again, the main stylized facts can be synthesized as follows.

- In accordance with the positive relation between the size and the depth of organizations documented in Chapter 3, *changes in size* lead to changes in the same direction in the number of hierarchical levels. There also is some evidence that this process may not be symmetric, even though the results on this issue are not unanimous.[23]

- In the 1980s and 1990s, a reduction in the number of hierarchical levels was more likely the greater *the depth of the organization*. In other words, all else equal, delayering seems to be more likely if firms have a more complex, more bureaucratic, less flat organization.

- Synergistic effects between the *adoption of PA technologies* and the flattening of the hierarchy seem to be sizable. In fact, the likelihood of the occurrence of this organizational change increases substantially with the extent of the use of a bundle of complementary PA technologies. Conversely, when individual PA technologies are adopted in isolation, the effects on the reduction of the number of levels are modest. This alleged complementarity extends to the adoption of *advanced ICTs* and of the *innovative organizational practices* mentioned above.

- The abundant availability of cheap skilled labor in the local market is found to favor delayering. This again confirms the argument of the skill-biased organizational change literature that there are complementarities between the organizational changes that we are considering here and the *human capital of workers*.

- *Stronger competitive pressures* connected with the globalization of markets and the entry of new players have increasingly forced firms to eliminate (allegedly unnecessary) intermediate hierarchical levels, in addition to adopting new organizational practices.

- Delayering has also been found to be significantly more likely the more heterogenous the business environment of firms and the closer they are to the technological frontier. In both these situations the *specific individual knowledge* of a firm's personnel is key in obtaining a sustainable competitive advantage. Delayering, when it is combined with increasing delegation of decision authority (see Chapter 2), may be instrumental in allowing firms to make better use of this knowledge.

- Lastly, there are powerful *inertial forces* that prevent firms from changing the number of hierarchical levels even though they have become unsuitable to changed environmental conditions. Two such forces have been clearly documented in this chapter. First, in accordance with real option theory (see Dixit and Pindyck 1994), the higher the *sunk costs* of a specific organizational design, the more difficult it is to change the depth of the organization. Accordingly, it has been shown that firms that adhere to a Tayloristic organization of production turn out to change their organizational depth more rarely than other firms. The reason is that in the former firms such changes involve substantial sunk costs, due to the formal specialization of the tasks performed by workers, the codification of procedures, and the rigid definition of authority relations and communication flows. Second, firms may abstain from changing the number of hierarchical levels so as to avoid *influence activities* on the part of employees (Milgrom 1988, Milgrom and Roberts 1990a). In fact, this change is likely to have redistributional consequences for firms' employees and they will spend time and energy to the detriment of productive activities, to exert pressures on the individuals endowed with decision authority so as to turn this change to their advantage. Structural inertia follows, as it allows firms to save on these influence costs.[24]

Appendix

4.A.1 Methodological issues

We classified plants depending on the evolution of their organizational depth. In particular, there are three possible cases, graphically presented in what follows: (a) plants that have not changed their organization over the observation period (i.e. from 1975 to 1996), (b) plants that have changed once, and (c) plants that have changed twice or more times.

(a) No change in organizational depth In this case the starting date of the observation period (t_0) is: (i) for Model I of Table 4.A1 (and Models IIIa and IIIb of Table 4.A3), the maximum between 1975 (the first year of observation of the empirical survey) and the date of plant's foundation (t_j^E); (ii) for Model II of Table 4.A1 (and Models IVa and IVb of Table 4.A3), the date of plant's foundation (t_j^E) or 1947 for plants established before the Second World War.

Observations are both left- and right-censored, since we do not know the exact date of the last organizational change and we impose a closing date given by 1996:

(b) One change in organizational depth In this case we divide the period under observation into two intervals. The first starts from t_0 and ends at the date of the change in organizational depth (t_1); observations are left-censored. The second is delimited by t_1 and 1996; observations are right-censored.

(c)   Two or more changes in organizational depth The period under observation is divided into two intervals. The first starts from the date of the
change in organizational depth before the last one (t_1) and ends at
the date of the last change (t_2). The second interval is delimited by t_2
and 1996; in this latter case observations are right-censored.

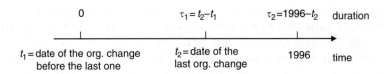

4.A.2   Definition and expected effects of the explanatory variables, and results of the econometric estimates

The explanatory variables are divided into three sets. The first set
includes variables that capture adoption by sample plants of technological and organizational innovations, having an expected positive impact
on organizational change.

For technological innovations, we consider AMTs belonging to the PA
paradigm to which the empirical literature on technological change has
devoted considerable attention (see, for instance, Dunne 1994). In particular we focus on the following AMTs: FMSs, machining centers, NC
and CNC stand-alone machine tools, and programmable robots (for
greater details see the Appendix of the book). As all such technologies
pertain to the production sphere, they directly affect production
processes and consequently the organization of plants. Both theoretical
(Milgrom and Roberts 1990b) and empirical (Bresnahan *et al.* 2002)
studies indicate that the introduction of such advanced technologies is
positively related to organizational change, resulting in the adoption of
a flatter organization – that is, one characterized by a smaller number of
layers. However, Qian (1994) suggests that the adoption of AMTs may
have an opposite effect on the direction of change: to the extent that
AMTs increase a plant's productivity, they may be associated with an
expansion of the corporate hierarchy. So whereas we expect a positive
impact of the AMT variables on the probability of change in organizational depth, the direction of such change is a matter of empirical test.

We also want to test the existence of a cluster effect: AMTs may affect
the organization of a plant especially when they are introduced together

rather than in isolation. For this purpose, we have defined four time-varying dummy variables: *DAMT1, DAMT2, DAMT3* and *DAMT4* equal one for plants which by year *t-1* had adopted one, two, three, and four AMTs, respectively. Doms *et al.* (1997), using a similar technology count for US manufacturing plants, find that the intensity of use of AMTs (that is, the level of intra-firm diffusion) is positively associated with the use of multiple technologies. So, we expect plants that have adopted a greater number of AMTs to be more inclined towards change in organizational depth, of whatever direction.

In addition, we consider time-dependent dummy variables concerning the introduction of IWPs and HRMPs. *Team, Rotation,* and *Incentive* equal zero for plants that by year *t* have not adopted teamwork and job rotation practices and individual incentive schemes (i.e. pay for quality and skills), respectively. In the year following adoption they are switched to one. It is often argued that the introduction of these organizational innovations is part of a new organizational paradigm characterized by greater decentralization of decision-making activities, multi-tasking (rather than specialization of tasks), and reduced bureaucratization, and that such new organizational practices positively affect productivity. Hence, we predict a positive impact of *Team, Rotation,* and *Incentive* on change in plants' organizational structure. As to the direction of change, the same reasoning as that made in relation to AMTs applies: again, we have no priors as to the net effect of the introduction of these new organizational practices.

The second group encompasses explanatory variables aimed at reflecting forces that oppose organizational change (i.e. favor structural inertia), namely the presence of sunk costs and the extent of influence activities within plants.

The characteristics of plants' production processes considerably affect the amount of sunk costs entailed by changing the organization, and thus the likelihood of change. The impact of sunk costs is examined through the time-varying dummy variable denoted *Line*. *Line* indicates whether at time *t* plants are involved in line production (*Line* = 1) or in job-shop operations (*Line* = 0). Line production is associated with the specialization of line workers in specific tasks, codification of organizational procedures, and rigid definition of communication flows and authority relations. Job shop operations, conversely, are linked to a less formalized, more flexible multi-task organization. Thus, plants involved in line production should be less likely to change their organizational depth, due to the higher sunk costs associated with such a change; such an argument applies to both an increase and a decrease in the number of tiers.

Turning attention to influence activities, we expect their extent within a plant to be closely linked with the characteristics of decision-making activities. Accordingly, we consider a number of variables that illustrate the allocation of decision-making power within the firm to which a given plant belongs. *PM Sup* is a time-varying dummy variable that equals one if at time t the plant manager's corporate superior has responsibility for decisions concerning the plant's organization. More specifically, *PM Sup* is set to one when authority over at least one of the decisions regarding plant's workforce (i.e. hiring and dismissal, definition of individual and collective incentive schemes, and decisions on the career paths of plant employees) is assigned to a plant manager's superior. Given that we do not have specific information as to the corporate level that takes the decision of changing the number of tiers, we assume that the likelihood of such decision being taken by a superior of the plant manager is greater if the superior is in charge of (some of the) decisions concerning plant personnel.

Further, we distinguish between single-unit and multi-unit firms. In the Italian economy the vast majority of firms is family-owned. This especially applies to single-plant (usually smaller) organizations. Therefore, in these latter firms the corporate superior of the plant manager generally is the owner–manager. Within a (usually larger) multi-unit corporation she likely is a salaried middle manager. In single-plant family-owned firms the owner–manager operates both inside and outside the plant and generally possesses discretionary power. Thus, in this case influence activities are likely to be very high, due to both the proximity between the plant's agents and the owner–manager and the discretionary nature of decision-making. In large multi-unit corporations where decision-making on the plant's organization is assigned to a salaried executive who works outside the production unit, however, influence activities are limited by both the distance between the decision-maker and the agents who are affected by her decisions and the existence of formal procedures that limit discretion.

In order to take into account these situations, we have defined three time-varying dummy variables: *Owner*, *PM*, and *External*.[25] *Owner* equals one if at time t decisions on plant organization are assigned to the plant manager's corporate superior (i.e. *PM Sup* = 1) and the plant is owned by a single-plant firm. In this case it is very likely that there are no intermediate levels between the plant manager and the owner–manager. Thus, *Owner* captures situations where the firm's owner–manager retains decision authority on the plant's organization, and is set to zero otherwise. *PM* equals one if at time t the plant manager is assigned responsibility for the decision of changing the plant's corporate hierarchy independently of the single or multi-plant ownership status (*PM Sup* = 0). *External* equals one when *PM Sup* is one (i.e. authority is centralized at the plant manager's corporate superior level) and the plant is owned by a multi-unit corporation. In this latter case the plant manager's corporate superior is probably a corporate officer who works outside the plant. On the basis of the theoretical considerations on influence activities illustrated in Section 4.2, we expect the following order as to the impact of the allocation of decision-making power upon the likelihood of organizational change: *Owner* < *PM* < *External*. We also expect these arguments to hold true independently of the direction of change.

Actually, case studies reveal that the owner–manager of a family business is often unwilling to change the organization. In (small) single-plant firms changing the organizational depth generally means both introducing new hierarchical levels and delegating power down the corporate hierarchy. Due to moral hazard problems and psychological motivations (i.e. aversion towards losing direct control of operations) owner–managers are usually reluctant to implement such change. It follows that the negative impact of *Owner* on the likelihood of changing the number of tiers (and especially of increasing it) might reflect factors that are not connected with influence costs. In order to control for such an effect, we have defined an additional explanatory variable denoted *Powerowner*. Such a variable aims to capture the propensity of owners of family-owned single-plant firms towards centralization of decision-making. It equals zero when *Owner* is zero. When *Owner* equals one, it is given by the number of decisions out of the six considered here which are taken at the level of the plant manager's superior (that is, by the owner-manager). So *Powerowner* is a proxy of the preference of owners for autocratic decision-making. Should the negative influence of *Owner* on the likelihood of organizational change be due to psychological reasons, *Powerowner* would be negatively (positively) associated with organizational change (structural inertia); such an argument applies in particular to the decision on expanding the corporate hierarchy. If the owner retains authority over all strategic decisions, an increase in the number of layers will almost inevitably lead to some delegation of power, a move that is likely to be opposed by an autocratic owner. Evidence that *Powerowner* is positively (negatively) related to organizational change (structural inertia), however, would be consistent with explanations that emphasize the role of influence costs. In a family-owned firm in which the owner–manager is directly responsible for decisions related to the organizational chart, the incentives for employees to engage in activities aimed at influencing the outcome of the owner–manager's decisions would be higher if she delegates some other strategic decisions down the organizational pyramid, as influence activities are more likely to be successful. In other words, partial delegation signals the possibility of influencing the owner–manager. Instead, if she keeps all decisions at the top, influence activities will be relatively discouraged.

The third category includes plant-, firm-, and industry-specific control variables. *Level* is the number of a plant's hierarchical levels at time *t*. It provides information on the complexity of the structure of agents' relations within the plant. On the one hand, the managerial literature suggests that during the 1980s and 1990s plants characterized by very bureaucratic structures changed their organization depth turning to a flatter hierarchy (Baharami 1992; Drucker 1988; Krafcik 1988; see also section 4.4.2). Hence, we expect *Level* to have a positive impact on the likelihood of shrinking the corporate hierarchy. On the other, organizational ecology theory (Hannan and Freeman 1984) predicts a different relation between *Level* and organizational change: complexity of organizations causes structural inertia and thus hinders organizational change, independently of its direction.

Size is the logarithm of the number of plant employees at June 1989. We do not have any priors as to the effect of such a variable based on theoretical considerations. However, previous empirical work on organizational change devoted considerable attention to firm size. On the one hand, Thompson (1983) shows that organizational change (i.e. the passage from a functional form to an M-form in large multi-plant companies) is positively related to firm size. On the other, more recent studies (see, for instance, Palmer *et al.* 1993) find that once we control for (product and geographic) diversification the effect of size vanishes. *Age* conveys information on a plant's age at time *t*. Young plants have less consolidated hierarchical structures in terms of procedural routines and authority relations than older ones. This should render it easier to change the organizational depth. In addition, in the early years after establishment it is often necessary to adjust a plant's organization as environmental conditions may differ from those that were expected at the time when the organizational chart was initially designed. Therefore, we expect *Age* to negatively affect change in the number of tiers in either direction. Lastly, in the model that distinguishes expansion from contraction of the corporate hierarchy, we also consider ΔSize. This variable measures the percentage growth rate in the number of plant employees between 1989 and 1996: it is a proxy of variations in plant size. Since the number of tiers is a positive function of plant size, we expect a change of the latter to end up in a change in the same direction as the former.[26]

For industry-specific characteristics, we considered the following variables. *I-Growth* is the value of the industry growth rate (three-digit NACE–CLIO classification) in the period 1981–91. To examine the impact of industry concentration on the likelihood of changing a plant's organization, we calculated the Herfindahl index at the three-digit NACE–CLIO classification in 1991 (*Herfindahl*). Finally, we included the variable *R&D*, which is the ratio of R&D expenses to industry turnover (two-digit NACE–CLIO classification) in 1994. Overall, we would expect plants in high-tech, fast-growing, and more competitive (i.e. less concentrated) industries to change the depth of their organizations more frequently, due to the need to quickly adapt the organizational design to an unstable and competitive environment.

Results of the four duration models on the effects of the explanatory variables on changes in organizational depth are reported in Tables 4.A1–4.A4.

Table 4.A1 Econometric models of change in organizational depth

Variables	I	II
p	1.2377 (0.1157)[b]	1.081 (.0887)
a_0 Constant	−5.0279 (.4075)[c]	−5.9255 (.4718)[c]
a_1 DAMT1	.6590 (.2123)[c]	1.2474 (.2452)[c]
a_2 DAMT2	.9589 (.2110)[c]	1.5507 (.2418)[c]
a_3 DAMT3	1.1870 (.2641)[c]	1.8365 (.3019)[c]
a_4 DAMT4	1.7710 (.3104)[c]	2.4550 (.3464)[c]
a_5 Team	.6240 (.1783)[c]	.7672 (.1989)[c]
a_6 Incentive	.1638 (.1574)	.2852 (.1788)
a_7 Rotation	.3573 (.1477)[b]	.6659 (.1752)[c]
a_8 Line	−.3465 (.1472)[b]	−.3872 (.1651)[b]
a_9 Owner	−.9523 (.3120)[c]	.7565 (.2545)[c]
a_{10} Powerowner	.7608 (.2986)[b]	.8300 (.2823)[c]
a_{11} External	−.2833 (.2381)	−.4453 (.2752)
a_{12} Level	.3576 (.0802)[c]	.3788 (.0889)[c]
a_{13} Size	−.1080 (.0816)	−.1061 (.0942)
a_{14} Age	.0035 (.0030)	.0029 (.0035)
a_{15} I-Growth	.4555 (.2261)[b]	.5460 (.2530)[b]
a_{16} R&D	1.6313 (2.0759)	2.0177 (2.3728)
a_{17} Herfindahl	−3.8202 (2.2986)[a]	−4.7165 (2.5873)[a]
Log-likelihood	−703.4120	−730.0693
LR χ^2-test	174.27 (17)[c]	278.43 (17)[c]

Continued

Table 4.A1 Continued

Variables	I	II
LR χ^2-tests on groups of explanatory variables:		
PA technologies: $a_1 = a_2$		
$= a_3 = a_4 = 0$	52.52 (4)[c]	85.75 (4)[c]
IWPs and HRMPs:		
$a_5 = a_6 = a_7 = 0$	26.34 (3)[c]	43.49 (3)[c]
Sunk costs: $a_8 = 0$	6.70 (2)[c]	6.32 (2)[b]
Influence activity:		
$a_9 = a_{10} = a_{11} = 0$	11.90 (3)[c]	16.12 (3)[b]
Industry: $a_{15} = a_{16}$		
$= a_{17} = 0$	10.76 (3)[b]	12.01 (3)[c]
No. of plants	438	438
No. of obs.	560	560
No. of records	8,169	8,169

Notes
Usual *t*-tests, except for *p*, where H_0: $p = 1$.
[a] Significance level greater than 10%.
[b] Significance level greater than 5%.
[c] Significance level greater than 1%.
Standard errors and degrees of freedom in parentheses.

Table 4.A2 Impact of technological complementarities on change in organizational depth

Intensity in the use of AMTs	Wald-tests on Model I of Table 4.A1	Wald-tests on Model II of Table 4.A1
DAMT4 > DAMT3	4.04 (1)[b]	4.42 (1)[b]
DAMT4 > DAMT2	9.09 (1)[c]	10.81 (1)[c]
DAMT4 > DAMT1	14.56 (1)[c]	16.54 (1)[c]
DAMT3 > DAMT2	0.96 (1)	1.27 (1)
DAMT3 > DAMT1	4.57 (1)[b]	5.10 (1)[b]
DAMT2 > DAMT1	2.34 (1)	2.29 (1)

Notes
[b] Significance level greater than 5%.
[c] Significance level greater than 1%.
Degrees of freedom in parentheses.

Table 4.A3 Econometric models of expansion and contraction of organizational depth

Variables	Expansion of organizational depth		Contraction of organizational depth	
	IIIa	IVa	IIIb	IVb
p	1.0144 (.1762)	0.8915 (.1363)	1.2430 (.1608)	1.1021 (.1267)
a_0 Constant	−3.4523 (.9420)[c]	−3.9644 (1.0593)[c]	−7.9263 (.8799)[c]	−8.8760 (.9151)
a_1 DAMT1	1.1731 (.4071)[c]	1.9538 (.4838)[c]	.3675 (.3352)	.8558 (.3741)[b]
a_2 DAMT2	1.2542 (.4405)30[c]	2.0019 (.5087)[c]	.9461 (.2851)[c]	1.4373 (.3237)[c]
a_3 DAMT3	1.6728 (.5507)[c]	2.4366 (.6185)[c]	1.0657 (.3643)[c]	1.6208 (.4103)[c]
a_4 DAMT4	1.6309 (.6856)[b]	2.3806 (.7667)[c]	1.9414 (.4116)[c]	2.5919 (.4614)[c]
a_5 Team	1.0357 (.4428)[b]	1.2031 (.4887)[b]	.5894 (.2204)[c]	.7174 (.2447)[c]
a_6 Incentive	−.0339 (.3160)	.1171 (.3523)	.1197 (.2176)	.2204 (.2434)
a_7 Rotation	.6270 (.3188)[b]	.9069 (.3676)[b]	.3836 (.2077)[a]	.6906 (.2370)[c]
a_8 Line	−.7861 (.3486)[b]	−.8759 (.3788)[b]	−.1521 (.2071)	.2108 (.2287)
a_9 Owner	−.9155 (.4868)[a]	−1.0310 (.5428)[a]	−.1199 (.3081)	−.1962 (.3485)
a_{10} Powerowner	1.0268 (.5359)[a]	1.1943 (.5937)[b]	.5126 (.3659)	.6320 (.4146)
a_{11} External	−.8957 (.6014)	−.9573 (.6780)	.0657 (.3074)	−.0624 (.3440)
a_{12} Level	−.9311 (.3040)[c]	−1.0784 (.3318)[c]	.8559 (.1541)[c]	.9383 (.1584)[c]
a_{13} Size	.2883 (.2060)	.2994 (.2320)	−.1066 (.1263)	−.1177 (.1405)
a_{14} ΔSize	.0038 (.0015)[b]	.0043 (.0017)[b]	.00004 (.0004)	.00001 (.0004)
a_{15} Age	.0032 (.0077)	.0019 (.0088)	.0011 (.0036)	−.0027 (.0040)
a_{16} I-Growth	.5224 (.4293)	.5779 (.4774)	.4661 (.3390)	.5854 (.3771)
a_{17} R&D	−6.0739 (6.0215)	−6.2940 (6.7593)	3.4833 (2.5610)	4.1818 (2.8778)
a_{18} Herfindahl	3.4216 (3.6565)	3.6375 (4.0894)	−7.5731 (4.3963)[a]	−8.4685 (4.8899)[a]

Continued

Table 4.A3 Continued

Variables	Expansion of organizational depth		Contraction of organizational depth	
	IIIa	IVa	IIIb	IVb
Log-likelihood	−357.2473	−366.9154	−395.7726	−411.5562
LR χ^2-test	105.75 (18)[c]	155.69 (18)[c]	214.41 (18)[c]	268.28 (18)[c]
LR χ^2-tests on groups of explanatory variables:				
PA technologies:				
$a_1 = a_2 = a_3 = a_4 = 0$	22.17 (4)[c]	41.40 (4)[c]	38.92 (4)[c]	52.14 (4)[c]
IWPs and HRMPs:				
$a_5 = a_6 = a_7 = 0$	17.10 (3)[c]	22.13 (3)[c]	14.40 (3)[c]	23.95 (3)[c]
Sunk costs: $a_8 = 0$	9.48 (1)[c]	9.22 (1)[c]	.66 (1)	1.00 (1)
Influence activity:				
$a_9 = a_{10} = a_{11} = 0$	11.26 (3)[b]	11.04 (3)[b]	2.46 (3)	2.71 (3)
Industry: $a_{16} = a_{17} = a_{18} = 0$	3.53 (3)	3.21 (3)	10.56 (3)[b]	11.63 (3)[c]
No. of plants	438	438	438	438
No. of obs.	494	494	505	505
No. of records	8,169	8,169	8,169	8,169

Notes
Usual t-tests, except for p, where H_0: $p = 1$.
[a] Significance level greater than 10%.
[b] Significance level greater than 5%.
[c] Significance level greater than 1%.
Standard errors and degrees of freedom in parentheses.

Table 4.A4 Impact of technological complementarities on the expansion and contraction of organizational depth

Intensity in the use of AMTs	Wald-tests on Model IIIa of Table 4.A3	Wald-tests on Model IIIb of Table 4. A3
DAMT4 > DAMT3	0.00 (1)	5.49 (1)[b]
DAMT4 > DAMT2	.34 (1)	9.54 (1)[b]
DAMT4 > DAMT1	.50 (1)	17.61 (1)[c]
DAMT3 > DAMT2	.85 (1)	.16 (1)
DAMT3 > DAMT1	1.28 (1)	4.04 (1)[b]
DAMT2 > DAMT1	.06 (1)	3.68 (1)[a]

Notes
[a] Significance level greater than 10%.
[b] Significance level greater than 5%.
[c] Significance level greater than 1%.
Degrees of freedom in parentheses.

5
The Effects of Organizational Design on Firm Performance

5.1   Introduction

It is conventional wisdom in the economic and managerial literature that a new organizational design was gaining ground in the 1980s and 1990s among firms in industrialized countries. Originally developed by large Japanese mass manufacturing firms (Womack *et al.* 1990), it has been rapidly diffusing since then in other countries and other sectors. This organizational design relies on a series of organizational practices whose purpose is to increase flexibility in the organization and take greater advantage of the creativity and skills of individual workers. These practices have been variously labeled by scholars as "high-performance," "flexible," "high-commitment," "innovative," "alternative," etc. In this book we have used the terms innovative work practices (IWPs) for practices that modify how employees perform their tasks, and human resource management practices (HRMPs) for practices aimed at eliciting effort and collaborative behavior from workers and at aligning their objectives to those of the organization (for a definition see Section 1.2.2 in Chapter 1). Moreover, this new organizational design is characterized by delegation of decision authority, an increase in the (horizontal) span of control, and a reduction in the number of levels of the corporate hierarchy (these dimensions of organizations have been called here structural organizational variables; for a definition, see Section 1.2.1 in Chapter 1).

In Chapter 1, we offered international evidence on the diffusion of organizational practices, the configuration of structural organizational variables (SOVs), and their evolution since the 1980s. Then we investigated the determinants of these latter aspects of organizational design (i.e. the allocation of decision authority in Chapter 2, and organizational depth in Chapter 3). Lastly, we analyzed in Chapter 4 the factors that shape organizational dynamics.

The purpose of this chapter is to extend the scope of the book to the examination of the existing quantitative empirical evidence on the effects of organizational design, and changes in it, on firm performance. We will focus on the effects on firms' productivity and profitability. It is important to note that this is only a portion, even though a prominent one, of the quantitative empirical literature on the effects of organizational variables on firms (or establishments) and their employees. Other related streams of literature that for the sake of synthesis will not be considered here include studies that have analyzed the effects of adoption of organizational practices and other changes in organizational design on firms' innovation (e.g. Michie and Sheehan 1999; Laursen and Foss 2003; Arundel *et al.* 2006). Moreover, we will not review work interested in the salary increases (e.g. Bailey *et al.* 2001; Bauer and Bender 2001; Forth and Millward 2004; Handel and Gittleman 2004; Osterman 2006) and greater job satisfaction of workers (e.g. Appelbaum *et al.* 2000; Freeman and Kleiner 2000; Godard 2001; Bauer 2004; see also Parent-Thirion *et al.* 2005) that allegedly arise from these organizational changes.

The chapter is organized as follows. Section 5.2 is devoted to methodological issues, regarding measurement of firm performance, the units of analysis, the characteristics of data sets, and econometric methodologies. In Section 5.3 we examine the effects of organizational design variables on firm productivity, while in Section 5.4 the focus of the analysis is firm profitability. In Section 5.5 we provide evidence as to the alleged complementarity between changes in organizational design and use of advanced technologies. Some concluding remarks in Section 5.6 end the chapter.

5.2 Methodological issues

Since the early 1990s a growing body of empirical literature has tried to assess the effects of organizational variables on firm performance.[1] These studies differ according to the performance indicator, the unit of analysis, and the estimation techniques. In this section we briefly discuss the methodological problems encountered by these studies and the advantages and disadvantages of different methodological approaches. We will postpone to subsequent sections a review of the empirical results obtained by this literature.

5.2.1 Measurement of performance

Studies in this stream of literature initially focused attention on productivity. In particular, studies that considered specific industries (or specific production processes within a given industry, see Section 5.3.1) were able to define reliable productivity indexes. The drawback is that these specific measures cannot be employed in other industries, and so the results of these studies can hardly be generalized.

Cross-sectoral studies, on the other hand, considered broader indicators of productivity, with the (log of the) ratio of total sales to total employment being the most popular (e.g. Huselid 1995; Black and Lynch 1996, 2001, 2004; Cappelli and Neumark 2001).

A limited number of studies analyzed the effects of organizational variables on firm profitability (Ichniowski 1990; Huselid 1995; Huselid and Becker 1996; Colombo *et al.* 2007). Consideration of firm profitability rather than productivity is a substantial step forward. In fact, there is a growing consensus that the introduction of new organizational practices (both IWPs and HRMPs) is associated with a rise in labor and other costs (e.g. Appelbaum *et al.* 2000; Cappelli and Neumark 2001; Bauer and Bender 2001; Bauer 2003; Black and Lynch 2004; for an opposite view, see Osterman 2000). So while these organizational changes may well lead to greater productivity, if the salary of employees and other costs also increase it is unclear whether they also are beneficial to firms' shareholders.

5.2.2   Unit of analysis

Depending on the unit of analysis, studies can be classified into two categories. Some studies used *firm-level* data. If the aim of the analysis is to assess the effects of organizational design on profitability, this is the unique option as plant-level profitability data are generally not available; at plant level profitability is even difficult to define unambiguously.

There are two drawbacks to this approach. First, the source of data on organizational variables generally is the Director for Human Resources (HR) or equivalently the senior HR professional. Therefore data on the actual use of organizational practices in production lines may be less accurate than in a situation in which data were directly collected from the line personnel in charge of production activity. Second, for multi-unit firms data on organizational variables need to be aggregated at firm level and firm-level data may hide substantial heterogeneity across different units that belong to the same firm.

The large majority of previous studies considered establishment-level data and analyzed the effects of organizational variables on productivity.

5.2.3   Characteristics of data sets

Almost all the studies that are surveyed in this chapter relied on surveys to collect data on organizational design. Hence they suffer from the typical shortcomings of this type of data.

First, only firms (or establishments)[2] having survived up to the survey date can participate in the survey. Hence a survivorship bias arises. If there is a (positive or negative) relation between organizational variables (e.g. the adoption of IWPs and HRMPs) and firm closure, the estimates of the performance effects of organizational design will be biased.

In addition, survey respondents self-select into samples. If they have not adopted any of the organizational practices under examination, they may not be interested in participating in the survey. Alternatively, depending on the complexity of the questionnaire, extensive users of these practices may not be willing to respond because of lack of time. Therefore, even if stratified samples (e.g. by size class, industry, or location) that are representative of the target population of firms are used in the empirical analysis, one cannot be sure that these samples do not suffer from a self-selection bias.[3]

Lastly, a small number of studies relied on repeated surveys. The main advantage is clearly the opportunity to build a longitudinal data set and to use the estimates of panel data models (see below). The drawback is the late-adopter problem. If the incidence of the organizational variables under consideration (e.g. use of a specific IWP or HRMP) is already quite high at the beginning of the observation period, estimates of their effects on firm performance will be dominated by the effects obtained by late adopters. As late adopters are likely to be those firms that benefit least from adoption, this may lead to a downward bias in the estimates.

5.2.4 Econometric methodology*[4]

With a few exceptions (e.g. the work by Ichniowski and his colleagues on the steel industry, see Section 5.3.1.1), most of the studies carried out in the 1990s used cross-sectional estimates and analyzed the association between organizational variables and firm performance, while inserting into the specification of the econometric models a set of control variables. These cross-sectional estimates suffer from several serious methodological problems (Huselid and Becker 1996; Bauer 2003). As a result, the findings of these studies cannot be interpreted as evidence of causality.

First, cross-sectional estimates may be affected by omitted-variable problems and be driven by unobserved heterogeneity. If there are unobserved factors that are positively correlated with both organizational variables and firm performance, the estimates of the effects of the former variables will be upwardly biased. This situation is likely to arise, for instance, if firms with a smarter managerial team and/or a more qualified workforce both enjoy better performance and are more rapid adopters of IWPs and HRMPs than other firms. Conversely, if unobserved factors are positively correlated with organizational variables and negatively correlated with firm performance or vice versa, a downward bias follows.

Second, a simultaneity or reverse causality problem may arise as changes of organizational variables cannot be assimilated to a random treatment.[5] In fact, organizational variables are endogenous: only those firms that expect to reap a positive payoff from a change in these variables (e.g. the adoption of a specific IWP) will indeed make that change. If this payoff is correlated with firm performance, cross-sectional estimates again will be distorted. For instance, previous studies have shown that there are greater incentives for the adoption of IWPs and HRMPs when firms perform poorly and there is a greater risk of closure (Ichniowski and Shaw 1995; Nickell *et al.* 2001). A downward bias is likely to follow. Conversely, if the payoff of a change of the organizational variables is greater among better-performing firms, the estimates will be upwardly biased.[6]

Estimates based on longitudinal data have several advantages. First, endogeneity problems may be alleviated simply through recourse to lagged independent variables. Moreover, if unobserved heterogeneity is engendered by a time-invariant firm-specific effect, then first-differencing solves the problem. Accordingly, in this situation fixed effects within-group (WG) panel data models provide consistent estimates of the effects of organizational variables on firm performance. Unfortunately, one cannot exclude that there are time-variant shocks that contextually influence organizational variables and firm performance. For example, firms that face transitory demand (e.g. a contraction of the market) or supply (e.g. an increase of unit labor costs) shocks may be more inclined to adopt IWPs and HRMPs in order to restore profitability conditions. Alternatively, an unexpected profitability increase may provide the firm with the financial resources necessary for workplace reorganization. As data on firm performance are generally serially correlated, lack of control for these time-varying shocks may again produce distorted estimates. Under these circumstances, one needs to find suitable instruments for organizational variables and to resort to dynamic panel data model estimation methods (i.e. General Method of Moments, GMM, see Arellano and Bond 1991, Blundell and Bond 1998, Bond 2002).

It is important to recognize that panel data models have their own limitations. First, the observation period may be too short for the use of dynamic panel data model estimation techniques.[7] Moreover, one has to carefully consider the duration of the treatment. In other words, the effects of organizational variables on firm performance are unlikely to show up immediately. Therefore, independently of the estimation technique, the observation period may be too short to detect these delayed effects. Lastly, WG panel data models exhibit great sensitivity to measurement errors (Huselid and Becker 1996). This holds true especially when the observation period is short, as in this situation the estimates are based on information provided by a small number of changers.

5.3 Effects of organizational design on productivity

In this section we review large-scale quantitative empirical work on the effects of organizational variables on labor (and/or capital) productivity. We first consider studies relating to specific industries; then we turn our attention to cross-sectoral studies. Actually, the studies that are described here are only part of the extant empirical literature on this issue. In particular, in accordance with the approach followed in this volume, we do not consider qualitative evidence provided by case studies, such as the well-known study of the NUMMI automobile assembly plant, jointly owned by General Motors and Toyota (see Krafcik 1988; Wilms 1995).[8]

5.3.1 Single-industry studies

5.3.1.1 Steel industry

Ichniowski *et al.* (1997) analyzed thirty-six steel finishing lines located in the US and owned by seventeen firms. They considered the impact on productivity of adoption by these lines of IWPs relating to teamwork and flexible job assignment, and several complementary HRMPs relating to incentive pay schemes, recruiting, employment security, skills training, and communication between management and labor. They measured productivity through production-line uptime – that is, the percentage of scheduled time that a line actually runs. They took advantage of a unique hand-collected longitudinal data set composed of 2,190 monthly observations and estimated pooled OLS and WG panel data models.

Because of the high correlation between the adoption of the different practices under consideration, they resorted to four "Systems of practices" (see Chapter 4, Section 4.3.1 for more details). A dummy variable for each system indicated whether a given line in a given month had adopted it, or not. In particular, System 4 corresponds to a very traditional work organization: lines in this category did not adopt any new practice. At the other extreme, in the System 1 category one finds lines with all the innovative practices under examination. Quite interestingly, transitions from one system to the other were extremely rare in their sample; changers accounted for only 13.8% of the total number of observations. In particular, there were no transitions to System 1. Unfortunately, this seriously limits the evidence provided by the WG models.

The authors considered several controls, including the year in which the lines under scrutiny were built, the time since a line's start-up, a series of specific technical parameters, the quality of lines' management, the threat of layoffs and of plant shut down, average pay rates, and yearly dummies. The key evidence provided by the pooled OLS estimates was that there is a clear order between the four systems of practices. The highest productivity level was associated with the adoption of System 1 and the lowest with the adoption of System 4, with Systems 2 and 3 being in intermediate positions. The same ranking between Systems 2, 3, and 4 was confirmed by the WG estimates. Moreover, the productivity increase obtained through the adoption of more advanced systems of practices was found to be of substantial economic magnitude. According to the WG estimates, should a line change from System 4 to System 2 it would obtain a 3.5% uptime increase, corresponding to an annual increase in operating profits greater than $1.1 million.[9]

The authors also estimated the effect on the productivity of sample lines of the adoption of individual organizational practices. First, they estimated fifteen models while adding a dummy variable for each of the fifteen organizational practices into the specification of the model that included three of the four System of practices dummies, with System 4 being the benchmark. The dummies relating to the individual practices were never statistically significant.[10] Moreover, they estimated a comprehensive model including the fifteen individual practice dummies and dummies for the three systems of practices. The three system of practices dummies exhibited positive and statistically significant coefficients, while the individual practice dummies were not significant. The authors deduced that it is the systems of practices that determine the productivity of the steel finishing lines, while adoption of individual practices has a negligible impact.

Ichniowski and Shaw (1999) replicated the analysis illustrated above while adding to the sample under examination five lines located in

Japan. As expected, Japanese lines turned out to have adopted a system of practices quite close to System 1. The GLS estimates of a pooled panel data model with correction for serial correlation of the error term showed that, on average, Japanese lines were more productive than US lines. Nonetheless, US lines that had adopted the innovative system of practices (i.e. System 1) had productivity levels very close to those of Japanese lines.

In a later work, Boning *et al.* (2001) considered rolling lines in thirty-four steel minimills located in the US, and estimated the effects on productivity of the adoption of problem-solving teams and group-based incentive schemes. The sample included five years of monthly observations. The authors resorted to several estimation techniques for panel data (pooled OLS, WG with line-specific autoregressive error). They also tried to correct for the endogeneity bias through a semi-parametric estimation procedure originally proposed by Andrews and Schafgans (1996). They found evidence that, all else equal, the use of incentive pay led to an increase of output, and use of problem-solving teams combined with incentive pay engendered an even greater output increase. The estimated magnitude of the average productivity increase when both practices are adopted corresponded to a $1.4 million increase in operating profits. Nonetheless, productivity increases were not homogenous across lines; they turned out to be greater in lines which produced more complex products and had more complicated production processes. For the lines with the most complex production process, the use of teams in conjunction with incentive schemes generated a yearly output increase worth approximately $2.4 million.[11]

These studies have a number of strengths. First, while focusing attention on a particular production process, Ichniowski and his colleagues were able to obtain a rather precise measure of production output, inputs, and productivity. An additional advantage is that, because of the homogeneity of the sample and the insertion of several controls in the specification of the econometric models, it is easier to detect the impact of IWPs and HRMPs on productivity than in cross-industry studies. The use of longitudinal data is another strength, even though the small number of changers prevented use of estimation methods that are more apt to take into account the endogenous nature of the organizational variables; this raises the question whether their results are possibly driven by a lack of proper controls for unobserved heterogeneity and reverse causality. The other disadvantage of their analysis is that one may wonder whether the evidence they provide is generalizable or not.

5.3.1.2 *Automobile assembly industry*

MacDuffie (1995) analyzed the impact of the use of systems of IWPs and complementary HRMPs on labor productivity based on survey data relating to sixty-two non-luxury automotive assembly plants located in the US, Europe, Japan, Australia, and some developing countries. Data were collected during 1989 and 1990. Labor productivity was measured through the hours of work effort needed to build a vehicle. The author considered a work systems index and a "HRM policies" index. Both were obtained as the sum of a series of standardized z-score variables. The former index included the extent of use by plants of formal teams and of employee involvement groups, the number of production related suggestions given by employees, the percentage of accepted suggestions, the extent of job rotation within and across teams, and the degree to which production workers carried out quality-related tasks. The latter index reflected the use of the following HRMPs: hiring criteria emphasizing willingness to learn new skills and ability to work with others, pay for performance compensation schemes, (low level of) status barriers between managers and production workers, level of training provided to newly hired personnel, and level of ongoing training.

The results of OLS cross-sectional estimates showed that the extent of use of a system of IWPs was positively associated with labor productivity, but only for plants that extensively used innovative HRMPs and/or resorted to a bundle of manufacturing practices aimed at the minimization of buffers.

5.3.1.3 *Machining*

Kelley (1996) analyzed survey-based data relating to a size-stratified random sample composed of 973 US manufacturing establishments in twenty-one industries involved in machining (i.e. precision metal cutting). Data were collected in 1991. The author used factor analysis to describe the characteristics of the work organization systems adopted by plants. She found three factors. The "Participative bureaucracy" factor reflected the use of joint labor–management problem-solving committees and of worker-run problem-solving groups, adoption of employee stock ownership plants (ESOP), and employer-provided technical classes. It also had high loading on a variable capturing conformance to formal standardized procedures in carrying out machining tasks. The other two factors distinguished unionized plants that relied on seniority for promotion and job assignment decisions, and plants with a craft apprenticeship training program, respectively.

As in the studies surveyed above, the author used a technology-specific indicator of labor productivity – that is, the number of machining hours it takes to produce one item of a given product type. She distinguished products according to the type of technology used in machining, either a conventional technology or programmable automation (PA, that is NC and CNC stand-alone machines, FMS). She collected productivity data on 1,301 observations, as some plants provided data relating to two types of products, one produced through PA and the other through conventional technologies.

In addition to the work organization factors, the set of covariates included variables mirroring the technology and operations strategy for the machining process at the plant, educational requirements and wage policies pertaining to the machining workforce, quality-related attributes of the machined products, and industry dummies. Again, OLS estimates were used.

The results of the estimates showed, quite surprisingly, that the Participative bureaucracy factor had no influence on productivity for the whole sample. Conversely, it had a positive statistically significant effect on the productivity of branch plants of (usually large) multi-unit enterprises. The same holds true for single-plant firms that used PA technologies. The econometric results therefore strongly supported the view that the benefits of organizational practices on productivity are contingent on the type of firms and the type of production technology in use.

5.3.1.4   Telecommunication services

Batt (1999) considered a stratified random sample composed of 223 residential service and sales representatives in numerous offices of a regional Bell operating company. In her study the dependent variable was the productivity of individual workers measured by the (log of) individual average monthly sales for the period January 1993–June 1994. A series of variables on the adoption of IWPs and HRMPs captured the effect of organizational design on productivity. For IWPs, she resorted to a TQM additive index reflecting participation in off-line QC, and individual discretion in the accomplishment of tasks, a dummy indicating participation in SMT, and two variables measuring time spent per month in QC and SMT. Other covariates measured the use of HRMPs relating to training, coaching support, advancement opportunity, and job security. Controls related to the adoption of automated technology, employment relations, service market location, and individual characteristics (i.e. age, gender, race).

The results of the OLS regressions can be synthesized as follows. First, the TQM index and the time spent in QC had no effect on labor productivity. Second, participation in SMT resulted in significantly greater productivity, even though the time spent in SMT had a significant negative coefficient but of small magnitude. Depending on the models, the average increase in labor productivity attributable to SMT was estimated between + 7.5% and + 9.3%. In addition, there was evidence of a large positive interaction effect between participation in SMT and the use of automated technologies: workers involved in SMT that used these technologies obtained an additional productivity increase estimated at + 17.4% on top of that attributable to SMT participation alone (on this issue, see Section 5.5). Conversely, there was no evidence of any interactive effect between TQM and the use of automated technologies. HRMPs did not exhibit any statistically significant positive effect on productivity, with the partial exception of coaching support.

5.3.1.5   Business services

Bertschek and Kaiser (2004) analyzed the labor productivity effects of work reorganization (see below) in a sample composed of 411 German firms that operated in the business-related service sectors. Data came from two waves of the *Service sector business survey* carried out in the first and third quarters of 2000. Their approach differs from that followed by the studies mentioned above in several respects. First, in addition to the adoption of teamwork they considered the flattening of firms' hierarchy (i.e. delayering) – that is, a change in a structural dimension of organizational design. Second, they relied on the key assumption that work reorganization does not only act as a shift parameter of the production function but, due to strategic complementarities, it changes the partial productivities of the other production inputs (i.e. labor, ICT capital, and non-ICT capital).

In accordance with this view, they resorted to the estimate of two endogenous switching regression models (i.e. for teamwork and delayering, respectively). In each model the parameters of a Cobb–Douglas production function were allowed to differ, depending on whether firms were involved in work reorganization or not. Moreover, firms were assumed to get involved in work reorganization if the labor productivity gain they obtained was greater than the reorganization costs per worker. Labor productivity was measured by the ratio of total sales to total employment. Unobservable reorganization costs per worker were assumed to be lower for exporting firms, firms that faced international competition, and firms that according to the interviewed managers were encountering difficulties in hiring qualified personnel. They were also assumed to vary with the business cycle. Controls in the production function equations included industry and location dummies.

The results of the estimates of the labor productivity equations indicated that neither adoption of teamwork practices nor delayering significantly modified the partial output elasticity of ICT investment, non-ICT investment, and labor input, even though the point estimates relating to the two latter inputs were somewhat larger with work reorganization. Nonetheless, when Kernel density estimates were used to compare the conditional log labor productivity distributions with and without work reorganization, things changed. In fact, if one focused attention on firms that adopted teamwork practices or eliminated some hierarchical layers, the log labor productivity distribution in the work reorganization regime was situated to the right of the corresponding distribution in the no-work reorganization regime. The mean differences in log labor productivity were equal to 0.9569 and 0.9171 for teamwork and delayering, respectively; both differences were found by a *t*-test to be statistically significant at conventional confidence levels.

The authors deduced that the firms that adopted teamwork practices and/or reduced the number of hierarchical layers were clearly better off compared with the hypothetical case with no work reorganization.

5.3.2   Cross-industry evidence

The decision to concentrate attention on a particular industry (or production process) allows us to define reliable productivity indexes and reduces problems of unobserved heterogeneity across firms. The drawback is that the results can hardly be generalized. A limited number of studies considered more representative cross-sectoral samples of firms and resorted to broader indicators of firm productivity. We will first survey work that relied on cross-section estimates; then we will turn our attention to studies based on estimates of panel data models.

5.3.2.1   Cross-section estimates

Ichniowski (1990) probably represents the first attempt to relate survey-based cross-sectoral data on the adoption of organizational practices including IWPs and HRMPs to business line-level productivity data. More precisely, the author estimated a standard Cobb–Douglas production function augmented through a series of nine dummies that reflected the adoption of different Systems of practices, on data relating to 126 US business lines observed in 1986. The system of practices dummies were obtained through a clustering algorithm, the purpose of which was to identify similar groupings of businesses in a multi-dimensional organizational practices space. The findings of OLS estimates supported the view that systems with flexible job design, formal employee training, merit-based promotions, and formal employee–management communication channels were associated with relatively higher levels of labor productivity than other systems. Systems that mixed old and innovative practices were those that exhibited the worst performances. Nonetheless, the author admits that "statistical models cannot determine whether the more progressive HRM system stimulates economic performance or whether this system is the appropriate choice for better performing businesses."[12]

Huselid (1995) analyzed a sample composed of 968 US listed firms. Data on IWPs and related HRMPs were obtained through a survey addressed to the firms' most senior HR official. Thirteen practices were considered; for each individual practice, the breadth of implementation throughout a firm (i.e. the percentage of firm's employees that were affected by the practice) was measured. The key idea of the study was that these practices are effective only when they are used in combination. Accordingly, in order to identify systems of complementary practices, data relating to the thirteen practices were factor analyzed through a PCA. Two factors emerged. The "Employee skills and organizational structures" factor included a broad range of practices aimed at enhancing the knowledge, skills, and abilities of employees, and at enabling them to exploit these abilities in performing their job. The second factor was named "Employee motivation": it included practices relating to employees' performance appraisal and compensation. The productivity indicator was the ratio of sales to the number of employees, and it was measured in the period July 1, 1991–June 30, 1992. A number of controls were inserted in the specification of the model, including firm size, recent growth of sales, capital intensity, R&D intensity, firm specific risk (i.e. the β), level of union coverage, and several industry-specific characteristics. The aim was to alleviate the omitted-variable problem from which cross-section estimates suffer.

When the Employee skills and organizational structures and Employee motivation factors were introduced individually in the estimates, they had a positive statistically significant coefficient. However, when both factors were entered simultaneously, only the latter was statistically significant. The estimated productivity increase was found to be of great economic magnitude: a standard deviation increase of the Employee motivation factor raised sales by about $27.000, corresponding to 16.4% of average sales per employee. Lastly, an interactive term between the two factors exhibited a positive, statistically significant coefficient, indicating the existence of superadditive effects from the use of a larger set of practices.

Black and Lynch (1996) used data from the Educational Quality of the Workforce National Employers' Survey (EQW–NES) that was administered by the US Bureau of the Census in 1994 to a nationally representative sample of private establishments with more than twenty employees. The sample considered in this study included 1,621 manufacturing and 1,324 non manufacturing establishments. The authors estimated a standard augmented Cobb–Douglas production function with constant returns to scale; output was proxied by 1993 sales. In addition to several controls, the explanatory variables included dummy variables for the use of TQM and benchmarking. Other explanatory variables reflected the extent and type of training of workers and the criteria used in recruiting personnel. The cross-sectional estimates failed to detect any positive effect of the IWPs under examination on current firm productivity. Conversely, for HRMPs, the proportion of time spent in formal training outside working hours and the use of grades as a priority in recruiting were found to have positive effects on the productivity of manufacturing and non-manufacturing establishments, respectively.

In a later work, Black and Lynch (2001) matched the EQW–NES data with annual data relating to production inputs and output provided by the Longitudinal Research Database. For a sample composed of 627 manufacturing plants, they exploited the longitudinal dimension of the data set to obtain more robust estimates of the Cobb–Douglas production function.[13] In addition to the two dummies mentioned above relating to the use of TQM and benchmarking, they considered the percentage of workers in SMT, other HRMPs, and SOVs. The latter variables included the number of managerial levels in plants (i.e. organizational depth) and the average number of workers per supervisor (i.e. the horizontal span of control). The former referred to the extent of training of workers and the use of profit-sharing compensation schemes. Unfortunately, all these variables were measured in 1993 only, so the authors were forced to resort to a two-step estimation procedure. In the first step, they used panel data estimation techniques (i.e. WG and GMM) to obtain estimates of the coefficients of capital, labor, and materials in the production function. These estimates were used to calculate the average value of the residual over the 1988–93 period for each plant. This value is an estimate of the plant-specific time-invariant component of the residual. In the second step it was regressed against IWPs, HRMPs,

SOVs, and a large set of control variables measured in 1993. Of course, this procedure does not assure that the cross-sectional estimates are not distorted.

Again, the econometric results were weak. Only benchmarking and, to a lesser extent, profit-sharing schemes for production, clerical and technical workers, and regular meetings among employees consistently had a positive statistically significant coefficient. TQM exhibited a negative coefficient, significant in the GMM estimates. All the remaining organizational variables turned out to have insignificant effects on plant productivity. In addition, the authors inserted in the specification of the model a wide range of interactive effects, but found no evidence of any synergistic gains from a combination of different organizational variables.

Bresnahan *et al.* (2002) collected survey-based perceptual data in 1995–6 from senior HR managers of 379 US firms. Data related to the importance of (i) IWPs as SMT and QC, (ii) HRMPs aimed at encouraging teamwork, and (iii) the decentralization of decision authority to plant workers at a firm's typical establishment. Based on these perceptual measures, they built an aggregate decentralizing decision-making to teams indicator. They considered the marginal impact on firm output measured by value added of this aggregate indicator in a standard production function framework. Even though they had longitudinal data on value added, labor and capital coming from Compustat, the work reorganization indicator was measured only at the end of the observation period. They found that this indicator was positively related to productivity and had a greater positive effect for IT-intensive firms (on this issue, see also Section 5.5).

5.3.2.2   Panel data estimates

As was highlighted in the previous subsection, cross-section estimates have serious shortcomings. A number of recent studies have used panel data estimation techniques. Unfortunately, in most of these studies only a small number of observations (i.e. generally two) on the use of IWPs, HRMPs, and SOVs are available over time for each firm. Hence, one may wonder whether the estimates are robust.

Cappelli and Neumark (2001) considered two subsequent waves of the EQW–NES survey administered in 1994 and 1997 and matched these data with data provided by the Longitudinal Research Database from 1977 onwards. They focused on manufacturing plants and built two panel data sets that included 433 plants observed in the years 1977 and 1993, and 660 plants observed in the years 1977 and 1996, respectively.

They considered SMT, job rotation, TQM, and benchmarking. They also considered HRMPs relating to pay for quality and skills and profit-sharing compensation schemes, and training. The implicit assumption they made was that in 1977 no plant had adopted any of the organizational practices under examination. Under this assumption, there was a substantial number of changers in the two data sets; this reduced the extent of the downward bias generated in the WG estimates by measurement errors. They estimated an augmented Cobb–Douglas production function that, in addition to IWP and HRMP variables, included several controls. They also investigated the presence of interactive effects between those practices that are intentionally designed to reinforce each other (e.g. SMT, job rotation, teamwork training, and incentive-based compensations schemes). Altogether, the econometric results were weak. There was no statistically significant evidence of a positive effect of individual organizational practices on labor productivity, even though the coefficients of these variables tended to be positive. Nor there was evidence of any synergistic effects between different practices, with the exception of a positive interaction between SMT and incentive-based compensation schemes (i.e. pay for skills and profit sharing).

Black and Lynch (2004) used the same data to build a two-year panel data set composed of the 284 manufacturing plants that participated in both EQW–NES surveys.[14] While first-differencing the data, they estimated whether changes in the use of IWPs (i.e. benchmarking, reengineering, the proportion of workers in SMT, the proportion of workers meeting regularly in groups), HRMPs (i.e. profit-sharing or stock options plans, importance of grades and communication skills in recruiting), and organizational depth over this period had any effect on changes in labor productivity. The only organizational design characteristic that appeared to have a significant effect on productivity in the panel estimates was that capturing reengineering. All the remaining organizational variables failed to exhibit any effect. Conversely, and quite surprisingly, the percentage of workers in SMT had a negative statistically significant coefficient.

Studies that considered firms located outside the US found evidence of a more positive effect of organizational design variables on productivity. Caroli and Van Reenen (2001) used a long-differenced production function to study the contribution of adoption of QC and delayering (i.e. a decrease in organizational depth) to the growth of the productivity of French establishments between 1992 and 1996. Organizational data were provided by the ER survey administered in 1992 to the senior managers of 2,500 French establishments. The questions on workplace reorganization related to the previous three years. Data on value added and capital stock came from the *Bilans industriels et commerciaux* (BIC) database. The authors showed that, all else equal, QC and delayering had a positive effect on productivity, with the coefficient of this latter variable being greater the higher the level of skills of plants' workforce.

Bauer (2003) linked survey-based data on changes in organizational design implemented by German establishments in the period 1993–5 that were provided by the IAB establishment panel to economic data relating to 1995 and 1997 provided by the Employment Statistics Register. The two-year panel data sets included 1,319 (1993–5) and 921 (1993–7) establishments, respectively. The two data sets were used to assess the short-run and long-run productivity effects of organizational changes. The focus here was on IWPs (i.e. teamwork) and SOVs (i.e. delayering and decentralization of decision authority to subordinates) captured by three dummy variables. These variables were combined through a PCA in a organizational change factor. Several controls were added to the specification of a standard Cobb–Douglas production function. In addition to cross-section estimates relating organizational changes that occurred in the 1993–5 period to end-of-period productivity levels (measured either in 1995 or in 1997), the authors used WG, GMM, and correlated random coefficient panel data estimates. This latter estimation technique aims to control for the different effects of organizational change across sample establishments (see, for instance, Wooldridge 1997; Heckman and Vytlacil 2000).

The coefficient of the organizational change factor, that was negative but insignificant in the cross-section estimates, was positive and statistically significant in the WG estimates, and it became more than four time greater in the GMM and random coefficient estimates. These results were interpreted by the author as an indication that cross-section estimates were downwardly biased, possibly because establishments that were performing poorly were more prone to organizational change than their better-performing counterparts (on this issue, see Chapter 4, Sections 4.3 and 4.4). In addition, when the estimates were replicated on the 1997 productivity data the positive effect engendered by organizational changes became even greater, in accordance with the view that it took some time (basically a couple of years) for organizational changes to display their positive effect on firm performance.

Janod and Saint-Martin (2004) departed from the methodology followed by most previous studies in that they used non-parametric estimates. In so doing, they relaxed the assumptions made by those studies as to the parametric form of the production function (i.e. Cobb–Douglas with constant returns to scale). Moreover, they also relaxed the assumption that the effects of organizational variables were homogenous across firms. They built a panel data set composed of 2,404 French manufacturing firms with twenty employees or more. Data on the introduction of thirteen organizational practices that included SMT, QC, and other changes in organizational design (e.g. delayering, greater versatility of the workforce) in the period 1994–7 were provided by the COI survey, administered in 1997. These data were matched with economic data from the DIANE (*DIsque pour l'ANalyse Economique*) (1995, 1997, and 1999 files). The authors built a work reorganization dummy variable indicating firms that were involved in two or more organizational changes. They also measured the number of organizational changes implemented by firms in the observation period. They assessed the effects of these variables on both labor and capital productivity (i.e. the ratios of value added to employees and value added to capital).

They used the propensity score method (see Rosenbaum and Rubin 1983) to match reorganized and non-reorganized firms. They first-differenced economic data to control for unobservable firm-specific time-invariant effects and used a Kernel-matching estimator to evaluate the causal effect of the work reorganization dummy on firm productivity. Then they extended the analysis to the examination of the effects engendered by the intensity of work reorganization through a pairwise comparison of firms with different levels of work reorganization (that is, firms having introduced a different number of organizational changes).

The findings of the estimates showed that work reorganization had a substantial, positive, statistically significant effect on both labor and capital productivity, while it did not affect the intensity of use of production factors. In other words, labor and capital seemed to be used more efficiently by reorganized firms. These effects were even more apparent for firms that introduced a larger number of organizational changes, possibly revealing the presence of complementarity between different aspects of organizational design.

As far as we know, Kato and Morishima's (2002) study is unique in that they did use a long (twenty years, from 1973 to 1992) panel data set relating to 126 Japanese listed manufacturing firms. The drawback is that they focused on specific practices reflecting employee participation in decisions (i.e. the set-up of joint labor–management committees and shop floor committees) and financial participation (i.e. ESOP and other general profit-sharing plans). This makes it difficult to compare their results with those of other studies. Moreover, all data on organizational practices were provided by the HRM survey of Japanese listed firms conducted at Keio University in 1993. As the period under consideration is longer than in other studies, the retrospective bias is likely to be more severe in their data on organizational changes.

The authors estimated both Cobb–Douglas and translog production functions augmented with variables capturing organizational changes. More precisely, following the approach originally proposed by Ichniowski and his colleagues, they defined four "Participation systems." System 4 (S4) firms are those that do not adopt any organizational practice. System 3 (S3) firms have adopted either employee participation practices or incentive compensation schemes, but not both, so they do not exploit potential complementarities between these two types of practices. System 2 (S2) firms lack either joint labor–management committees or shop floor committees, while System 1 (S1) firms have adopted all the practices under examination. They used both WG and IV estimators.[15] Moreover, they inserted in the specification of the model lagged (up to ten years) organizational variables to capture delayed effects on firm productivity. The results of the estimates indicated that the S3 and S2 dummies had no effect on productivity, either in the short or in the long term. Conversely, a positive effect of S1 on productivity of around + 9% showed up when this variable was lagged seven or more years. The authors deduced that while use of individual organizational practices basically had no influence on firm performance, positive effects could be obtained, but only in the long run, when these different aspects of organizational design were used in combination.

5.4 Effects of organizational design on firm profitability

5.4.1 Previous empirical evidence

Again, the first study of the relation between organizational variables and firm profitability is Ichniowski (1990). Profitability was measured by Tobin's q, defined as the ratio of the expected discounted value of firm's net income to the replacement cost of its assets. The results of OLS estimates indicated that the adoption of a system of practices including enriched job design was associated with higher financial performance. Nonetheless, the small size of the sample (composed of only 65 US firms) made it difficult to draw robust conclusions from these results.

Huselid (1995) considered two indicators of firm profitability: Tobin's q, defined as the ratio of the market value of the firm to the replacement cost of its assets, and the gross rate of return on capital (GRATE), given by the ratio of cash flow to the gross capital stock. These indicators were regressed against the Employee skills and organizational structures and Employee motivation factors and the controls that were described in Section 5.3.2.1. The two factors exhibited a positive statistically significant effect on Tobin's q, both individually and jointly. Conversely, in the GRATE equation, only the former factor had a positive statistically significant coefficient, while the latter one was insignificant. Moreover, there again was evidence of a positive interactive effect between the two factors in both the Tobin's q and GRATE equations.

In a later work, Huselid and Becker (1996) attempted to evaluate the magnitude of the bias that arises from unobserved heterogeneity in these estimates. For this purpose, they replicated their analysis on a panel dataset composed of 218 firms observed in 1991 and 1993. They defined a new independent variable capturing the adoption of new organizational practices (*HRTOTAL*), defined as the sum of the values of the two above-mentioned factors. This variable exhibited a positive statistically significant coefficient in the OLS pooled estimates; conversely, this positive effect largely vanished in the WG estimates. The authors also estimated a random effects model: in this specification, the coefficient of *HRTOTAL* was positive and significant, even though its magnitude was around 70% lower than in the pooled estimates. They deduced that while cross-section estimates were probably upwardly biased due to a lack of control for factors that positively affect both the organizational variables under scrutiny and firm performance (e.g. the quality of firms' management), WG estimates suffered from an opposite (i.e. downward) bias as first-differencing amplified the effects of measurement errors in the organizational variables, especially if the observation period was short and so there were few changers. Lastly, the authors also provided evidence of the existence of a lag between implementation of organizational changes and the appearance of economic benefits. In fact, the positive effects of *HRTOTAL* on firm profitability were greater when the 1992 and 1993 values of Tobin's q and GRATE replaced the values measured in 1991.

5.4.2 Evidence based on the new empirical methodology

As far as we know, Colombo *et al.* (2007) is the only study of the effects on firm profitability of changes in organizational design that relies on a sufficiently long longitudinal data set. Another strength of this work is consideration of both the adoption of IWPs and HRMPs and changes in SOVs (see below).

More precisely, the plant-level data from FLAUTO (see the Appendix of this book for a detailed description) relating to organizational design variables in Italian manufacturing plants described in Chapter 1 were matched with firm-level data on profitability from the AIDA database (the database of the Italian Chambers of Commerce). Profitability was measured by returns on investment (i.e. ROI), defined as the ratio of operating profits (i.e. earnings from continuing operations before interest expenses and taxes) to the sum of equity and debt capital.[16] Data on profitability were available for the period 1991-7. In particular, the study concentrated on plants owned by single-plant firms, so as to construct a panel data set of information at the same level of analysis. This reduced the sample size from 438 to 338 units. In addition, since AIDA contains information only on the 30,000 largest Italian firms (in terms of sales), the matching between the two data sets further reduced the number of firms to 109.

In spite of the relatively small number of firms in the data set, this study has a number of strengths. First, there is repeated yearly information on organizational variables over a long period (1975-96), so the authors were able to deal with unobserved heterogeneity, endogeneity, and measurement error problems more effectively than in previous studies. Of course, as the organizational data are provided by an individual survey, the usual drawback relating to the possible presence of a retrospective bias applies. Moreover, as was mentioned above the data on organizational changes included both the adoption of IWPs (i.e. SMT, job rotation, and TQM practices) and HRMPs (i.e. pay for quality and skills and profit-sharing compensation schemes), and changes in SOVs (i.e. changes in organizational depth and the allocation of authority over strategic and operating decisions). For the allocation of decision authority, the authors used an aggregate decentralization index that was calculated as minus the mean value of the two indicators of centralization of strategic and operating decisions described in Chapter 1, Section 1.2.1. Consideration of different aspects of organizational design made it possible to assess the presence in a proper panel data framework of synergistic effects from the introduction of mutually reinforcing organizational changes.

The author started the econometric analysis from the estimate of a random effects panel data model specification in which variables capturing the adoption of new organizational practices were inserted individually.[17] Adoptions of profit-sharing schemes and TQM practices were found to have positive, statistically significant effects on firm profitability, while the other organizational practice variables were insignificant. The number of hierarchical levels and the decentralization index were then added to the model specification. The coefficient of this latter indicator, though positive, was insignificant. The former variable exhibited an inverted U-shaped relation with firm profitability, with the best performance being obtained in correspondence of a number of levels between three and four.[18]

The authors then used factor analysis to obtain an aggregate indicator of the adoption of the bundle of IWPs and HRMPs under consideration. The resulting HPWP index explained 32.8% of the total variance: all organizational practices had a positive factor loading. When this index replaced the individual practice variables it exhibited a positive highly significant coefficient, with the effect of the other variables remaining unchanged. This result supports the view that firm profitability increases with the extent of the use of a bundle of (allegedly) complementary and mutually reinforcing organizational practices.

Moreover, in order to assess the existence of synergistic effects between the adoption of new organizational practices and of a flatter, more decentralized organization, the authors added to the model specification the interactive terms *HPWP × Decentralization, HPWP × Level*, and *HPWP × Level²*. The results were quite interesting. While the coefficients of the linear and squared terms of *Level* were almost unchanged, the two interactive terms that included this variable were insignificant. So there is no evidence that for rather bureaucratic firms delayering has a more positive effect on firm profitability if these firms are using a bundle of new organizational practices rather than traditional practices. For the other organizational variables, the coefficients of *HPWP* and *Decentralization* were positive, though insignificant. Conversely, their interactive term *HPWP × Decentralization* exhibited a positive, highly significant coefficient. This result points to the complementarity inherent in the adoption of a set of mutually reinforcing organizational practices from one side, and the delegation of decision authority down the corporate hierarchy from the other. Note also that this synergistic effect on firm profitability was found to be of great economic magnitude. In fact, with all controls at their mean values, a standard deviation increase of both *HPWP* and *Decentralization* above their mean values led to a 64.4% profitability increase (i.e. from 5.7% to 9.3%). A model specification that included the interactive terms *Decentralization × Level* and *Decentralization × Level²* was also considered. Both these interactive terms were found not to be statistically significant at conventional confidence levels. So there was no evidence of any superadditive effects between delayering and decentralization of decision authority.

Lastly, the authors used a GMM-system estimator to estimate a version of the model that contained an autoregressive profitability term, with the additional benefit of better control for the endogeneity of the organizational variables. The results were very close to those described above.

5.5   More on the complementarity between technological and organizational innovations

Several studies have given considerable attention to the *joint effects* on firm performance of the adoption of technological innovations relating to PA technologies and ICTs and changes in organizational design.[19] If complementarity indeed exists between technological and organizational innovations, one should observe a positive effect on firm performance when they are used in combination over and above the effects that can be obtained by use of each individual type of innovation in isolation.

Again, econometric studies in this stream of literature originally focused on specific industries and/or firms.[20] For instance, Kelley (1994, 1996) considered machining operations of a large sample of US plants. She found that a job redesign strategy giving greater autonomy to line workers had a positive effect on productivity only for products made through PA equipment. Moreover, small firms were found to derive substantial benefits from reliance on group-based participative HRMPs only if they also used PA technologies. Similarly, Batt (1999) showed that in telecommunication services, team practices boosted the productivity of the customer service employees of a regional Bell operating company, especially when they were associated with the use of advanced technologies (see Section 5.3.1.4).

Econometric work based on large cross-industry data sets is rare, and the findings are far from robust. Caroli and Van Reenen (2001) showed that the positive impact on productivity growth of greater use of IT (of delayering) was greater in French plants where some internal managerial layers had been eliminated (IT was used by a greater proportion of workers). However, in their regressions the interaction of the organizational change and technology variables was not significant at conventional confidence levels.

Bresnahan *et al.* (2002) highlighted that, in a production function framework, the decentralizing decision-making to teams aggregate indicator and the variable measuring the stock of IT capital contributed to output separately, but they were more productive when the level of the other variable was also high. Similar results were obtained when firm performance was measured differently; for instance, Brynjolfsson *et al.* (2000) showed that the stock market value of a dollar of IT capital was considerably greater in decentralized firms than in centralized ones.

Greenan and Mairesse (2004) estimated a long-differenced augmented production function relating to the period 1992–8; they inserted in the model specification a series of dummies taking into account high or low use of IT and of innovative organizational practices in 1997 and changes in them in the period 1994–7. The econometric findings suggested that there were superadditive effects on productivity growth arising from use of organizational innovations in conjunction with IT (i.e. static complementarity). Conversely, there was no evidence of dynamic complementarity. In fact, the effect on productivity growth of switching to a high use of IT (organizational innovations) seemed not to depend on whether in 1994 the establishment under scrutiny was in the high organizational innovations (IT) category. Nor there were any synergistic gains from simultaneous increases in the use of both types of innovations over and above those that could be obtained by changing the intensity of use of each individual innovation in isolation.

Lastly, Colombo *et al.* (2007), in their analysis of the impact of organizational design variables on the profitability of Italian manufacturing firms, considered among control variables the count of the PA technologies used by sample plants (AMT).[21] This variable exhibited a positive, though insignificant, coefficient. Furthermore, in order to check for the existence of superadditive effects from the introduction of both technological and organizational innovations they proceeded to insert in the model specification four additional interactive terms: *AMT × HPWP*, *AMT × Decentralization*, *AMT × Level*, and *AMT × Level²*. The null hypothesis that *AMT* has no effect on firm profitability, either alone or in combination with organizational changes, was rejected by a Wald-test, even though only at 10%. In particular, the interactive term *AMT × HPWP* was found to have a positive coefficient significant at 5%, indicating that the effects on profitability of the use of PA technologies become more positive when they are accompanied by the introduction of supposedly complementary HPWPs. Moreover, the interactive terms *AMT × Level* and *AMT × Level²* exhibited positive and negative statistically significant (at 5%) coefficients, respectively. Hence, for very bureaucratic firms (i.e. number of levels greater than four) the elimination of intermediate layers leads to a greater profitability increase the greater is the number of PA technologies in use.

5.6 Concluding remarks

The aim of this chapter was to analyze empirically the effects on firm performance of organizational design variables. In particular, in accordance with the definition of organizational design adopted in this book, we considered both the adoption of organizational practices (i.e. IWPs and HRMPs) and structural dimensions of organizational design (i.e. SOVs – that is, organizational depth and the allocation of decision authority).

The empirical literature is quite complex and articulated; Tables 5.1a and 5.1b summarize the main findings and methodologies of cross-industry studies.[22]

Empirical studies that analyzed specific industries starting from the inside-econometric work by Ichniowski and colleagues in the steel industry, documented sizable productivity gains from the introduction of bundles of complementary organizational innovations, even though the impact of individual organizational practices was generally found to be negligible.

Conversely, quantitative cross-industry studies provided more articulated evidence. For US firms, work at firm level showed a positive effect of the adoption of bundles of complementary organizational changes on firm performance (Ichniowski 1990; Huselid 1995; Huselid and Becker 1996). Nonetheless, with a few exceptions (e.g. Bresnahan *et al.* 2002), these results were not replicated by studies at establishment level that focused attention on productivity (e.g. Cappelli and Neumark 2001, Black and Lynch 1996, 2001, 2004). Studies that considered firms located outside the US offer a more positive view. Firms involved in organizational changes were generally found to outperform their non-reorganized counterparts. Moreover, the effects of these changes on productivity seemed to become stronger in the longer term.

Only a few studies considered firm profitability. This is unfortunate as there is a growing consensus that the use of organizational variables often results in an increase of wages and other costs (e.g. Appelbaum *et al.* 2000; Cappelli and Neumark 2001; Bauer and Bender 2001; Bauer 2003; Black and Lynch 2004; for an opposite view see Osterman 2000). So while organizational innovations may well lead to greater productivity, if the salary of employees and other costs also increase it is unclear whether there are any benefits to firm shareholders. Even though the

Table 5.1a Cross-industry studies on the effect of organizational design on firm (or plant) performance: characteristics of the empirical methodology

	Country	Sector	Sample	Performance indicator	Methodology
Ichniowski (1990)	US	Manufacturing sectors	US lines of production. 126 lines observed in 1986.	Sales per employees. Tobin's q.	Cross-section.
Huselid (1995)	US	All sectors	US listed firms with more than 100 employees. 968 firms observed in 1991.	Sales per employees. Tobin's q. GRATE.	Cross-section.
Huselid and Becker (1996)	US	All sectors	US listed firms with more than 100 employees. 826 firms observed in 1991, out of which 218 observed also in 1993.	Tobin's q. GRATE.	Cross-section. Panel (2 years: 1991–3). WG and random effects.
Black and Lynch (1996)	US	All sectors	EQW–NES (1994). 1,621 manufacturing and 1,324 non-manufacturing establishments observed in 1993.	Sales per employees. Augmented Cobb–Douglas production function with constant returns to scale.	Cross-section.
Black and Lynch (2001)	US	Manufacturing	EQW–NES (1994), Longitudinal Research Database. 627 plants with twenty employees or more observed in 1993.	Unobserved time-invariant plant-specific effect of a Cobb–Douglas production function with constant returns to scale, average over the 1988–93 period.	Cross-section.
Cappelli and Neumark (2001)	US	Manufacturing	EQW–NES (1994 and 1997), Longitudinal Research Database. Manufacturing plants with twenty employees or more. 433 in the 1977–93 panel, 660 in the 1977–96 panel. 663 in the 1993 cross-section.	Log of sales per employee. Augmented Cobb–Douglas production function.	Cross-section. Panel (2 years, 1977–93 and 1977–96). WG.
Caroli and Van Reenen (2001)	French, UK	All sectors	French: ER survey (1992) matched with BIC database. UK: WIRS survey (1984 and 1990).	Production function.	Panel (2 years).
Bresnahan et al. (2002)	US	All sectors	379 US firms observed in 1995–6.	Production function.	Cross-section

Continued

Table 5.1a Continued

	Country	Sector	Sample	Performance indicator	Methodology
Kato and Morishima (2002)	Japan	Manufacturing	Japanese listed firms. 126 firms in 1973–92.	Augmented Cobb–Douglas and translog production functions.	Panel (twenty years, 1973–92). WG and IV estimators.
Bauer (2003)	Germany	All sectors (excl. agriculture, mining, non-profit)	IAB Establishment Panel. Employment Statistics Register. 1,319 firms in the 1993–5 panel. 921 firms in the 1993–7 panel.	Log of sales per employee.	Cross-section. Panel (2 years: 1993–5 and 1993–7). WG, GMM, random coefficient.
Black and Lynch (2004)	US	All sectors	EQW-NES (1994 and 1997), Longitudinal Research Database. Manufacturing plants with twenty employees or more. 284 in the 1993–6 panel. 1,493 in the 1996 cross-section.	Log sales per employees. Augmented Cobb–Douglas production function.	Cross-section. Panel (2 years, 1993–6).
Janod and Saint-Martin (2004)	France	Manufacturing	COI survey, DIANE. French manufacturing firms with twenty employees or more. 2,404 firms observed in 1994–9.	Value added/employees. Value added/capital.	Panel. Kernel matching estimator.
Colombo *et al.* (2007)	Italy	Metalworking sectors	FLAUTO database, AIDA. Italian single-plant firms. 109 firms observed in 1991–7.	ROI	Panel (7 years: 1991–7). WG, random effects and GMM.

Table 5.1b Cross-industry studies on the effect of organizational design on firm (or plant) performance: effects of organizational variables

	IWPs	HRMPs	SOVs	Bundles of organizational variables	Results of organizational variables
Ichniowski (1990)	Flexible job design, formal employee–management communication channels	Formal employee training, merit-based promotions		Cluster analysis (9 dummies)	Mixing old and innovative practices produces bad performance
Huselid (1995)	% workers in teams	% workers with compensation schemes, training, recruitment		Factor analysis (2 factors: skill and organization structure, and motivation)	Productivity: significant effect of employee motivation factor; existence of synergistic effects Profitability: significant effect of both factors; existence of synergistic effects
Huselid and Becker (1996)	Teams	Compensation schemes, training, recruitment		Factor analysis	Weak positive effect of work practices; existence of a lag between implementation of practices and performance
Black and Lynch (1996)	TQM, benchmarking	Training, recruitment		Interactive effects	No effect
Black and Lynch (2001)	% workers in teams, TQM, benchmarking	Profit sharing, training, recruitment	Organizational depth, (avg.) span of control	Interactive effects	Only benchmarking has a systematic positive effect; no effect of other organizational variables (TQM negative)
Cappelli and Neumark (2001)	Teams, job rotation, TQM, benchmarking	Compensation schemes, training		Interactive effects	No statistically significant effect with the exception of the interaction between teams and incentive compensation schemes
Caroli and Van Reenen (2001)	QC		Delayering		Positive effect on productivity. Larger in establishments with highly skilled workforce

Continued

Table 5.1b Continued

	IWPs	HRMPs	SOVs	Bundles of organizational variables	Results of organizational variables
Bresnahan et al. (2002)	SMT, QC	Team promoting practices	Decentralization of decisions	Aggregate indicator	Positive impact of organizational variables considered in combination
Kato and Morishima (2002)	Decision committees	ESOP and profit-sharing schemes		Dummies (four systems)	Long run positive effect of the system of innovative practices
Bauer (2003)	Teams		Organizational depth (delayering), decentralization of decisions	Factor analysis (1 factor: organizational change)	Positive effect of organizational change
Black and Lynch (2004)	% workers in teams, TQM, benchmarking, reengineering	Profit-sharing	Organizational depth	Interactive effects	Only reengineering has a positive effect; no effect of other organizational variables (teams negative)
Janod and Saint-Martin (2004)	Teams, TQM, job rotation		Delayering	Dummy (work reorganization: 2 or more organizational changes)	Positive effect of work reorganization
Colombo et al. (2007)	Teams, job rotation, TQM	Profit-sharing, pay for skills schemes	Organizational depth, decentralization of decisions	Factor analysis (1 organizational practice factor) Interactive effects with SOVs	Positive synergistic effects of practices and decentralization of decisions Inverted U-shaped effect of organizational depth

available econometric evidence suggests a positive effect on firm profitability, it is fair to recognize that this evidence awaits further corroboration.

Actually, in this chapter we emphasized that the studies that tried to detect the effects of organizational design on firm performance suffer from several methodological problems. On the one hand, cross-sectional estimates are likely to be distorted because of a lack of proper control for unobserved heterogeneity and endogeneity bias. On the other hand, short panel data sets can deal effectively with the bias engendered by time-invariant unobserved factors, through first-differencing. However, if the number of changers is low, estimates are likely to be downward biased because of measurement errors. In addition, these data sets are unsuitable to the use of estimation techniques (i.e. GMM) that control for endogeneity bias. These methodological weaknesses may explain why results sometime are discordant.

As a matter of fact, without panel data sets with a sufficiently long longitudinal dimension it will be very difficult to ascertain whether use of IWPs, HRMPs, and changes in the structural dimensions of organizational design (i.e. delayering, delegation of decision authority) have positive effects on firm performance or not. Hence, the collection of this type of data clearly is a crucial priority in this field. As a corollary, this points to the need to focus attention on a limited number of key aspects of organizational design that can be measured through quantitative indicators, as we have done in this volume, so as to make this type of data collection effort manageable.

In fact, empirical studies often suffer from problems related to the definition of organizational variables (see Section 1.2.2 in Chapter 1 for a discussion of this issue for IWPs and HRMPs). This is particularly true for the structural dimensions of organizational design that are very often analyzed through the use of rather crude (dummy) variables that are the results of (too) simple questions (such as: "has the firm reduced the number of levels?"). Consequently, as explanatory variables often are rough indicators of organizational dimensions, the poor performance of regressors comes as no surprise. Again we have tried in this volume to suggest directions for improvements of research work in this area.

In spite of the existence of some open issues, the quantitative empirical literature that has been surveyed in this chapter has highlighted some interesting stylized facts on the relation between organizational design and firm performance.

There is general agreement in the literature that organizational variables, when they are changed in isolation, fail to exert any positive effect on the performance of firms. Conversely, several studies have clearly documented that there are synergistic gains from combining complementary changes in a cluster of organizational variables. In other words, the effects on firm performance of changes in organizational design are positive and of great economic magnitude only when firms adopt a bundle of coherent, mutually reinforcing organizational innovations. Early studies confined this effect to the adoption of Systems of practices (both IWPs and HRMPs), while more recent research has suggested that this synergistic gain extends to changes in the structural dimensions of organizations (i.e. the delegation of decision authority down the corporate hierarchy and delayering).

Synergistic gains may also possibly originate from the adoption of PA technologies and ICTs in conjunction with these changes in organizational design, even though it is fair to acknowledge that the empirical evidence on this issue still is rather weak.

These considerations have the obvious implication that changes in organizational design are no panacea for firms. However, they also show that when these changes are carefully designed and executed, taking into account the complementarities between different aspects of a firm's organization, they can generate great economic value for both firms and their employees. This remark offers an important justification for this book. In fact, it highlights how crucial it is to study the determinants and evolution of firms' organizational design, as we did in Chapters 1–4 of this book.

Conclusions

Scholars in management and economics and most practitioners probably agree that the choice of organizational design is a crucial activity of firms' managers.[1] Accordingly, the main objective of this book was to extend our understanding of the determinants of organizational design, its evolution over time and its effects on firm performance.

As was illustrated in previous chapters (in particular in Chapter 1), important changes have taken place since the 1980s in the organization of firms, especially large-sized ones. These changes have involved, among other things, the elimination of some intermediate hierarchical levels (i.e. delayering), the delegation of decision authority down the corporate hierarchy, and the adoption of new organizational practices concerning such aspects as the content of work, compensation schemes, recruitment, and training. At a macro-level, it is argued that these changes have been triggered by the inducement engendered by globalization and the associated stronger competitive pressures on firms, and the opportunity offered by new more versatile production technologies and more efficient information and communication technologies. As was documented in Chapter 5, adoption of this new organizational design has generally been beneficial to both firms and their employees.

Nonetheless, several fundamental questions on firms' organizational design remain unanswered. How ubiquitous are these organizational changes? Is the new organizational design a panacea for all firms, or are its virtues confined to large, complex firms which are the ones that benefit the most from greater responsiveness, faster decision-making, and a more proactive attitude of workers? Under what circumstances is the "old" organizational design still more efficient? And if the new organizational design is superior to the old, why is it not diffusing more rapidly? After all, several firms are still very hierarchical, centralize decision authority at the top of the hierarchy, and use rather traditional, Tayloristic organizational practices.

In our view, two serious obstacles have so far slowed down progress in this field. First, the empirical evidence on these issues is rather fragmented and most studies use qualitative investigations. In fact, the main source of evidence in this field is represented by business history and management case studies. Large-scale quantitative studies are relatively less numerous; moreover, they have been produced by scholars in disciplines as diverse as management, organization science, industrial economics, personnel economics, and sociology. Scholars were interested in different aspects of organizational design; they used different indicators and different methodologies. This has largely prevented cumulative learning and cross-fertilization between different studies.

Second, since the 1980s a growing body of theoretical work in economics has analyzed different aspects of firms' organizational design. Even though this literature is also rather fragmented, it has provided important insights. As was highlighted in the Introduction to this book, the information processing stream has emphasized the need for firms to choose an organizational design that economizes on information processing and communication costs. Conversely, the decentralization of incentive stream has considered the influence exerted on this choice by the need to take advantage of the specific knowledge dispersed among firms' personnel and to elicit effort from workers. Other streams of the theoretical literature have argued that, for several reasons, substantial adjustment costs are incurred by firms when they decide to change their organizational design. In spite of the interest of these works, they suffer from a serious shortcoming in that, partly as a consequence of the nature of the available empirical evidence, they have often abstained from developing testable (and eventually confutable) theoretical hypotheses as to how firms should over time design and modify their organization.

In this book we have tried to contribute to removing these obstacles. For this purpose, we have first of all systematized the findings offered by the quantitative empirical literature on organizational design. This was a necessary preliminary step to being able to give a more precise and comprehensive answer to the following question:

- what do we know about the determinants of organizational design and its evolution?

In addition, we have proposed a new empirical methodology that, taking inspiration from the seminal research work conducted in the 1960s by the Aston group, focuses attention on a limited number of key dimensions of organizational design: the *configuration* of corporate hierarchy (i.e. depth and span of control), the delegation of *decision authority*, and the adoption of (a limited number of) well defined *organizational practices* (IWPs and HRMPs). All these dimensions are measurable through quantitative indicators that can be applied in a standardized way to different samples of firms. Even though there are other important aspects of organizational design that have been neglected here, and other indicators can be defined, we are convinced that selectivity is a necessary condition to render large-scale empirical analysis of these issues manageable. In addition, these indicators are theoretically driven, so that they have then been used to test through econometric techniques the predictions derived by the theoretical literature. The attempt was to go beyond the blend of (sometime rather abstract) theory and qualitative evidence that has so far been dominant in this field. In so doing, we hope that this book paves the way for further research work along these lines.

As a final contribution, we think that it is useful to condense here the key stylized facts about organizational design that have been described in the volume, their relation to economic theory, and open issues that in our view need further research.

First, the different dimensions of organizational design have been found to covariate. This is in line with the intuition of the Aston group that there are empirically identifiable profiles of organizational design (see Pugh *et al.* 1963). In a static perspective, the depth of the organization and the delegation of decision authority are positively correlated. In a dynamic perspective, IWPs and HRMPs are generally adopted in bundles; when they are used in isolation, their contribution to firm performance is negligible. In addition, their adoption goes hand in hand (and the benefits from adoption increase) with the decentralization of authority over decisions (especially operating ones). This evidence has important implications for economic theory. In fact, what one needs is a structural theoretical model which is able to explain the simultaneous choices by firms of the different dimensions of organizational design. Conversely, failure to incorporate this interdependency into a model limits its explanatory power. This will undoubtedly be an important challenge for future theoretical work in this field.

Second, the depth of the hierarchy, the decentralization of decision authority, and the extent of use of new organizational practices, all increase with firm size. In other words, in small firms there is generally a smaller number of hierarchical layers and decision authority tends to be more concentrated at the top of the hierarchy than in their larger counterparts. Moreover the likelihood of adoption of IWPs and HRMPs is lower in the former than in the latter firms. This pattern is in line with arguments advanced by different streams of the theoretical literature. The information processing stream emphasizes the greater amount of information that needs to be processed and transmitted in larger firms, and the advantage in effective decision-making enjoyed by a hierarchical, decentralized organizational design. The decentralization of incentive stream highlights the difficulty of monitoring a large number of subordinates, which constraints the maximum span of control. Scholars in both streams (though with different modelling strategies) argue that delegation allows firms' workers to use their specific local knowledge to the advantage of firm performance.

Third, in all types of firms strategic decisions are more centralized than operating ones. On the one hand, the dispersed local knowledge of firms' workers is more pertinent to operating decisions than to strategic ones. On the other, externalities and close coordination are more important for the latter decisions than for the former. More generally, whenever locally optimal decisions are unlikely also to be optimal for the firm as a whole, centralization follows. In particular, this explains why, all else equal, decision authority tends to be more centralized in multi-unit firms that in single-unit ones.

Fourth, we have noticed above that large firms have undergone a quite radical modification of their organizational design. More precisely, what has happened is a flattening of their hierarchy (i.e. delayering), with no corresponding increase in the centralization of (strategic) decision-making. In other words, there has been a modification of the trade-off between organizational depth and centralization of decision authority in large firms. There is no evidence, however, that delayering extends to smaller firms.

Fifth, the decentralization of decision authority and the adoption of IWPs and HRMPs are favored in environments where cheap skilled labor is largely available in the local market and effective use of workers' specific knowledge plays a relatively more important role in assuring a sustainable competitive advantage (e.g. in a heterogenous business environment with high technological obsolescence). Again, this evidence clearly shows that there is no one best way to design the organization.[2] It also points to the complementarity between organizational design and the human capital of the workforce, in accordance with the arguments proposed by the skill-biased organizational change literature (e.g. Caroli and Van Reenen 2001). From this perspective, the competencies and incentives of workers are two sides of the same coin, and need to be studied in combination.

Sixth, in accordance with Woodward's (1958) claim that there exists a technological imperative, there is compelling evidence that technological innovations do indeed affect firms' organizational design. Nonetheless, this relation is fairly complex. In particular, it depends both on the type of technology (PA as opposed to ICT technologies, early-vintage technologies as opposed to later-vintage ones), and the specific use firms make of a given technology. For instance, while early mechanization of production resulted in greater centralization of decision authority, diffusion of PA technologies turned out to have an opposite effect. Moreover, these latter technologies are complementary to and favor the adoption of IWPs, HRMPs, and a more decentralized organizational design, but only when they are adopted in bundles; isolated adoption of individual PA technologies has basically no effect on organizational design. In addition, firm-specific characteristics are found to moderate the effect of technology on organizational design, as is clearly illustrated by the different effects of ICTs in small firms as opposed to large ones, and in independent units as opposed to units that are parts of larger groups. Different technologies have different impacts on the information processing, communication, and monitoring costs incurred by different firms. They also affect firms' productivity and versatility differently. Their effects on organizational design are the result of the rather unique combination of these factors. Consequently, in order to gain further insights into the relation between technology and firms' organizational design there is a need for a fine-grained, micro-level analysis aimed at disentangling, both conceptually and empirically, these different forces.

Lastly, we have shown in this volume that organizational design is shaped by, and adapts to, the contingent characteristics of firms and their business environment. Quite unsurprisingly, adaptation is more rapid the stronger the competitive pressures to which firms are subject. Nonetheless, adaptation is far from being smooth. On the contrary, we have clearly documented here that firms' organizational design is sticky. Firms are rather resistant to add or eliminate layers of their hierarchy, even over a long period of time. Moreover, the speed of diffusion of profitability-enhancing IWPs and HRMPs is much slower than that typical of technological innovations. Theoretical work suggests that there are powerful inertial forces that oppose changes in organizational design. In Chapter 4 we have documented three sources of structural inertia.

For one thing, sizable investments are generally tied up with a specific organizational design. As is claimed by real option theory (Dixit and Pindyck 1994), the associated sunk costs prevent a radical reorganization which would diminish the value of these investments. In accordance with this view, it has been shown that firms that adhere to a Tayloristic organization of production turn out to change their organizational depth more rarely than other firms. In addition, firms may decide to abstain from modifying their organizational design so as to avoid influence costs. In fact, this kind of change is likely to have redistributional consequences on the firm's employees: they will spend time and energy to the detriment of productive activities to influence decision-makers so as to turn any organizational change to their advantage. Structural inertia follows. This argument points to the importance of the allocation of decision authority, the ownership and governance of firms, and the way in which decisions are made (in particular, the extent of discretionary decision-making) to promote or prevent rapid adjustment of organizational design to changing environmental conditions. Lastly, because of the routinized behavior of individuals, in order for a new organizational design to be effective, the firm's workers and managers need first to learn how to operate it, and to unlearn old organizational practices. This learning process requires both committed and competent personnel, and adjustment costs have been consistently shown to be higher in firms that have an older, less educated workforce.

Appendix: Data Set and Empirical Methodology

The aim of this research project was to find robust evidence on structural organizational variables (SOVs) such as the allocation of decision-making, the span of control, the depth of the corporate hierarchy, and the adoption of organizational practices (i.e. IWPs and HRMPs) and technological innovations (e.g. PA technologies and ICTs). In Italy, there are no institutional sources that provide data on such features of business organizations. We thus designed and conducted – with the valuable help of researchers of the Politecnico di Milano and Univeristà di Pavia – a questionnaire analysis directed at collecting information on the organization of Italian manufacturing plants. This Appendix provides details of the methodology of the empirical survey. In addition, each chapter of the book contains further information on the organizational, technological, and other plant-specific variables that comprise the data set.

A.1 The sample

The current data set derives from the FLAUTO database developed in 1989 at the Politecnico di Milano. The sample was originally composed of 810 plants and was stratified by industry, geographical area, and plant size so as to faithfully represent the universe of all Italian metalworking plants with more than ten employees which were in operation in 1989 (for a detailed description of the FLAUTO database, see Cainarca *et al.* 1989). For each sample plant, the updated 1997 version of FLAUTO (i.e. FLAUTO97) provided information as to whether the plant was shut down during the period June 1989–June 1997. Plant closure was distinguished from situations where a plant had changed either its ownership structure as a consequence of merger and acquisition (M&A) activity or its location. We were thus able to avoid possible measurement errors resulting from localization, ownership, and other administrative changes (e.g. change of the name of the parent firm) which are quite usual in this type of exercise (for a discussion of such problems, see Dunne *et al.* 1988). Out of the 810 plants, 708 turned out to be still in operation in 1997.[1] The current data set constitutes an update and an extension of the old database.

In June 1997, a questionnaire was mailed to the plant managers of the 708 plants of the initial sample that were still in operation. The response rate was 62%, so that the current database includes 438 plants. The plant managers provided all the information relating to the organization of plants and its changes during the 1980s and 1990s. For each plant of the final sample, the plant manager was directly contacted by phone in order to check that answers were accurate and to complete the questionnaire if needed.

The current sample may thus contain some biases with respect to the Italian universe of metalworking plants from which it was originally drawn in 1989. However, we have important reasons to justify the use of FLAUTO97. The statistical robustness of questionnaire analyses closely depends on firms' response rate. In particular, empirical investigations that build on low response rates are very likely to suffer from sample selection-bias problems. Industrial practitioners know very well the difficulties in reaching a high response rate. A means of obtaining a high level of managers' collaboration is to link the fieldwork with a previous survey. In our case, the very high response rate was due to two reasons. First, we already knew the person (the plant manager) to contact within each of the 708 sample plants. Second, managers knew the institution, Politecnico di Milano, and they usually remembered the previous survey as well. Indeed, we found that the cooperation of most plant managers led not only to a high response rate but also to clean and reliable answers.[2] Even more importantly, the FLAUTO database provides information over a very long length of time (1975–97). Lastly, the very low failure rate of sample plants during the period 1989–97 (see n. 1) caused the exclusion of a very small proportion of sample plants.

As regards the conduct of the fieldwork, we started the survey in autumn 1996 with the definition of the questionnaire, which involved the active support of statisticians, sociologists, economists, and managers. In March 1997, we conducted ten personal pilot interviews with managers of plants of very different size and industry within the metalworking sector, so as to test the questionnaire's effectiveness. These interviews included managers of ABB, Alenia, Ansaldo, Contraves, Electrolux, FIAT Ferroviaria, Mannesmann, Merloni, Romana Lamiere, and Semikron. In April and May 1997, we personally contacted each plant manager of the 708 sample plants of FLAUTO that were in operation, in order to inform them of the research. Then, in June, we sent the questionnaire by mail with an introductory letter in which we further explained the objectives of the research and the links with the previous investigation. Finally, telephone follows-up aiming to check the

Table A.1 Size and geographical distribution of sample plants

	Final sample no. of plants	%	Initial sample no. of plants	%
Small plants (n. of employees < 100)	247	56.4	–	–
Medium plants (n. of empl. 100 – 500)	157	35.8	–	–
Large plants (n. of employees > 500)	34	7.8	–	–
North-west of Italy	248	56.6	390	55.1
North-east of Italy	111	25.4	173	24.4
Middle of Italy	54	12.3	91	12.9
Southern Italy and islands	25	5.7	54	7.6
Total	438	100.0	708	100.0

accuracy of the answers and to complete the questionnaires when needed were made during the summer.

Table A.1 shows the geographical and size distribution of sample plants. Concerning the size distribution, most plants have a number of employees lower than 100. This clearly reflects the overall size distribution of the Italian manufacturing sector, which is characterized by the presence of small and medium-sized firms. Similarly, the sample plants are mainly located in the industrialized northern part of Italy. Lastly, if we compare the geographical distribution of the initial sample composed of 708 plants to that of the final sample (438), it is evident that there is no manifest localization bias.[3]

In sum, FLAUTO97 is a comprehensive and reliable database that includes dynamic information over a large spectrum of plants' characteristics (see the next paragraph). It derives from a preceding survey conducted by the Politecnico di Milano in 1989. A possible source of bias of the current version concerns the exclusion of closed plants. However, the very high response rates of both investigations counterbalances this potential problem.[4] Furthermore, FLAUTO97 covers a period of time of almost twenty years, with detailed information at the plant level.

A.2 The industry

The metalworking sector includes the following nine two-digit industries (NACE–CLIO classification): production of metals (NACE–CLIO 27), fabricated metals (NACE–CLIO 28), non-electrical machinery (NACE–CLIO 29), computers and office equipment (NACE–CLIO 30), electrical machinery and electronics (NACE–CLIO 31), communication equipment (NACE–CLIO 32), scientific, precision, medical and optical instruments (NACE–CLIO 33), automotive industry (NACE–CLIO 34),

Table A.2   Industry distribution of sample plants

	No. of plants	%
NACE–CLIO 27	38	8.7
NACE–CLIO 28	127	29.0
NACE–CLIO 29	153	34.9
NACE–CLIO 30	2	0.5
NACE–CLIO 31	45	10.3
NACE–CLIO 32	23	5.3
NACE–CLIO 33	15	3.4
NACE–CLIO 34	19	4.3
NACE–CLIO 35	16	3.7
Total	438	100.0

and other transportation equipment (NACE–CLIO 35). In 1996 such industries accounted for 45% and 36% of total employment and number of firms of the Italian manufacturing sector, respectively (see *Censimento Intermedio dell'Industria e dei Servizi, Istat*). The distribution of sample plants by industry is shown in Table A.2.

Generally speaking, metalworking industries are ones that make most use of ICTs and PA technologies. Moreover, in the 1980s and 1990s these industries were rapid adopters of new technologies in the spheres of production (e.g. NC and CNC machine tools, FMS), design and engineering (CAD, CAM, and CAD–CAM), and communication (LANs), and of innovative production and logistic techniques (e.g. JIT). Finally, as is noted in the management literature (see Kenney and Florida 1988; Womack *et al.* 1990), the lean production model has been developed and initially applied in (some of) these industries. So, they constitute an ideal testbed to analyze quantitatively the organization of plants and firms and its evolution. In sum, the metalworking macro-sector covers almost half of the Italian manufacturing sector and in particular those industries that are of basic importance in the study of technological and organizational change.

A.3   FLAUTO97

The current version of the database, FLAUTO97, contains technological, organizational, and other plant-specific variables (see the list of all variables in Table A.3).

Plant-specific variables relate to: the number of employees in 1989 and 1997, the plant's location and industry, and its ownership status. In

Table A.3   List of the variables of FLAUTO97

General plant- and firm-specific variables:
- activity (NACE–CLIO three-digit code)
- location
- date of establishment
- number of employees (size)
- legal form of business
- ownership status (and characteristics of parent firm, if applicable)
- proportion of total production as a subcontractor
- production structure (job shop or line)
- use of JIT manufacturing

Performance variables:
- return on investment (ROI), ratio of operating profits (i.e. earnings from continuing operations before interest expenses and taxes) to the sum of equity and debt capital (period 1991–7)

Technology: date of first adoption of
- NC and CNC machine tools
- machining centers
- programmable robots
- inflexible manufacturing systems (IMS)
- flexible manufacturing systems and cells (FMS)
- intra-firm network: local area network (LAN) and/or on-line connection with headquarter
- intercompany network: electronic data interchange (EDI) with customers, suppliers, and/or subcontractors
- mainframe
- personal computer (PC)
- internet/intranet

Organization:
1. date of first adoption of the following IWPs and HRMPs:
- SMT and QC
- job rotation
- total quality management (TQM)
- incentive pay scheme (i.e. non-traditional individual pay for quality and skills incentive schemes)
- profit-sharing
2. structural organization variables:
- number of hierarchical levels of plant's organization (depth)
- average span of control (see Chapter 1)
- allocation of real and formal authority over a number of plant strategic and operating decisions (see Chapter 1)
- date of change (in the period 1975–96) of the number of levels and the allocation of authority, and eventually the characteristics of the previous organization

particular, individual plants are assigned to the industry which accounts for the largest share of production. For ownership status, we know if the plant is owned by a single- or multi-unit firm. Further, we can distinguish between foreign and Italian business groups as well as between state and private ownership. We know the nationality of the group, its size (in terms of number of employees), and other information that we derived from institutional sources (such as Hoover *et al.* 1998a and 1998b) and company reports.

Information relating to technological change concerns the date of first adoption of the following technologies: intrafirm network (LAN), interfirm network (EDI), internet/intranet, machining centers, NC and CNC stand-alone machine tools, FMS, programmable robots, IMS, personal computers (PCs), and mainframes.[5] We can therefore distinguish between technologies pertaining to the production and network spheres. Further, we may be interested in looking at the differences between plants that adopt old Tayloristic technologies (such as IMS) and those that make use of innovations that belong to the PA paradigm (such as FMS).

The data on the organization of plants represent the main novelty. First, we know the date of first adoption of the following IWPs and HRMPs: job rotation, team work, TQM, non-traditional individual pay incentive plans (i.e. pay for quality and skills), and profit- sharing.

In addition, we collected information that allows us to define quantitatively some structural characteristics of the organization (i.e. SOVs). These are the number of hierarchical levels that comprise the plant's organization and the allocation of decision authority over the plant's strategic and operating decisions. For each sample plant we have data on the current organizational structure. Moreover, we know if plants have changed their organization during the 1980s and 1990s, meaning that they changed one of or both these aspects of the organization. If the answer is affirmative, we have also information on the "old" organization, the organizational architecture that was in operation before the current one. Chapter 1 has a more detailed description of these organizational variables and their use in order to analyze quantitatively the organizational design of businesses and its dynamics.

Notes

Introduction: A New View of Organizational Design

1. On this issue see also the work by Simon (1945) on bounded rationality.
2. See Radner (1992) and Van Zandt (1999a) for a survey of this literature.
3. "Since transmission of information is costly in the sense of using resources, especially the time of individuals, it is cheaper and more efficient to transmit all the pieces of information once to a central place than to disseminate each of them to everyone" (Arrow, 1974, p. 68).
4. For a survey of this literature see Laffont and Martimort (1997); Poitevin (2000); Mookherjee (2006).
5. See Myerson (1982) and Williamson (1985) for an extended discussion.
6. For a survey of studies that analyzed decentralization (i) under the assumptions of the Revelation Principle, or (ii) with collusion among agents, see again Mookherjee (2006). The drawback of this literature is that it is difficult to obtain testable predictions on the determinants of decentralization.
7. For a similar attention to the interdependency of firms' decisions regarding organizational design, though in a different setting that does not include incentive considerations, see Morita (2005).
8. They consider a situation with a principal and two agents. There are two tasks that need to be performed. In addition, investment opportunities arise, each of which is discovered by one of the agents. Given agents' effort, each project modifies the gross returns of both tasks. Two noisy measures (with both a common noise and a task-specific one) are used by the principal to determine the rewards of the two agents.
9. Routines are the memory of the organization, being responsible for the preservation of distinctive capabilities in spite of the fact that individual employees come and go (Winter 1988). See also the analysis by Nelson and Winter (1982). For a critical review of the concept of routines and its relation to firms' distinctive capabilities, see Cohen *et al.* (1996).

1 A New Quantitative Empirical Methodology for the Analysis of Organizational Design and Dynamics

1. For instance, the sample originally analyzed by the Aston group included fifty-two organizations.
2. This subsection is based on Colombo and Delmastro (1999).
3. See Smeets and Warzynski (2006) for a relevant exception. In order to gather dynamic data on the span of control of each manager, the authors had however to focus only one firm.

4. If for instance the number of employees is eighty-five and the hierarchy is composed of four levels, then *Span* equals four. This means, in turn, that on average within the organization each superior has four subordinates.

5. To our knowledge, no comparable large-scale evidence exists for Japanese companies and companies located in other countries.

6. Unfortunately, these aspects were captured by categorical variables based on perceptual data. Strategic decisions refer to aspects such as long-term strategic planning and appraisal of major investments; operating decisions include decisions about such issues as the choice of main suppliers and the organization of production processes. See Ruigrok *et al.* (1999, p. 60).

7. Note, however, that delayering, even though prevalent, proved not to be ubiquitous among sample firms. In fact, 20% of firms declared that they had augmented the number of hierarchical levels between 1992 and 1996.

8. Technical section.

9. Values of the $\chi2$ tests are 5.79 (4 d.o.f.), 11.54 (4), and 14.13 (3) for small, medium, and large plants, respectively.

10. The data set on which this exercise is based (see the Appendix to the book) encompassess data on the level at which an Italian manufacturing plant takes the following six strategic decisions: (i) purchases of stand-alone machinery, (ii) purchases of large-scale capital equipment, (iii) introduction of new technologies, (iv) hiring and dismissals, (v) individual and collective incentives, and (vi) career paths. In addition, we also know what level of plant hierarchy is assigned responsibility for the following five operating activities: (a) daily plan of production, (b) weekly plan of production, (c) definition of employees' tasks, (d) control of results, and (e) modification of plan of production after sudden shocks. Technical section.

11. Indeed, only 3% of small plants belong to a group, while the same percentages are 39% and 76% for medium and large plants, respectively.

12. *t*-tests show that these differences are statistically significant at the 1% level.

13. For an interesting discussion of this issue that highlights the difficulties of translating in French such Anglo-Saxon terms as "job rotation," "multi-tasking," "multi-skilling," and "employee involvement practices," see Greenan and Mairesse (1999).

14. These methodological problems are probably responsible for most cross-country heterogeneity in diffusion levels. For instance, at the end of the 1990s, QC were reportedly adopted by 57% of US establishments and by 30% of UK establishments, while they seemed to be almost non-existent in Denmark with a diffusion level as low as 3%.

15. Note that there are well-known examples of companies in which internal reorganization lasted for many years, being obstructed by high-level corporate officers; in the end a drastic change of the top management was needed for the restructuring to take place (see, for instance, the cases of Du Pont in Chandler *et al.* 1996, of General Motors in Chandler 1962, of Mitsubishi in Moriwaka 1970, and of Siemens in Kocha 1971). In other instances, organizational changes were implemented only when a crisis threatened the very survival of the firm (see, for instance, Baker and Wruck 1989 and Wruck 1994, mentioned in Schaefer 1998).

2   The Determinants of the Allocation of Decision Authority

1. It is worth noticing that the term "monitoring" is used here quite broadly to include both the direct observation of the agents' actions and the availability of good performance measures on which efficient incentive schemes can be based. See for instance Milgrom and Roberts (1992, Chapters 6 and 7).
2. For instance, Marxist scholars have argued that the introduction of technical innovations has often served the purpose of placing labor in a weaker bargaining position (see Dow 1985). Had these decisions been delegated, these innovations would never have been introduced.
3. This argument is consistent with the claim originally made by contingency organizational theorists (see for instance Burns and Stalker 1961; Lawrence and Lorsch 1967) that increasing changeability and uncertainty in the business environment would lead to increasing decentralization of decision-making.
4. An alternative interpretation in the decentralization of incentive stream is provided by Raith (2005): the more urgent a decision, the more unlikely that the agent will have time to transmit to the principal her private information, and so the larger the knowledge gap of the principal. Delegation of decision authority follows.
5. The cost of using information about the environment is not simply the cost of collecting the information, but also the human cost of processing and understanding it (Van Zandt 1998, p. 25).
6. The cost of communication within an organization includes the receiver's processing cost and the sender's cost of formulating the message (van Zandt 1998, p. 25).
7. These arguments are also in line with the remark originally made by Leavitt and Whisler (1958) that the use of ICTs tends to make the process of recentralization of decisions easier. On this issue see also Whisler (1970, Chapter 4).
8. A similar reasoning applies to subcontractors: the need for close coordination with customers hinders decentralization of decision authority.
9. Concerning the use of ICTs, it has been argued by previous studies on the organization of firms that the sign of their net effects on the decentralization of decision authority depends very much on the level at which they are implemented. In particular, contrary to the expectations of earlier studies (see in particular Leavitt and Whisler 1958, Whisler 1970), starting in the 1970s, the lowering of the level at which ICTs are adopted drove a tendency towards decentralization (see Carter 1984, p. 251). For instance, Child (1984, p. 219) argues that "the improved analytical facilities provided by information technologies ... could be used to enhance the capacity of local units to make 'sound' judgments in their decision-making." According to the same logic, if there are differences across firms (e.g. small and large) in the level of the corporate hierarchy at which ICTs are implemented, the net effect of ICTs on the decentralization of authority may well differ across firms. For the sake of simplicity, this latter argument is not considered in Table 2.1.

10. The methodological framework on which these studies rely is described in Pugh *et al.* (1963). See also Inkson *et al.* (1970) for a parsimonious replication of the earlier studies. For a synthesis see Pugh and Hickson (1976).

11. The number of hierarchical levels was one of the measured indicators. This aspect will be analyzed in Chapter 3, where its relation to the delegation of decision authority will also be considered.

12. "Authority to make decisions was ascertained by asking 'Who is the last person whose assent must be obtained before *legitimate action* is taken – even if others have subsequently to confirm the decision?' This identified the level in the hierarchy where executive action could be authorized, even if this remained subject to a routine confirmation later" (see Pugh *et al.* 1968, p. 76).

13. Note, however, that this result was greatly affected by the presence of governmental bodies within the sample.

14. The association between technology and organizational design variables was originally analyzed by Woodward (1958, 1965). Her approach, confined to manufacturing organizations, was based on a classification of production methods ranging from the production of single units, through small batches, large batches, mass production, up to a continuous flow process production. For more details see Chapter 3, Section 3.3.2.

15. Child (1973) considered the following industries: chocolate & sweets, electronics, daily newspaper, pharmaceuticals, advertising, and insurance. For a detailed description of the sample see also Child (1972).

16. For a meta-analysis of empirical work on the relation between technological routineness reflected by workflow integration, production continuity, and the allocation of decision authority see Miller *et al.* (1991).

17. They also considered the assignment of decision authority in personnel matters. Results were in line with those illustrated above, but correlations with the technology variables were considerably weaker.

18. The argument that the allocation of decision authority depends on the nature of the decision under scrutiny is not new in the organizational empirical literature. See, for instance, Grinyer and Yasai-Ardekani (1980) and Carter (1984).

19. In addition to decision authority, Collins *et al.* (1999) also analyzed the determinants of the decentralization of *decision influence*, with this latter notion referring to the provision of information and advice useful for decision-making.

20. In each organization, six hierarchical levels were considered, from the company headquarters to operatives. For each decision "the lowest level (*in the organization*) that has the authority to decide ... to take action on the decision without waiting for confirmation from above" was recorded (Marsh 1992, p. 264).

21. Japanese plants seem to constitute an exception. In fact, Donaldson's (1986) meta-analysis showed that although most studies suggest a positive effect of size on the decentralization of decision authority, the one Japanese study reviewed (Azumi and Mc Millan 1981) was one of the two that did not find any positive relation.

22. In addition to Woodward's indicators, the authors considered the Aston workflow rigidity scale and an indicator of the level of automation based on Amber and Amber (1962).

23. Following Inkson *et al.* (1970), dependence of a bank was measured by summing three scales indicating the impersonality of its origin, its status, and its size relative to that of the parent organization (see Wong and Birnbaum-More 1994, p. 118).

24. For further information on these databases, see Chapter 1.

25. Firm-specific controls included, among others, firms' size, market share, diversification, ownership status, number of sites, capital intensity, skill level and age of workers, and percentage of employees working with computers. Industry-specific controls reflected capital and IT intensity and the level of competition (proxied by the Lerner index). The estimates showed that firms that had a younger and more skilled workforce had a greater percentage of workers using computers, and operated in IT-intensive industries and in a more competitive environment were more decentralized. The same holds true for larger, foreign-owned, multi-unit, and more diversified firms. Conversely, capital intensity seemed to play a negligible role.

26. Results relating to the decentralization measure obtained from the COI database were more robust for the subsample of firms that were part of larger groups.

27. Note that this indicator can also be regarded as a proxy for the urgency of decisions.

28. The indicators measuring workers' opportunism, managers' opportunism, and environmental uncertainty were provided by PCAs of a series of perceptual individual constructs.

29. This section is based on Colombo and Delmastro (2004). Technical sections are indicated by an asterisk (*).

30. Both decisions (ii) and (iii) concern investments in new capital equipment, with the main difference being the greater amount of financial resources involved on average by the former decision.

31. It is worth noticing that fixed effects models cannot be estimated since most of the independent variables are plant-specific and do not vary across types of decision.

32. In accordance with this view, note that the sum of the coefficients of *Network × Multi-plant* and *Multi-plant* (either *diversified* or *dominant business*) is found to be null at conventional levels. In other words, with the use of advanced ICTs the negative effect on delegation of decision authority of multi-plant ownership vanishes (see also the marginal effects reported in Table 2.A3).

33. In fact, the value of a Wald-test relating to the sum of the coefficients of *Size* and the interactive term *Network × Size* is not significant at conventional levels. The negligible effect of *Size* on the allocation of decision authority when *Network* equals one also is apparent from the values of the marginal effects reported in Table 2.A3.

34. Indeed, the null hypothesis of joint equality to zero of their coefficients is rejected by a LR test at the 1% level.

35. The negative relation of the Lerner index to decentralization of decision authority highlighted by Acemoglu *et al.* (2006) can be interpreted as evidence that delegation is more likely for firms that operate in a more competitive environment. In fact, for the corporate headquarters of these firms monitoring the decisions taken by managers at division or plant level is easier due to both benchmarking against competitors and the disciplining effects of greater competition.

36. For similar evidence in a very different context (i.e. US daily newspapers in the early 1980s) of the moderating role of organizational size on the effects of the use of computers on the allocation of decision authority, see Carter (1984). For opposing evidence, see Zeffane (1989).
37. The evidence provided by Acemoglu *et al.* (2006) that competition favors delegation of decision authority may also be interpreted as supporting the view that easier monitoring facilitates delegation.
38. Data are derived from Hoover *et al.* (1998a, 1998b), and Company Reports.
39. Of course, there are exceptions to this general rule relating to specific decisions. For instance, the plant manager is likely to care more about an investment decision which may make her job trivial than about whom to hire for office cleaning. Nevertheless, the point we want to make here is that lack of power as regards decisions that concern the management of the labor force is generally perceived by a plant manager as a serious impediment to the exercise of her function and a potential source of personnel problems.

3 The Determinants of the Corporate Hierarchy

1. As was mentioned in the Introduction to this volume, a hierarchical design saves on information processing and communications costs. On this issue see Arrow (1974, p. 68), Williamson (1975, Chapter 3).
2. Define N as the number of firm's employees which is the sum of the number of non-manual workers k and the number of line workers h. Then $k = N/(1 + h/k)$. The number of non-manual workers at Siemens was 370 in 1890 and 12,667 in 1913. If we assume a constant span of control equal to s, the number of hierarchical levels l, with the exclusion of the line worker layer, can be derived from $k = 1 + s + s^2 + \ldots + s^{l-1}$.
3. Note that this positive correlation between depth and delegation is not at odds with the tendency of firms, especially large-sized ones, in the last two decades to adopt a "flatter" and more decentralized organizational design (see Chapter 1, section 1.3.1 for a synthesis of evidence of this process). To put it simply, given size, (large) firms have reduced the number of layers of their organization, thus becoming flatter, without reducing accordingly the extent of the decentralization of decision authority. In other words, the depth–centralization frontier has moved downwards.
4. This argument echoes the view originally proposed by Leavitt and Whisler's (1958) seminal article that the diffusion of computers leads to the downsizing of middle management, and thus to a reduction of the number of hierarchical levels. On this issue see also Whisler (1970); Child (1984).
5. Management scholars generally argue that adoption of PA leads to flatter hierarchies (see, for instance, Zuboff 1988; Huber 1990; Goldhar *et al.* 1991).
6. According to Lindbeck and Snower (1996), advances in ICTs have had a similar effect on firm organization.
7. This is the intuition behind the claim that there exist archetypes of organizations. See Pugh *et al.* (1969a).

8. This indicator captured the level in the hierarchy to which power over thirty-seven recurrent decisions was formally assigned. A more precise definition of this indicator was provided in Chapter 2, Section 2.3.1.
9. Actually, the depth of the corporate hierarchy was measured here by the number of hierarchical levels between the CEO and divisional managers. In turn, a division was defined as the lowest level of profit center responsibility for a business unit that engineers, manufactures, and sells its own products.
10. Note that in this study the authors resorted to fixed effects (i.e. within-group) panel data estimates of the determinants of organizational depth. Hence, properly speaking, their results indicate that when a firm grows larger (downsizes), the number of levels increases (decreases).
11. Other studies that examined Japanese organizations found different results. For instance, Lincoln *et al.* (1986) compared fifty-one Japanese manufacturing plants with fifty-five US plants that operated in the same industries. Quite interestingly, the number of hierarchical levels was significantly higher in the Japanese plants (for similar findings see Azumi and McMillan 1981). Nonetheless, *F*-tests were not able to reject the equality of country-specific regressions. Moreover, in both the US and Japanese regressions the (log) size of plants exhibited a positive statistically significant coefficient.
12. These functions spanned activities as diverse as marketing and distribution, purchases, R&D, and human resource management (HRM). The activities in which computers were mostly used were administrative support of production and marketing and distribution. Note that nearly two-thirds of the sample plants did not have any data processing facilities at their own site. Most of them relied on off-site computers at division or corporate headquarter levels, or on time-sharing services.
13. The tendency of computer automation to be associated with an increase in the number of hierarchical levels had already been observed in US governmental agencies by Blau and Schoenherr (1971, pp. 74–7).
14. For documented evidence of this relation see, for instance, Rajan and Wulf (2006, Table 6).
15. This section is based on Delmastro (2002). Technical sections are indicated by an asterisk (*).
16. Actually, in the data set there is no precise information on the number of levels of plants that have six or more levels; see Chapter 1.
17. We have also introduced into the econometric model the number of employees in a linear form. The coefficient of the size variable is still positive, but insignificant. More specifically, a LR test shows that one can drop the linear form. This result mimics those of the earlier studies surveyed in Section 3.3.1.
18. This result is confirmed by Wald-tests of the difference between the coefficients of the AMT variables. While the coefficients of *AMT1*, *AMT2*, and *AMT3* are not statistically different from each other, that of *AMT4* is significantly different from the others at conventional levels. Note that we have also estimated a model in which we specify the effect of every single AMT (i.e. machining centers, robots, computerized numerically controlled stand-alone machine tools, and flexible manufacturing systems and cells) and of all possible technological combinations (consisting of clusters of two, three, and four flexible technologies). For the sake of synthesis, the estimates are not

reported here. The main finding can be summarized as follows. No single AMT displays a significant effect on the size of the corporate hierarchy, neither does a combination of two or even three flexible technologies. Only when all (four) types of AMT are introduced is the effect of PA on organizational depth large and significant.

19. Of course, we cannot rule out that corporate culture and other country-specific institutional factors determine differences in the organizational structure among firms of different nationality (e.g. Kreps 1985, Lincoln *et al.* 1986).

20. Evidence of complementary effects between PA technologies and innovative work practices is illustrated in Chapters 4 and 5.

21. For a description of these technologies see the Appendix to the book.

22. See again the Appendix to the book.

23. More precisely, *Just in time* is intended to reflect the adoption of JIT production schedule methods with clients and/or suppliers aimed at the reduction of a plant's stocks.

4　Evidence on the Determinants of Organizational Dynamics

1. There exists robust empirical evidence that demonstrates that the adoption of new technologies has a positive impact upon a firm's productivity (see, for instance, Stoneman and Kwon 1996; Brynjolfsson and Hitt 2003). The evidence on the impact on productivity of adoption of IWPs and HRMPs will be surveyed in Chapter 5 (see Section 5.3).

2. Colombo and Mosconi (1995); and Åstebro *et al.* (2006) analyze the diffusion of PA manufacturing and design technologies among Italian and US metal-working plants. They provide evidence that consistently with the above argument, the adoption of any one of the two technologies positively influences the subsequent adoption of the other. In addition, Colombo and Mosconi (1995) shows that adoption of both types of technologies is positively associated with use of new organizational practices such as total quality management (TQM) practices.

3. Note that while the arguments inspired by both Milgrom and Roberts (1990b) and Qian (1994) suggest that organizational change is stimulated by the adoption of advanced production technologies and new organizational practices, the authors differ as to the direction of the expected change. Milgrom and Roberts (1990b) predicts a decrease in the number of tiers of the corporate hierarchy; according to Qian (1994), conversely, one would expect an increase.

4. For a theoretical model of real-time decentralized information processing which shows how the need to base decisions on timely information leads to increasing reliance on small managerial teams, see van Zandt (1999b).

5. For a definition of organizational practices (i.e. IWPs and HRMPs) and international evidence on their adoption, see Chapter 1.

6. For details about the data sets used in these works, see Chapter 1, Section 1.3.3 (in particular, Table 1.15).

7. The organizational data on British establishments used by Caroli and Van Reenen (2001) were provided by different waves of the British Workplace Industrial Relations Survey (WIRS) administered in 1980, 1984, and 1990. More precisely, establishment managers were asked whether in the previous three years substantial changes in work organization affected either manual or non-manual workers. Even though the precise nature of organizational changes remained unspecified, evidence from the 1984 wave suggests that most organizational changes involved the assignment of greater responsibility to workers and a widening of the range of tasks they performed.

8. For a definition of structural organizational variables and international evidence on their recent evolution see Chapter 1; in addition, Chapters 2 and 3 deal with the static determinants of SOVs.

9. Quite surprisingly, in Collins *et al.*'s (1999) estimates, plant size measured at the beginning of the observation period exhibited a positive statistically significant effect on the increase in the number of levels over the observation period, after controlling for the initial number of levels. Similar results were obtained by Wang (2006) when no account was taken of the interaction effect of size and ownership status (see below). Nonetheless, the size of organizations is closely associated with the number of hierarchical levels; so these results may suffer from multi collinearity problems. They may also indicate that organizations with a number of employees in excess of the optimal one conditional on the number of levels are induced to increase the depth of the organization.

10. As was mentioned in Chapter 3 (see n. 4), this argument was originally proposed by Leavitt and Whisler (1958). It is based on the idea that the key role of middle managers is to collect and transmit information, and that this role can be more effectively performed by computers. See Pinsonneault and Kraemer (1997) for a more thorough discussion of this issue.

11. Further details on these studies are provided below. The measures of competition considered by Caroli and Van Reenen (2001) included import prices, concentration indexes, and managers' assessment of the number of competitors faced by their establishments.

12. Effective governance was proxied by the extent of institutional shareholdings in a firm and the governance index compiled by Gompers *et al.* (2003).

13. "Educated workers" were defined as workers having a college degree or any *baccalaureat*.

14. See again Section 2.3.4 in Chapter 2 for further details.

15. A similarly negligible effect of firm age on the likelihood of both a decrease and an increase in organizational depth was found by Wang (2006).

16. This section is based on Colombo and Delmastro (2002). Technical sections are indicated by an asterisk (*).

17. Another solution to left-censoring problems is to base the estimates only on uncensored observations and disregard the information provided by censored ones; in other words, data can be handled as if they were left-truncated. Nonetheless, this way of analyzing the data is not efficient (see again Andersen *et al.* 1993). In addition, in our sample left-censored observations largely outnumber left-uncensored ones.

18. Actually, for plants that were established before the Second World War, t_f^E was conventionally assumed to equal 1947.

19. We also tried different functional forms, with very similar results (see n. 20).

20. As was mentioned earlier, estimates with other functional forms (i.e. logistic, normal, and exponentional) have also been performed. In all models, results were very close to those presented in this chapter. They have been omitted for reasons of space.

21. Nonetheless, it is fair to recognize that the above results may also reflect unobserved heterogeneity across plants: plants that adopt multiple PA technologies may be more likely to change the organization due to differences in plants' employees skills (see DiNardo and Pischke 1997 for a similar issue, but in another empirical context) or to an attitude more prone to both technological and organizational innovation. It is also worth noticing that, unlike AMTs, there is no cluster effect for IWPs and HRMPs. This result is confirmed by Wald-tests on organizational practices, similar to those on AMTs.

22. For example Lindbeck and Snower (1996) note that "the organizational structure of firms is becoming flatter: the new structure is built around teams that report to the central management, with few if any intermediaries."

23. For instance, compare the findings of Wang (2006) mentioned in Section 4.4.2 with those of the econometric analysis described in Section 4.4.3.

24. Of course, there are other means beyond structural inertia to limit influence costs such as restricting the exercise of discretionary decision authority (see Milgrom 1988).

25. Note that these variables are mutually exclusive and exhaustive, thus one has to be chosen as the baseline of the estimates. In particular, we chose *PM*, which thus does not appear in the estimates of the econometric models.

26. Note that unfortunately we know only the number of plant employees in 1989 and 1996; *ΔSize* is a time-invariant variable. In particular, we do not have information as to the number of plant employees before 1989. While the dependent variable is observed over the period 1975–96 (except for plants that changed the number of tiers twice or more times) the variable *ΔSize* measures a plant's growth rate in a shorter period. So this variable is a rough proxy of plants' growth rate for the overall period under observation.

5 The Effects of Organizational Design on Firm Performance

1. Here, we generally refer to organizational variables, even though most studies concentrate on the effects of the adoption of IWPs and HRMPs. Of course, there are important exceptions that will be presented in depth in the following sections. See, for instance, the work of Black and Lynch (2001) and of Colombo *et al.* (2007) presented in Sections 5.3.2.1 and 5.4.2, respectively).

2. For the sake of simplicity, in the remaining of this section we will use the term "firm" to refer to both firms and establishments.

3. Obviously, this self-selection bias also affects the estimates of the extent of use of IWPs and HRMPs and of other characteristics of firms' organizational design.

4. Technical section.
5. This problem has been extensively analyzed in the econometric literature interested in assessing the effect of a treatment. See, for instance, Heckman *et al.* (1999).
6. As a correction for this problem, one may resort to a two-step instrumental variable (IV) estimation procedure where the organizational variables, if they are continuous, are replaced by their predicted values (see Greene 2003). If the organizational variables are dummies, in accordance with the "endogenous treatment effect" literature (see Heckman 1990; Vella and Verbeek 1999), a selection equation can be first specified to explain changes in the organizational variable under consideration. Then, the predicted adoption probabilities are computed and inserted in the performance equation in place of the values of the original dummy variable. Alternatively, the control function (CF) method proposed by Heckman (1978, 1979) can be used. According to this approach, the selection equation is used to calculate an inverse Mill's ratio type of variable (actually, the generalized residual of the selection probit model, see Gourieroux *et al.* 1987) that is included as a control in the performance equation.
7. In particular, in GMM-system estimates other than using lagged levels of the series as instruments for first differences (as in GMM-DIF), additional information is extracted using first differences as instruments for variables in levels. Considering organizational variables as endogenous implies the use of instruments dated t-2 for the equations in first differences and t-1 for the equations in levels.
8. For a review of this literature see for example Huselid (1995); Cappelli and Neumark (2001); Ichniowski and Shaw (2003). See Appelbaum *et al.* (2000) for a thorough analysis based on qualitative data of the performance effects of IWPs and HRMPs in the medical electronic instruments and imaging, steel, and apparel industries. On these latter two industries see also Arthur (1994), and Bailey (1993) and Berg *et al.* (1996), respectively.
9. Based on the pooled OLS estimates, the annual operating profit increase that would be generated by the transition from System 4 to System 1 is as great as $2.2 million (see Ichniowski and Shaw 2003). The authors note that these estimates are conservative as they do not take into account the substantial quality increases generated by these transitions.
10. They also estimated the fifteen different models while omitting the "System of practices" dummies. In this case, all the dummies relating to individual practices exhibited a positive statistically significant coefficient.
11. Correction for the endogeneity bias resulted in a slight increase in the coefficient of the team variable for both the "average treatment effect" and the "treatment effect of the treated." This result was interpreted by the authors as evidence of a downward bias in OLS and WG estimates generated by a lack of proper control for the complexity of production processes. In fact, complexity reduces productivity and is positively related to the adoption of team problem-solving practices.
12. Actually, in order to correct for the endogeneity bias, the author resorted to several IV estimators. The point estimates of the effects on labor productivity

of the different systems of practices were very imprecise and discordant across the different methods, possibly because of the poor quality of the instruments.

13. More precisely, they used both WG and GMM estimation techniques. The WG estimates eliminated the bias that may arise from the correlation between the inputs of the production function and the firm-specific time-invariant component of the error term. The GMM estimates also controlled for the endogeneity bias engendered by the plants' simultaneous choice of capital, labor, materials, and output.

14. They also replicated their earlier 1996 and 2001 studies on the 1996 data using a sample of 1,496 observations.

15. IV estimates were used to correct for the endogeneity of labor and capital. Conversely, organizational variables were assumed to be exogeneous.

16. Use of data on operating profits allowed to avoid distortions that may be created by fluctuations over time of net profits engendered by non-recurrent events (e.g. short-term write offs, such as those associated with big changes in a plant's labor force due to layoffs and forced retirements or changes in the tax regime).

17. WG panel data models were also estimated, with similar results.

18. In the estimates, all organizational variables were lagged one period so as to alleviate endogeneity problems. Two- and three-period lagged organizational variables were also inserted into the model specification so as to check for the existence of a positive but lagged effect. The estimates provided no evidence of this effect.

19. A further stream of literature concerned with skill-biased technological and organizational changes has analyzed the joint effects of technological and organizational innovations on firms' demand for skilled labor. See, for instance, Caroli *et al.* (2001); Bresnahan *et al.* (2002); Piva *et al.* (2005, 2006); and the studies mentioned there.

20. For a survey of qualitative work in this domain, see Brynjolfsson and Hitt (2000).

21. The following PA technologies were considered: FMS, CNC stand-alone machine tools, machining centers, and programmable robots.

22. As was explained in Section 5.3, the results of single-industry studies can hardly be generalized and are difficult to compare as they often use industry-specific performance indicators.

Conclusions

1. "The traditional search for competitive advantage in terms of specific products, technology, markets, or production processes is obsolete. You won't find it anymore. The only real sustainable source of competitive advantage lies, instead, in an organization's 'architecture'" (Nadler and Tushman 1997, p. viii).

2. "The value of an organizational design depends completely on how well it matches the particular environment and strategy ... The key is in finding and establishing a fit among strategy, organization, and the environment and then maintaining the fit over time in the face of change " (Roberts 2004, p. 20).

Appendix: Data Set and Empirical Methodology

1. This corresponds to a 12.6% failure rate over an eight-year period. Previous empirical work found considerably lower survival rates among newly established units. For instance, Dunne *et al.* (1988) found that only between one-quarter and one-third of US manufacturing plants owned by single-plant firms survive fifteen years. However, the likelihood of survival is substantially higher for large establishments owned by multi-plant firms. Mata *et al.* (1995) showed that more than 20% of new Portuguese plants closed within two years from birth and only 30% survived seven years. Nonetheless, our sample includes plants in existence in 1989, which were at least three years old. In addition, smaller units (i.e. those which, in 1989, had fewer than ten employees) were excluded. As hazard rates are usually found to rapidly decline with both age and size, the value of the average failure rate in our sample is not surprising.

2. Note that we were able to control some answers with the information provided by FLAUTO89. For instance, we knew if a plant had already adopted, during 1970–89, some advanced manufacturing technologies (such as FMS, LAN, and robots).

3. Of course, we have no data concerning the number of plant employees in 1997 for plants that did not answer to the questionnaire. So, we can confront only the geographical distribution of the two samples.

4. In this respect, it is worth noticing that in 1989 the response rate was nearly 100%, since the analysis was conducted with the cooperation of the Association of Italian Manufacturing Firms.

5. Numerical control (NC) machines are controlled by numerical commands punched on paper or plastic tape, whereas CNC machines are controlled through internal computer. Machining centers are CNC machine tools which integrate a series of operations, as opposed to stand-alone NC (and CNC) machine tools, which instead are able to perform just one of them. Flexible manufacturing systems and cells (FMS) are manufacturing equipment composed of two or more machine tools or programmable robots connected through material handling devices and controlled by computers, which render them capable of performing a variety of operations in a variable sequence. Automated inflexible manufacturing line systems (IMS) differ from production technologies included in the previous category due to the absence of computerized control and programmable equipment; as the sequence of performed operations is fixed, they are specialized in the production of a pre-specified output. Finally, robots are reprogrammable, multifunctional manipulators designed to move materials, parts, tools, or specialized devices through variable programmed motions. Intra- and interfirm network technologies are defined as follows. Intra-firm network: LAN technologies are to exchange technical data and general information with other departments, (on-line connection) with headquarters and between different points on the factory floor (within the plant). Interfirm network: intercompany computer network linking the plant to subcontractors, suppliers, and/or customers.

References

Acemoglu, D., P. Aghion, C. Lelarge, J.V. Reenen, and F. Zilibotti (2006) "Technology, Information and the Decentralization of the Firm." NBER Working Paper n.W12206, forthcoming in the *Quarterly Journal of Economics*.

Aghion, P. and J. Tirole (1995) "Some implications of growth for organizational form and ownership structure." *European Economic Review* 39, 440–455.

Aghion, P. and J. Tirole (1997) "Formal and Real Authority in Organizations." *Journal of Political Economy* 105, 1–29.

Alchian, A.A. and H. Demsetz (1972) "Production, Information Costs, and Economic Organization." *American Economic Review* 62, 777–795.

Aldrich, H.E. (1972) "Technology and Organizational Structure: A Reexamination of the Findings of the Aston Group." *Administrative Science Quarterly* 17, 26–43.

Amber, G.H. and P.S. Amber (1962) *Anatomy of Automation*. Englewood Cliffs, NJ: Prentice Hall.

Andersen, P., O. Borgan, R. Gill, and N. Keiding (1993) *Statistical Methods Based on Counting Processes*. New York: Springer.

Andrews, D.W.K. and M.A. Schafgans (1996) "Semiparametric Estimation of a Sample Selection Model." Cowles Foundation, Yale University, Cowles Foundation Discussion Papers 1119.

Aoki, M. (1986) "Horizontal vs. Vertical Information Structure of the Firm." *American Economic Review* 76, 971–983.

Appelbaum, E., T. Bailey, P. Berg, and A.L. Kalleberg (2000) *ManufacturingAdvantage: Why High-performance Work Systems Pay Off*. Ithaca, NY and London: Cornell University Press, ILR Press.

Arellano, M. and S. Bond (1991) "Some Tests of Specification for Panel Data: Monte Carlo Evidence and an Application to Employment Equations." *Review of Economic Studies* 58, 277–297.

Arrow, K. (1974) *The Limits of Organization*. New York: Norton.

Arthur, J.B. (1994) "Effects of Human Resource Systems on Manufacturing Performance and Turnover." *Academy of Management Journal* 37, 670–687.

Arundel, A., E. Lorenz, B.Å. Lundvall, and A. Valeyre (2006) "The Organization of Work and Innovative Performance: A Comparison of the EU–15." Copenhagen: Druid Working Paper Series 14.

Åstebro, T. (2002) "Noncapital Investment Costs and the Adoption of CAD and CNC in US Metalworking Industries." *RAND Journal of Economics* 33, 672–688.

Åstebro, T., M.G. Colombo, and R. Seri (2006) "The Diffusion of Complementary Technologies: An Empirical Test." Politecnico di Milano, mimeo.

Athey, S. and J. Roberts (2001) "Organizational Design: Decision Rights and Incentive Contracts." *American Economic Review* 91, 200–205.

Azumi, K. and C.J. McMillan (1981) "Management Strategy and Organization Structure: A Japanese Comparative Study." In D.J. Hickson and C.J. McMillan (eds.), *Organisation and Nation: The Aston program IV*. Westmead: Gower, 115–172.

Bahrami, H. (1992) "The Emerging Flexible Organization: Perspectives from Silicon Valley." *California Management Review* 34, 33–51.

Bailey, T. (1993) "Organizational innovation in the apparel industry." *Industrial Relations* 32, 30–48.

Bailey, T., P. Berg, and C. Sandy (2001) "The Effect of High-Performance Work Practices on Employee Earnings in the Steel, Apparel, and Medical Elecronics and Imaging Industries." *Industrial & Labor Relations Review* 54, 525–543.

Baker, G., R. Gibbons, and K.J. Murphy (1999) "Informal Authority in Organizations." *Journal of Law, Economics & Organization* 15, 56–73.

Baker, G.P. and K.H. Wruck (1989) "Organizational Changes and Value Creation in Leveraged Buyouts: The Case of The O.M. Scott & Sons Company." *Journal of Financial Economics* 25, 163–190.

Barron, J.M. and K.P. Gjerde (1996) "Who Adopts Total Quality Management (TQM): Theory and an Empirical Test." *Journal of Economics and Management Strategy* 5, 69–106.

Batt, R. (1999) "Work Organization, Technology, and Performance in Customer Service and Sales." *Industrial and Labor Relations Review* 52, 539–564.

Bauer, T.K. (2003) "Flexible Workplace Practices and Labor Productivity." IZA DP 700.

Bauer, T.K. (2004) "High Performance Workplace Practices and Job Satisfaction: Evidence from Europe." Working Paper, IZA DP 1265.

Bauer, T.K. and S. Bender (2001) "Flexible Work Systems and the Structure of Wages: Evidence from Matched Employer–Employee Data." IZA DP 53.

Becker, B. and B. Gerhart (1996) "The Impact of Human Resource Management on Organizational Performance: Progress And Prospects." *Academy of Management Journal* 39, 779–801.

Beckmann, M.J. (1977) "Management Production Functions and the Theory of the Firm." *Journal of Economic Theory* 14, 1–18.

Berg, P., E. Appelbaum, T. Bailey, and A.L. Kalleberg (1996) "The Performance Effects of Modular Production in the Apparel Industry." *Industrial Relations* 35, 356–373.

Bertschek, I. and U. Kaiser (2004) "Productivity Effects of Organizational Change: Microeconometric Evidence." *Management Science* 50, 394–404.

Black, S.E. and L.M. Lynch (1996) "Human-capital Investments and Productivity." *American Economic Review* 86, 263–267.

Black, S.E. and L.M. Lynch (2001) "How to Compete: The Impact of Workplace Practices and Information Technology on Productivity." *Review of Economics and Statistics* 83, 434–445.

Black, S.E. and L.M. Lynch (2004) "What's Driving the New Economy?: The Benefits of Workplace Innovation." *Economic Journal* 114, 97–116.

Blau, P.M., C.M. Falbe, W. McKinley, and P.K. Tracy (1976) "Technology and Organization in Manufacturing." *Administrative Science Quarterly* 21, 20–40.

Blau, P.M. and R.A. Schoenherr (1971) *The Structure of Organizations.* New York: Basic Books.

Blundell, R. and S. Bond (1998) "Initial Conditions and Moment Restrictions in Dynamic Panel Data Models." *Journal of Econometrics* 87, 115–143.

Bolton, P. and M. Dewatripont (1994) "The Firm as a Communication Network." *Quarterly Journal of Economics* 109, 809–839.

Bond, S.R. (2002) "Dynamic Panel Data Models: A Guide to Micro Data Methods and Practice." *Portuguese Economic Journal* 1, 141–162.

Boning, B., C. Ichniowski, and K. Shaw (2001) "Opportunity Counts: Teams and the Effectiveness of Production Incentives." National Bureau of Economic Research. NBER Working Papers 8306.

Bresnahan, T.F., E. Brynjolfsson, and L.M. Hitt (2002) "Information Technology, Workplace Organization, and the Demand for Skilled Labor: Firm-Level Evidence." *Quarterly Journal of Economics* 117, 339–376.

Brews, P.J. and C.L. Tucci (2004) "Exploring the Structural Effects of Internetworking." *Strategic Management Journal* 25, 429–451.

Brynjolfsson, E. and L.M. Hitt (2000) "Beyond Computation: Information Technology, Organizational Transformation and Business Performance." *Journal of Economic Perspectives* 14, 23–48.

Brynjolfsson, E. and L.M. Hitt (2003) "Computing Productivity: Firm-Level Evidence." *Review of Economics & Statistics* 85, 793–808.

Brynjolfsson, E., L. Hitt, and S.K. Yang (2000) "Intangible Assets: How the Interaction of Information Systems and Organizational Structure Affects Stock Market Valuations." Cambridge. MA: MIT and Wharton, mimeo.

Burns, T. and G.M. Stalker (1961) *The Management of Innovation*. London: Tavistock.

Cainarca, G.C., M.G. Colombo and S. Mariotti (1989) "An Evolutionary Pattern of Innovation Diffusion. The Case of Flexible Automation." *Research Policy* 18, 59–86.

Calvo, G.A. and S. Wellisz (1978) "Supervision, Loss of Control, and the Optimum Size of the Firm." *Journal of Political Economy* 86, 943–952.

Calvo, G.A. and S. Wellisz (1979) "Hierarchy, Ability, and Income Distribution." *Journal of Political Economy* 87, 991–1010.

Cappelli, P. and D. Neumark (2001) "Do 'High-Performance' Work Practices Improve Establishment-Level Outcomes?" *Industrial and Labor Relations Review* 54, 737–775.

Caroli, E., N. Greenan, and D. Guellec (2001) "Organizational Change and Skill Accumulation." *Industrial & Corporate Change* 10, 481–506.

Caroli, E. and J. Van Reenen (2001) "Skill-biased Organizational Change? Evidence from a Panel of British and French Establishments." *Quarterly Journal of Economics* 116, 1449–1492.

Carter, N.M. (1984) "Computerization as a Predominate Technology: Its Influence on the Structure of Newspaper Organizations." *Academy of Management Journal* 27, 247–270.

Chandler, A.D. (1962) *Strategy and Structure: Chapters in the History of the Industrial Enterprise*. Cambridge, MA: MIT Press.

Chandler, A.D. (1977) *The Visible Hand: The Managerial Revolution in American Business*. Cambridge, MA: Belknap Press of Harvard University Press.

Chandler, A.D., T.K. McCrow, and R.S. Tedlow (1996) *Management Past and Present*. Cincinnati: South-Western College Publishing.

Child, J. (1972) "Organization Structure and Strategies of Control: A Replication of the Aston Study." *Administrative Science Quarterly* 17, 163–177.

Child, J. (1973) "Predicting and Understanding Organization Structure." *Administrative Science Quarterly* 18, 168–185.

Child, J. (1984) "New Technology and Developments in Management Organization." *Omega* 12, 211–223.

Child, J. and R. Mansfield (1972) "Technology, Size, and Organization Structure." *Sociology* 6, 369–393.

Christie, A.A., M.P. Joye and R.L. Watts (2003) "Decentralization of the firm: theory and evidence". *Journal of corporate Finance* 9, 3–36.

Cohen, M.D., R. Burkhart, G. Dosi, M. Egidi, L. Marengo, M. Warglien, and S. Winter (1996) "Routines and Other Recurring Action Patterns of Organizations: Contemporary Research Issues." *Industrial & Corporate Change* 5, 653–688.

Collins, P.D., L.V. Ryan, and S.F. Matusik (1999) "Programmable Automation and the Locus of Decision-Making Power." *Journal of Management* 25, 29–53.

Colombo, M.G. and M. Delmastro (1999) "Some Stylized Facts on Organization and Its Evolution." *Journal of Economic Behavior and Organization* 40, 255–274.

Colombo, M.G. and M. Delmastro (2002) "The Determinants of Organizational Change and Structural Inertia: Technological and Organizational Factors." *Journal of Economics & Management Strategy* 11, 595–635.

Colombo, M.G. and M. Delmastro (2004) "Delegation of Authority In Business Organizations: An Empirical Test." *Journal of Industrial Economics* LII, 53–80.

Colombo, M.G. and R. Mosconi (1995) "Complementarity and Cumulative Learning Effects in the Early Diffusion of Multiple Technologies." *Journal of Industrial Economics* 43, 13–48.

Colombo, M.G., M. Delmastro and L. Rabbiosi (2007) "High performance work practices, Decentralization and profitablity: Evidence from Panel Data." *Industrial and Corporate Change*, 16.

Cox, D.R. and D. Oakes (1984) *Analysis of Survival Data*. New York, NY: Chapman & Hill.

Cully, M., S. Woodland, A. O'Reilly, G. Dix, N. Millward, A. Bryson, and J. Forth (1998) *The 1998 Workplace Employee Relations Survey: First findings*. London: DTI.

Cyert, R.M. and J.G. March (1963) *A Behavioral Theory of the Firm*. Englewood Cliffs, NJ: Prentice Hall.

David, P. (1975) *Technical Choice, Innovation and Economic Growth*. London: Cambridge University Press.

Dean Jr., J.W., Y. Se Joon, and G.I. Susman (1992) "Advanced Manufacturing Technology and Organization Structure: Empowerment or Subordination?" *Organization Science* 3, 203–229.

Delmastro, M. (2002) "The Determinants of the Management Hierarchy: Evidence from Italian Plants." *International Journal of Industrial Organization* 20, 119–137.

Dessein, W. and T. Santos (2006) "Adaptive Organizations." *Journal of Political Economy* 114, 956–995.

DiNardo, J.E. and J.-S. Pischke (1997) "The Returns to Computer Use Revisited: Have Pencils Changes The Wage Structure Too?" *Quarterly Journal of Economics* 112, 291–303.

Dixit, A.K. and R.S. Pindyck (1994) *Investment under Uncertainty*. Princeton, NJ: Princeton University Press.

Doms, M., Dunne, T. and Troske, K., (1997) "Workers, Wages and technology," *Quartely Journal of Economics* 112, pp. 253–290.

Donaldson, L. (1986) "Size and Bureaucracy in East and West: A Preliminary Meta-analysis." In S. Clegg, D. Dunphy, and S.G. Redding (eds.), *The Enterprise and Management in East Asia*. Hong Kong: University of Hong Kong Press, 67–91.

Dosi, G., D.A. Levinthal, and L. Marengo (2003) "Bridging Contested Terrain: Linking Incentive-based and Learning Perspectives on Organizational Evolution." *Industrial & Corporate Change* 12, 413–436.

Dow, G.K. (1985) "Internal Bargaining and Strategic Innovation in the Theory of the Firm." *Journal of Economic Behavior and Organization* 6, 301–320.

Dow, G.K. (1987) "The Function of Authority in Transaction Cost Economics." *Journal of Economic Behavior and Organization* 8, 13–38.

Drucker, P.F. (1988) "The Coming of the New Organization." *Harvard Business Review* 66, 45–53.

Dunlop, J.T. and D. Weil (1996) "Diffusion and Performance of Modular Production in the US Apparel Industry." *Industrial Relations* 35, 334–355.

Dunne, T. (1994) "Plant Age and Technology Use in US Manufacturing Industries." *RAND Journal of Economics* 25, 488–499.

Dunne, T., M.J. Roberts, and L. Samuelson (1988) "Patterns of Firm Entry and Exit in US Manufacturing Industries." *RAND Journal of Economics* 19, 495–515.

Elger, H.J. (1975) "Industrial Organizations." In J.B. McKinley (ed.), *Processing People*, pp. 91–149. New York: Holt, Rhinehart & Winston.

Emerson, R.M. (1962) "Power–Dependence Relations." *American Sociological Review* 27, 31–41.

Eriksson, T. (2003) "How Common Are the New Compensation and Work Organization Practices and Who Adopts Them?" Working Paper, Aarhus School of Business.

Eriksson, T. and J. Ortega (2004) "The Adoption of Job Rotation: Testing the Theories." Working paper: Department of Economics, Aarhus School of Business.

Forth, J. and N. Millward (2004) "High-involvement Management and Pay in Britain." *Industrial Relations* 43, 98–119.

Freeman, R.B. and M.M. Kleiner (2000) "Who Benefits Most from Employee Involvement: Firms or Workers?" *American Economic Review* 90, 219–223.

Galbraith, J.R. (1973) *Designing Complex Organizations*. Boston, MA: Addison-Wesley Longman.

Garicano, L. (2000) "Hierarchies and the Organization of Knowledge in Production." *Journal of Political Economy* 108, 874–904.

Garicano, L. and E. Rossi-Hansberg (2006) "Organization and Inequality in a Knowledge Economy". *The Quarterly Journal of Economics* 121, 1383–1435.

Geanakoplos, J. and P. Milgrom (1991) "A Theory of Hierarchies Based on Limited Managerial Attention." *Journal of the Japanese and International Economies* 5, 205–225.

Gittleman, M., M. Horrigan, and M. Joyce (1998) " 'Flexible' Workplace Practices: Evidence from a Nationally Representative Survey." *Industrial and Labor Relations Review* 52, 99–115.

Godard, J. (2001) "High Performance and the Transformation of Work? The Implications of Alternative Work Practices for the Experience and Outcomes of Work." *Industrial & Labor Relations Review* 54, 776–805.

Goldhar, J.D., M. Jelinek, and T.W. Schlie (1991) "Flexibility and Competitive Advantage – Manufacturing Becomes a Service Business." *International Journal of Technology Management* 33, 243–259.

Gompers, P., J. Ishii, and A. Metrick (2003) "Corporate Governance and Equity Prices." *Quarterly Journal of Economics* 118, 107–155.

Gourieroux, C., A. Monfort, E. Renault, and A. Trognon (1987) "Generalised Residuals." *Journal of Econometrics* 34, 5–32.

Greenan, N. and J. Mairesse (1999) "Organizational Change in French Manufacturing: What Do We Learn From Firm Representatives and From Their Employees?" National Bureau of Economic Research. NBER Working Papers 7285.

Greenan, N. and J. Mairesse (2002) "How Do New Organizational Practices Change the Work of Blue Collars, Technicians and Supervisors? Results From Matched Employer–Employee Survey For French Manufacturing." Working Paper, Centre d'Etudes de l'Emploi, CREST–NBER.

Greenan, N. and J. Mairesse (2004) "A Firm Level Investigation of the Complementarity between Information and Communication Technologies and New Organizational Practices." Working Paper, Centre d'Etudes de l'Emploi.

Greene, W. (2003) *Econometric Analysis*. Upper Saddle River, NJ: Prentice Hall.

Grinyer, P.H. and M. Yasai-Ardekani (1980) "Dimensions of Organizational Structure: A Critical Replication." *Academy of Management Journal* 23, 405–421.

Hall, R.H. (1972) *Organizations: Structure and Process*. Englewood Cliffs, NJ: Prentice Hall.

Handel, M.J. and M. Gittleman (2004) "Is There a Wage Payoff to Innovative Work Practices?" *Industrial Relations* 43, 67–97.

Hannan, M.T. and J. Freeman (1984) "Structural Inertia and Organizational Change." *American Sociological Review* 49, 149–164.

Harris, M. and A. Raviv (2002) "Organization Design." *Management Science* 48, 852–865.

Hart, O. and J. Moore (2005) "On the Design of Hierarchies: Coordination versus Specialization." *Journal of Political Economy* 113, 675–702.

Heckman, J. (1990) "Varieties of Selection Bias." *American Economic Review* 80, 313–318.

Heckman, J.J. (1978) "Dummy Endogenous Variables in a Simultaneous Equation System." *Econometrica* 46, 931–959.

Heckman, J.J. (1979) "Sample Selection Bias as a Specification Error." *Econometrica* 47, 153–161.

Heckman, J.J., R.J. Lalonde, J.A. Smith, O. Ashenfelter, and D. Card (1999) "The Economics and Econometrics of Active Labor Market Programs." In *Handbook of Labor Economics. Volume 3A*, pp.1865–2097 *Handbooks in Economics* 5. Amsterdam, New York, and Oxford: Elsevier Science, North-Holland.

Heckman, J.J. and E.J. Vytlacil (1998) "Instrumental Variables Methods for the Correlated Random Coefficient Model: Estimating the Average Rate of Returns to Schooling when the Return is Correlated with Schooling." *Journal of Human Resources 33*, 974–987.

Hickson, D.J., C.R. Hinings, C.J. McMillan, and J.P. Schwitter (1974) "The Culture-free Context of Organization Structure: A Tri-National Comparison." *Sociology* 8, 59–80.

Hickson, D.J. and C.J. McMillan (1981) *Organization and Nation: The Aston Programme IV*. Westmead: Gower.

Hickson, D.J., C.J. McMillan, K. Azumi, and D. Horvath (1979) "Grounds for Comparative Organization Theory: Quicksands or Hardcore?" In C.J. Lammers and D. J. Hickson (eds.), *Organizations Alike and Unlike*. London: Routledge & Kegan Paul, 25–41.

Hickson, D.J., D.S. Pugh, and D.C. Pheysey (1969) "Operations Technology and Organization Structure: An Empirical Reappraisal." *Administrative Science Quarterly* 14, 378–397.

Hölmstrom, B. and P. Milgrom (1994) "The Firm as an Incentive System." *American Economic Review* 84, 972–991.

Hoover, G., A. Campbell, and P.J. Spain (eds.) (1998a) *Profiles of Over 500 Major Corporations*. Austin: TX Reference Press, Inc.

Hoover, G., A. Campbell, and P.J. Spain (eds.) (1998b) *Profiles of Over 500 Major US Corporations*. Austin: TX Reference Press, Inc.

Horvath, D., C.J. McMillan, K. Azumi, and D.J. Hickson (1976) "The Cultural Context of Organizational Control: An International Comparison." *International Studies of Management & Organization* 6, 60–86.

Hubbard, T.N. (2000) "The Demand for Monitoring Technologies: The Case of Trucking." *Quarterly Journal of Economics* 115, 533–560.

Huber, G.P. (1990) "A Theory of the Effects of Advanced Information Technologies on Organizational Design, Intelligence, and Decision Making." *Academy of Management Review* 15, 47–71.

Huselid, M.A. (1995) "The Impact of Human Resource Management Practices on Turnover, Productivity, and Corporate." *Academy of Management Journal* 38, 635–672.

Huselid, M.A. and B.E. Becker (1996) "Methodological Issues in Cross-sectional and Panel Estimates of the Human Resource–Firm Performance Link." *Industrial Relations* 35, 400–422.

Ichniowski, C. (1990) "Human Resource Management Systems and the Performance of US Manufacturing Businesses." National Bureau of Economic Research. NBER Working Papers 3449.

Ichniowski, C., T.A. Kochan, D. Levine, C. Olson, and G. Strauss (1996) "What Works at Work: Overview and Assessment." *Industrial Relations* 35, 299–333.

Ichniowski, C. and K. Shaw (1995) "Old Dogs and New Tricks: Determinants of the Adoption of Productivity-enhancing Work Practices." *Brookings Papers on Economic Activity*, 1–65.

Ichniowski, C. and K. Shaw (1999) "The Effects of Human Resource Management Systems on Economic Performance: An International Comparison of US and Japanese Plants." *Management Science* 45, 704–721.

Ichniowski, C. and K. Shaw (2003) "Beyond Incentive Pay: Insiders' Estimates of the Value of Complementary Human Resource Management Practices." *Journal of Economic Perspectives* 17, 155–180.

Ichniowski, C., K. Shaw, and G. Prennushi (1997) "The Effects of Human Resource Management Practices on Productivity: A Study of Steel Finishing Lines." *American Economic Review* 87, 291–313.

Inkson, J.H.K., D.S. Pugh, and D.J. Hickson (1970) "Organization Context and Structure: An Abbreviated Replication." *Administrative Science Quarterly* 15, 318–329.

Jaffe, A.B. (1986) "Technological Opportunity and Spillovers of R&D: Evidence from Firms' Patents, Profits, and Market Values." *American Economic Review* 76, 984–1001.

Jaikumar, R. (1986) "Postindustrial Manufacturing." *Harvard Business Review* 64, 69–76.

Janod, V. and A. Saint-Martin (2004) "Measuring the Impact of Work Reorganization on Firm Performance: Evidence from French Manufacturing, 1995–1999." *Labour Economics* 11, 785–798.

Jensen, M.C. and W.H. Meckling (1992) "Specific and General Knowledge, and Organizational Structure." In Lars Werin and Hans Wijkander (eds.), *Contract Economics*. Cambridge, MA and Oxford: Blackwell, 251–274.

Johnson, H.T. (1975) "Management Accounting in an Early Integrated Industrial: E.I. duPont de Nemours Powder Company." *Business History Review* 49, 184–204.

Johnson, H.T. (1978) "Management Accounting in an Early Multidivisional Organization: General Motors in the 1920s." *Business History Review* 52, 490–517.

Johnston, H.R. and M.A. Vitale (1988) "Creating Competitive Advantage With Interorganizational Information Systems." *MIS Quarterly* 12, 152–165.

Kalbfleisch, J.D. and R.L. Prentice (1980) *The Statistical Analysis of Failure Data.* New York: Wiley.

Kandel, E. and E.P. Lazear (1992) "Peer Pressure and Partnerships." *Journal of Political Economy* 100, 801–817.

Karshenas, M. and P.L. Stoneman (1993) "Rank, Stock, Order, and Epidemic Effects in the Diffusion of New Process Technologies: An Empirical Model." *RAND Journal of Economics* 24, 503–528.

Kato, T. and M. Morishima (2002) "The Productivity Effects of Participatory Employment Practices: Evidence from New Japanese Panel Data." *Industrial Relations* 41, 487–520.

Kelley, M.R. (1994) "Productivity and Information Technology: The Elusive Connection." *Management Science* 40, 1406–1425.

Kelley, M.R. (1996) "Participative Bureaucracy and Productivity in the Machined Products Sector." *Industrial Relations* 35, 374–399.

Kenney, M. and R. Florida (1988) "Beyond Mass Production: Production and the Labor Process in Japan." *Politics and Society* 16, 121–158.

Keren, M. and D. Levhari (1979) "The Optimum Span of Control in a Pure Hierarchy." *Management Science* 25, 1162–1172.

Keren, M. and D. Levhari (1983) "The Internal Organization of the Firm and the Shape of Average Costs." *Bell Journal of Economics* 14, 474–486.

Keren, M. and D. Levhari (1989) "Decentralization, Aggregation, Control Loss and Costs in a Hierarchical Model of the Firm." *Journal of Economic Behavior and Organization* 11, 213–236.

Kersley, B., C. Alphin, J. Forth, A. Bryson, G. Dix and S. Oxenbridge (2006). *Inside the Workplace. Findings from the 2004 Workplace Employment Relations Survey.* London: Routledge.

Khandwalla, P.N. (1974) "Mass Output Orientation of Operations Technology and Organizational Structure." *Administrative Science Quarterly* 19, 74–97.

Kiefer, N.M. (1988) "Economic Duration Data and Hazard Functions." *Journal of Economic Literature* 26, 646–679.

Kocha, J. (1971) "Family and Bureaucracy in German Industrial Management 1850–1914." *Business History Review* 45, 133–156.

Kogut, B. and D. Parkinson (1998) "Adoption of the Multidivisional Structure: Analyzing History from the Start." *Industrial & Corporate Change* 7, 249–273.

Koike, K. (1990) "Intellectual Skill and the Role of Employees as Constituent Members of Large Firms in Contemporary Japan." In M. Aoki, B. Gustafsson and O.E. Williamson (eds), *The Firm as a Nexus of Treaties.* London, Newbury Park, CA, and New Delhi: Sage, 85–208.

Krafcik, J.F. (1988) "Triumph of the Lean Production System." *Sloan Management Review* 30, 41–52.

Kreps, D. (1985) "Corporate Culture and Economic Theory." Stanford University, mimeo.

Kuc, B., D.J. Hickson, and C. McMillan (1980) "Centrally Planned Development: A Comparison of Polish Factories with Equivalents in Britain, Japan, and Sweden." *Organization Studies* 1, 253–370.

Laffont, J.-J. and D. Martimort (1997) "The Firm as a Multicontract Organization." *Journal of Economics & Management Strategy* 6, 201–234.

Lancaster, T. (1990) *The Econometric Analysis of Transition Sata.* Cambridge: Cambridge University Press.

Laursen, K. and N.J. Foss (2003) "New Human Resource Management Practices, Complementarities and the Impact on Innovation Performance." *Cambridge Journal of Economics* 27, 243–263.

Lawrence, P.R. and J.W. Lorsch (1967) *Organization and environment: Managing differentiation and integration.* Boston, MA: Harvard Business School Press.

Lazear, E.P. (1995) *Personnel Economics.* Cambridge, MA and London: MIT Press.

Leavitt, H.J. and T.L. Whisler (1958) "Management in the 1980s." *Harvard Business Review* 36, 41–48.

Leijonhufvud, A. (1986) "Capitalism and the Factory System." In R. N. Langlois (ed.), *Economics as a Process: Essays in the New Institutional Economics.* Cambridge; New York, and Melbourne: Cambridge University Press, 203–223.

Levin, J. (1988) "Multiple Group Factor Analysis of Multitrait–Multimethod Matrices." *Multivariate Behavioral Research* 23, 469–479.

Lin, X. and R. Germain (2003) "Organizational Structure, Context, Customer Orientation, And Performance: Lessons From Chinese State-Owned Enterprises." *Strategic Management Journal* 24, 1131–1151.

Lincoln, J.R., M. Hanada, and K. McBride (1986) "Organizational Structures in Japanese and U.S. Manufacturing." *Administrative Science Quarterly* 31, 338–364.

Lindbeck, A. and D.J. Snower (1996) "Reorganization of Firms and Labor-market Inequality." *American Economic Review* 86, 315–321.

MacDuffie, J.P. (1995) "Human Resource Bundles and Manufacturing Performance: Organizational Logic and Flexible Production Systems in the World Auto Industry." *Industrial and Labor Relations Review* 48, 197–221.

Maddala, G.S. (1983) *Limited-dependent and Qualitative Variables in Econometrics.* Cambridge: Cambridge University Press.

Mahajan, V., S. Sharma, and R.A. Bettis (1988) "The Adoption of the M-Form Organizational Structure: a Test of Imitation Hypothesis." *Management Science* 34, 1188–1201.

Mansfield, E. (1968) *Industrial Research and Technological Innovation.* New York: Norton.

March, J.G. and H. Simon (1958) *Organizations.* New York: Wiley.

Marglin, S.A. (1974) "What Do Bosses Do? The Origins and Functions of Hierarchy in Capitalist Production." *Review of Radical Political Economics* 6, 60–112.

Marschak, J. and R. Radner (1972) *Economic Theory of Teams*. New Haven, CT: Yale University Press.

Marsh, R.M. (1992) "A Research Note: Centralization of Decision-making Japanese Factories." *Organization Studies* 13, 261–274.

Marsh, R.M. and H. Mannari (1981) "Technology and Size as Determinants of the Organizational Structure of Japanese Factories." *Administrative Science Quarterly* 26, 33–57.

Marsh, R.M. and H. Mannari (1988) *Organizational Change in Japanese Factories*. Greenwich, CT and London: JAI Press.

Mata, J., P. Portugal, and P. Guimaraes (1995) "The Survival of New Plants: Start-up Conditions and Post-entry Evolution." *International Journal of Industrial Organization* 13, 459–482.

McMillan, C.J., D.J. Hickson, C.R. Hinings, and R.E. Schneck (1973) "The Structure of Work Organizations Across Societies'." *Academy of Management Journal* 16, 555–569.

Meagher, K and A. Wait (2007) "Delegation of Decision Making, Competition and Business Strategy", University of New South Wales, Working Paper.

Menard, C. (1997) "Internal Characteristics of Formal Organizations." In C. Menard (ed.), *Transaction Cost Economics: Recent Developments*. Cheltenham, UK and Lyme, NH: Edward Elgar, 30–58.

Michie, J. and M. Sheehan (1999) "HRM Practices, R&D Expenditure and Innovative Investment: Evidence from The UK's 1990 Workplace Industrial Relations Survey (WIRS)." *Industrial & Corporate Change* 8, 211–234.

Milgrom, P.R. (1988) "Employment Contracts, Influence Activities, and Efficient Organization Design." *Journal of Political Economy* 96, 42–70.

Milgrom, P. and J. Roberts (1990a) "Bargaining Costs, Influence Costs, and the Organization of Economic Activity." In James E. Alt and Kenneth A. Shepsle (eds.), *Perspectives on Positive Political Economy. Political Economy of Institutions and Decisions Series*. Cambridge, New York, and Melbourne: Cambridge University Press, 57–89.

Milgrom, P. and J. Roberts (1990b) "The Economics of Modern Manufacturing: Technology, Strategy and Organization." *American Economic Review* 80, 511–528.

Milgrom, P. and J. Roberts (1992) *Economics, organization and management*. Englewood Cliffs, NJ: Prentice Hall.

Milgrom, P. and J. Roberts (1995) "Complementarities and Fit: Strategy, Structure, and Organizational Change in Manufacturing." *Journal of Accounting & Economics* 19, 179–208.

Miller, C.C., W.H. Glick, Y.-d. Wang, and G.P. Huber (1991) "Understanding Technology-Structure Relationships: Theory Development and Meta-analytic Theory Testing." *Academy of Management Journal* 34, 370–399.

Montgomery, D. (1987) *The Fall of the House of Labor: The Workplace, the State, and American Labor Activism, 1865–1925*. Urbana, IL: University of Illinois Press.

Mookherjee, D. (2006) "Decentralization, Hierarchies, and Incentives: A Mechanism Design Perspective." *Journal of Economic Literature* 44, 367–390.

Morikawa, H. (1970) "The Organizational Structure of the Mitsubishi and Mitsui Zaibatsu, 1868–1922: A Comparative Study." *Business History Review* 44, 62–83.

Morita, H. (2005) "Multi-skilling, Delegation and Continuous Process Improvement: A Comparative Analysis of US–Japanese Work Organizations." *Economica* 72, 69–93.

Mosconi, R. and R. Seri (2006) "Non-causality in bivariate binary time series." *Journal of Econometrics* 132, 379–407.

Mukhopadhyay, T., S. Kekre, and S. Kalathur (1995) "Business Value of Information Technology: A Study of Electronic Data Interchange." *MIS Quarterly* 19, 137–156.

Myerson, R.B. (1982) "Optimal Coordination Mechanisms in Generalized Principal–Agent Problems." *Journal of Mathematical Economics* 10, 67–81.

Nadler, D.A. and M.L. Tushman (1997) *Competing by Design*. New York and Oxford: Oxford University Press.

Nelson, R. and S. Winter (1982) *An Evolutionary Theory of Economic Change*. Cambridge, MA: Harvard University Press.

Nickell, S., D. Nicolitsas, and M. Patterson (2001) "Does Doing Badly Encourage Management Innovation?" *Oxford Bulletin of Economics & Statistics* 63, 5–28.

O'Donnell, C. (1952) "The Source of Managerial Authority." *Political Science Quarterly* 67, 573–588.

Osterman, P. (1994) "How Common Is Workplace Transformation and Who Adopts It?" *Industrial & Labor Relations Review* 47, 173–188.

Osterman, P. (2000) "Work Reorganization in an Era of Restructuring: Trends in Diffusion and Effects on Employee Welfare." *Industrial and Labor Relations Review* 53, 179–196.

Osterman, P. (2006) "The Wage Effects of High Performance Work Organization in Manufacturing." *Industrial & Labor Relations Review* 59, 187–204.

Palmer, D., R. Friedland, P.D. Jennings, and M.E. Powers (1987) "The Economics and Politics of Structure: The Multidivisional Form and the Large US Corporation." *Administrative Science Quarterly* 32, 25–48.

Palmer, D.A., P.D. Jennings, and X. Zhou (1993) "Late Adoption of the Multidivisional Form by Large US Corporations: Institutional, Political, and Economic Accounts." *Administrative Science Quarterly* 38, 100–131.

Parent-Thirion, A., E. Fernández Macías, J. Hurley, and G. Vermeylen (2005) "Fourth European Working Conditions Survey, European Foundation for the Improvement of Leaving and Working Conditions." Loughlinstown, Ireland.

Perri, T.J. (1994) "Influence Activity and Executive Compensation." *Journal of Economic Behavior and Organization* 24, 169–181.

Pettigrew, A.M. (1973) *The Politics of Organizational Decision-making*. London: Tavistock.

Pil, F.K. and J.P. MacDuffie (1996) "The Adoption of High-involvement Work Practices." *Industrial Relations* 35, 423–455.

Pinsonneault, A. and K.L. Kraemer (1997) "Middle Management Downsizing: An Empirical Investigation of the Impact of Information Technology." *Management Science* 43, 659–679.

Piva, M., E. Santarelli, and M. Vivarelli (2005) "The Skill Bias Effect of Technological and Organisational Change: Evidence and Policy Implications." *Research Policy* 34, 141–157.

Piva, M., E. Santarelli, and M. Vivarelli (2006) "Technological and Organizational Changes as Determinants of the Skill Bias: Evidence from the Italian Machinery Industry." *Managerial and Decision Economics*, 63–73.

Poitevin, M. (2000) "Can the Theory of incentives Explain Decentralization?" *Canadian Journal of Economics* 33, 878–906.

Pugh, D.S. and D.J. Hickson (1976) *Organizational Structure in its Context: The Aston Programme I.* Hants: Saxon House.

Pugh, D.S., D.J. Hickson, and C.R. Hinings (1969a) "An Empirical Taxonomy of Structures of Work Organizations." *Administrative Science Quarterly* 14, 115–126.

Pugh, D.S., D.J. Hickson, C.R. Hinings, and C. Turner (1969b) "The Context of Organization Stuctures." *Administrative Science Quarterly* 14, 91–114.

Pugh, D.S., D.J. Hickson, C.R. Hinings, K.M. Macdonald, C. Turner, and T. Lupton (1963) "A Conceptual Scheme for Organizational Analysis." *Administrative Science Quarterly* 8, 289–315.

Pugh, D.S., D.J. Hickson, C.R. Hinings, and C. Turner (1968) "Dimensions of Organization Structure." *Administrative Science Quarterly* 13, 65–105.

Qian, Y. (1994) "Incentives and Loss of Control in an Optimal Hierarchy." *Review of Economic Studies* 61, 527–544.

Radner, R. (1992) "Hierarchy: The Economics of Managing." *Journal of Economic Literature* 30, 1382–1415.

Radner, R. (1993) "The Organization of Decentralized Information Processing." *Econometrica* 61, 1109–1146.

Radner, R. (1996) "Bounded Rationality, Indeterminacy, and the Theory of The Firm." *Economic Journal* 106, 1360–1373.

Raith, M. (2005) "Specific Knowledge and Performance Measurement." Simon School Working Paper FR 04–02.

Rajan, R.G. and J. Wulf (2006) "The Flattening Firm: Evidence from Panel Data on the Changing Nature of Corporate Hierarchies." *Review of Economics & Statistics* 88, 759–773.

Reimann, B.C. (1980) "Organization Structure and Technology in Manufacturing: System Versus Work Flow Level Perspectives." *Academy of Management Journal* 23, 61–77.

Roberts, J. (2004) *The Modern Firm: Organizational Design for Performance and Growth.* New York and Oxford: Oxford University Press.

Romeo, A.A. (1975) "Interindustry and Interfirm Differences in the Rate of Diffusion of an Innovation." *Review of Economics and Statistics* 57, 311–319.

Rosen, S. (1982) "Authority, Control, and the Distribution of Earnings." *Bell Journal of Economics* 13, 311–323.

Rosenbaum, P.R. and D.B. Rubin (1983) "The Central Role of the Propensity Score in Observational Studies for Causal Effects." *Biometrika* 70, 41–55.

Ruigrok, W., A. Pettigrew, S. Peck, and R. Whittington (1999) "Corporate Restructuring and New Forms of Organizing: Evidence from Europe." *Management International Review* 39, 41– 64.

Sah, R.K. and J.E. Stiglitz (1986) "The Architecture of Economic Systems: Hierarchies and Polyarchies." *American Economic Review* 76, 716–727.

Sah, R.K. and J.E. Stiglitz (1988) "Committees, Hierarchies and Polyarchies." *Economic Journal* 98, 451–470.

Schaefer, S. (1998) "Influence Costs, Structural Inertia, and Organizational Change." *Journal of Economics & Management Strategy* 7, 237–263.

Shleifer, A. (1998) "State versus Private Ownership." *Journal of Economic Perspectives* 12, 133–150.

Simon, H. (1962) "The architecture of complexity." *Proceedings of the American Philosophical Society* 106, 467–482.

Simon, H.A. (1945) *Administrative Behavior*. New York: Macmillan.

Smeets, V. and F. Warzynski (2006) "Testing models of Hierarchy: Span of Control, Compensation and Career Dynamics", Aarhus School of Business WP, 06–10.

Starbuck, W.H. (1971) *Organizational Growth and Development*. Harmondsworth, UK: Penguin Books.

Stoneman, P. and M.-J. Kwon (1994) "The Diffusion of Multipurpose Process Technologies." *Economic Journal* 104, 420–431.

Stoneman, P. and M.J. Kwon (1996) "Technology Adoption and Firm Profitability." *Economic Journal* 106, 952–962.

Stoneman, P. and O. Toivanen (1997) "The Diffusion of Multiple Technologies: an Empirical Study." *Economics of Innovation & New Technology* 5, 1–17.

Taylor, F.W. (1967) *The Principles of Scientific Management*. New York: Norton.

Thompson, R.S. (1983) "Diffusion of the M-Form Structure in the UK." *International Journal of Industrial Organization* 1, 297–315.

Van den Steen, E. (2006) "The Limits of Authority: Motivation versus Coordination." Working Paper, MIT Sloan School of Management.

Van Zandt, T. (1998) "Organizations that Process Information with an Endogenous Number of Agents." In M. Majumdar (ed.), *Organizations with Incomplete Information*. Cambridge: Cambridge University Press.

Van Zandt, T. (1999a) "Decentralized Information Processing in the Theory of Organizations." In M. Sertel (ed.), *Contemporary Economic Issues*. London, 125–160.

Van Zandt, T. (1999b) "Real-time Decentralized Information Processing as a Model of Organizations with Boundedly Rational Agents." *Review of Economic Studies* 66, 633–658.

Vázquez, X.H. (2004) "Allocating Decision Rights on the Shop Floor: A Perspective from Transaction Cost Economics and Organization Theory." *Organization Science* 15, 463–480.

Vella, F. and M. Verbeek (1999) "Estimating and Interpreting Models with Endogenous Treatment Effects." *Journal of Business and Economic Statistics* 17, 473–478.

Venkatraman, N., L. Loh, and J. Koh (1994) "The Adoption of Corporate Governance Mechanisms: A Test of Competing Diffusion Models." *Management Science* 40, 496–507.

Walton, E.J. (2005) "The Persistence of Bureaucracy: A Meta-analysis of Weber's Model of Bureaucratic Control." *Organization Studies* 26, 569–600.

Wang, L. (2006) "Ownership Structure and Size Dynamics: Implications for Architectural Change in Organizations." Working Paper, Graduate School of Business, Columbia University.

Weber, M. (1946) "Bureaucracy." *From Max Weber: Essays in Sociology*. Oxford: Oxford University Press.

WES "Workplace and Employee Survey," Statistics Canada 1999–2001.

Whisler, T.L. (1970) *The Impact of Computers on Organizations*. New York: Praeger.

Whittington, R., A. Pettigrew, S. Peck, E. Fenton, and M. Conyon (1999) "Change and Complementarities in the New Competitive Landscape: A European Panel Study, 1992–1996." *Organization Science* 10, 583–594.

Williamson, O.E. (1967) "Hierarchical Control and Optimum Firm Size." *Journal of Political Economy* 75, 123–138.

Williamson, O.E. (1975) *Markets and Hierarchies: Analysis and Antitrust Implications.* New York: Free Press.

Williamson, O.E. (1985) *The Economic Institutions of Capitalism.* New York: Free Press.

Wilms, W. (1995) *NUMMI: An Ethnographic Study.* New York: Free Press.

Winter, S.G. (1988) "On Case, Competence, and the Corporation." *Journal of Law, Economics & Organization* 4, 163–180.

Womack, J., D. Jones, and D. Roos (1990) *The Machine that Changed the World.* New York: Rawson Associates.

Wong, G.Y.Y. and P.H. Birnbaum-More (1994) "Culture, Context and Structure: A Test on Hong Kong Banks." *Organization Studies* 15, 99–123.

Woodward, J. (1958) *Management and Technology.* London: HMSO.

Woodward, J. (1965) *Industrial Organization: Theory and Practice.* New York: Oxford University Press.

Wooldridge, J.M. (1997) "On Two Stage Least Squares Estimation of the Average Treatment Effect in a Random Coefficient Model." *Economics Letters* 56, 129–133.

Wruck, K.H. (1994) "Financial Policy, Internal Control, and Performance Sealed Air Corporation's Leveraged Special Dividend." *Journal of Financial Economics* 36, 157–192.

Zabojnik, J. (2002) "Centralized and Decentralized Decision-making in Organizations", *Journal of Labor Economics* 20, 1–22.

Zeffane, R. (1989) "Computer Use and Structural Control: A Study of Australian Enterprises." *Journal of Management Studies* 26, 621–648.

Zuboff, S. (1988) *In the Age of the Smart Machine: The Future of Work and Power.* New York: Basic Books.

Index

The abbreviation 'C-D' is used in the index to refer to M.G. Colombo and M. Delmastro in the context of their research presented in this book.